WOMEN AFTER COMMUNISM

The East German Experience

Helen H. Frink

University Press of America,® Inc.
Lanham · New York · Oxford

Copyright © 2001 by
University Press of America,® Inc.
4720 Boston Way
Lanham, Maryland 20706

12 Hid's Copse Rd.
Cumnor Hill, Oxford OX2 9JJ

Library of Congress Cataloging-in-Publication Data

Frink, Helen
Women after communism : the East German
experience / Helen H. Frink.
p.   cm
Includes index.
1. Women—Germany (East)—Social conditions. I. Title.
HQ1630.5 .F764   2000   305.42'0943'1—dc21   00-048863 CIP

ISBN 0-7618-1894-4 (cloth : alk. paper)

⊖™The paper used in this publication meets the minimum
requirements of American National Standard for Information
Sciences—Permanence of Paper for Printed Library Materials,
ANSI Z39.48—1984

Contents

Acknowledgments

There are countless people who have contributed to the making of this book since its inception in 1992. First and foremost, thanks are due to the East German women who shared their stories with me: Andrée Fischer-Marum, Barbara Teuber, Jutta Freiberg, Gudrun Israel, Bärbel Garche, Frau Debbert and Frau Ullendorf, Sabine Meise, Elke Goltz, Sonja Richter, Kerstin Kiok, Gerlinde Lipfert, Dr. Christa Anders, Maggie Hofmann, Andrea Guth, Dr. Margit Quilitz, Susanne Fähnrich, Birgit Graumann, Regina Werner, Frau Krumm, Ria and Liane Schwaß. Some of these women were interviewed by Robert Jay Cook in my stead, and some have chosen to appear in the text under a pseudonym. Many others spoke with me at roundtable conversations in Berlin at the Gesellschaft zum Schutz von Bürgerrecht und Menschenwürde, the Verein Miteinander Wohnen, and the Mecklenburg-Vorpommern Bildungswerk der Wirtschaft at Schloß Hasenwinkel. Others permitted me to seek them out and interview them in the offices where they work: Christina Schenk, Dr. Karin Aleksander, Hanne Hammer, and Barbara Hömberg. Dr. Wolfgang Richter, Professor Dr. Hanna Behrend, and Dr. Christa Anders encouraged me to pursue the publication of this work. Professor Dr. Helmut Voigt provided my contacts with the women entrepreneurs of Hasenwinkel, and to his wife, Ursula Voigt, who translated a portion of the manuscript into German, I owe a special debt of gratitude.

I thank Keene State College for its considerable financial support through the years, in the form of professional development money and Faculty Development Grants. My colleagues in Women's Studies likewise offered some financial support, and were always eager to share the highs and lows of feminist research. The Marion and Jasper Whiting Foundation funded my first visit to East Germany in 1985 and a return trip in spring 2000 which enabled me to complete my research.

Heartfelt thanks also to my family, Dr. Frederick James Wolf, Annaliese Hiller Wolf, and Laura O'Shea Wolf, who listened and waited for me to come home, and offered suggestions and moral support at every step of the way.

Finally, this project would not have borne fruit without the tireless efforts of Gisela Meise, who collected material, telephoned, made contacts, offered encouragement, and never flagged in her insistence that the story of East German women should be told in America. Last but by no means least, my warmest thanks to Robert Jay Cook, my former student who has also become my teacher.

Introduction: Behind the Wall

Growing up in the northeastern United States in the 1950s and 1960s, I learned that my country and its *allies* in the free world were democratic and good. The Soviet Union and its *satellites* were communist and bad. The small brick library building in my town bore a black and yellow sign reading "Fallout Shelter." Schoolchildren learned to put their hands over their heads and duck beneath their desks in air raid drills. Radio stations periodically broadcast piercing signals called Norad alerts. The enemy threat that prompted small New Hampshire towns to move chicken coops and ramshackle sheds onto high points of land to serve as airplane spotting towers during the Second World War continued to frighten Americans for decades afterwards.

Matters grew more complex when I began studying German as a junior in high school in the early sixties. My teacher had visited Germany shortly after the Berlin Wall rose overnight to divide the city into communist East and democratic West, her travel funded by the National Defense Education Act. Our national government told us we needed to be protected, and that education was a key link in our defense, but what were we being defended against?

The question continued to trouble me as I studied German in college. I lived in West Germany from August 1966 until July 1967, spending a junior year abroad in the small, ancient university town of Marburg an der Lahn. Among the special courtesies shown to foreign students in those days was a cheap week in the divided city of Berlin. Our bus drove along the concrete wall dividing the city and through Checkpoint Charlie into East Berlin. Two sights impressed me above all: pigeons flew in and out of the ruined domes which had once capped the city's cathedral, a mammoth Baroque edifice with soot-blackened walls. And inside a state-run department store I wandered among racks of housewares, all the saucepans the same monotonous steel gray. I concluded that what I had been taught must be true: East Germany preached that God was dead and refused to repair its bomb-damaged churches. Its people lived without free choices; communism was ugly, drab, and shoddy, its evil as plainly visible as the wickedness of ugly witches in Grimm's fairy tales.

But was the contrast really that simple? Working in Washington, D.C. after graduation and continuing on to graduate school in Chicago, I found America's inner cities ugly, drab, and shoddy as well.

I lived in Germany again during the 1972-1973 academic year, this time in the prosperous Black Forest city of Freiburg im Breisgau. Again I benefited from a discounted week in Berlin, sponsored this time by the German Academic Exchange Service, which lodged a busload of foreign students in West Berlin's elegant Schweizerhof Hotel. This time the contrast to the unrelieved ugliness of the East was even more striking. And yet there were other things to see: the coppery windows of East Berlin's Palace of the Republic caught the brilliant sunset over the city. Tickets at the State Opera House on Unter den Linden cost only a few marks, and inside the theater chandeliers and plush red seats had been richly restored. We heard a glorious production of Puccini's Madame Butterfly, sung in German. I toured the Pergamon Museum on Unter den Linden, peering into the dusty, ill-lighted display cabinets at the treasures of classical antiquity. Some of Germany's cultural heritage had received generous funding, and some had not.

In the years that followed, I revised my earlier ideas about democracy being good and communism being bad. Was it accurate to compare democracy, a political system, with communism, an economic system? To be fair, shouldn't we be measuring communism against capitalism, its economic opposite? When I began teaching college German in 1974, I tried to explain this distinction between economic systems and systems of government to my students, many of them baffled to hear that the German *Democratic* Republic meant the communist "satellite" of the Soviet Union.

In 1985 I enrolled in a three-week seminar on social life in the German Democratic Republic for teachers of German "from the capitalist West" held at the Dr. Theodor Neubauer College of Education in the city of Erfurt. By then I spoke the language well enough to pass for German, and had learned in my travels that such a facility would give me a unique opportunity for insight into a radically different, non-capitalist society.

My journey began in early August of 1985. The train which carried me east from Frankfurt am Main seated eight passengers in a compartment instead of the usual six. Its windows were streaked with grime, and the curtains woven with the initials DR, *Deutsche*

Reichsbahn, the name of Germany's national railroads during the Hitler era. During an interminable wait at the border, West German guards confiscated my Frankfurt newspaper, taking even the furniture advertising insert I had kept as teaching material. My fellow passengers explained that the East German government did not want its citizens reading world news (often defamed as *Kriegshetzerei*, or war-mongering) nor advertisements for capitalist goods. The incident was my first inkling of what life was like in East Germany behind the *anti-faschistische Schutzmauer* (the anti-fascist protective wall). Would it be more accurate to call it the Iron Curtain, or was that term equally misleading? Most Germans, East and West, simply called it the Wall, and meant all that divided them.

My fellow travelers' attitude toward such restrictions as the confiscation of my newspaper was difficult to interpret. Older people were allowed to travel to the West, and if they chose to stay there, the West German government would pay their retirement pensions. The loss of older citizens was simply a financial gain for the East. But most chose to go west and return east, their valises bulging with presents for those they had left behind: clothing, coffee, chocolate, oranges, and bananas. They scrupulously kept in touch with second cousins, nieces, nephews, anyone whose invitation might authorize another journey West. They shrugged at the newspaper incident; they knew, since nearly all East Germans could receive West German television, the true state of affairs East and West, but little could be done. When our train screeched to a halt in Erfurt, they pulled down the windows and peered out. "Ach," they exclaimed, "isn't it wonderful to be home again!"

Erfurt, a city of about 216,000, reminded me instantly of Marburg two decades before; the same post-war shabbiness, the same odor of coal smoke and shared toilets and stale beer hung in the air. Everything mechanical seemed hopelessly out-of-date. The streetcar which took me from the train station to the dormitory where I would stay rattled and swayed and shook. An elderly widow on the train had given me a paper ticket worth about a nickel, but the stamping machine used to punch a hole in it had to be clamped by hand; in contrast the ticket punches in Frankfurt's streetcars or subways were electronically triggered, instantaneous, and stamped the date, time, and route on the ticket. Routes marked on the front of Erfurt's streetcars bore names like Alma Ata and Ulan Bator, evidence, I learned later, of the government's desire to promote feelings of solidarity with workers in Kazakhstan and Mongolia.

I arrived at the Straße der Völkerfreundschaft (the street of peoples' friendship) near the college's gray Stalin-era high rise dormitories and got off at a shopping center comprised of a post office, grocery store, hairdresser, a few shops, and a café called Stadt Vilnius (named for the capital of Lithuania) which was always closed. A mural of larger-than-life farm workers decorated one wall, reminding me of Cesar Chavez and his United Farm Workers. A feeble trickle of water splashed in a fountain basin, surrounded by figurines wearing folk costumes that looked as if they came from Guatemala, Vietnam, and Africa.

Inside the dormitory an official from the seminar checked my documents and handed me over to a young man, a student at the College of Education, who presented me with a bouquet of asters and carried my suitcase up several flights of stairs; the elevator wasn't working. As I followed him up six flights, I studied his brown corduroy pants, meticulously pieced fore and aft, so that little remained of the original garment save the waistband and zipper. Only after many similar observations did I understand that zippers were so precious, and jeans so completely out of reach, that a good woman, probably his mother, found it more efficient to replace pieces of what he had than go in search of new pants.

My room in the college dormitory contained six bunks, a single writing table, a clothes closet, and an enormous radio. An adjoining room, furnished identically, was occupied by a Portuguese teacher of German, with whom I shared the foul-smelling bathroom and an adjoining utility room complete with cupboards, a sink, and a hot plate. Had we been ordinary students at the College of Education, twelve of us would have shared this space, encumbered by our food, clothing, and books. I could only imagine the chaos, the clamor, and the reek.

In the weeks that followed my roommate and I cleaned the bathroom, walked together to the seminar classes, and talked. One afternoon we sat in a café over coffee and Kuchen while she told me about her childhood in Angola. A man who had sat down at our table, customary behavior in any part of Germany, seemed to follow our conversation. Maria Augusta described the war in Angola, and wanted to say that many people fled into the bush. She apologized for using the English word "jungle," not knowing the German word. "Oh, it's 'Dschungel,' the same word," the young man offered. Another seminar participant pointed out that we were always being observed. *Betreuer*, young caretakers attached to our group, conferred with our seminar leaders and made notes on a clipboard. Were these the ill-famed informants (*informelle Mitarbeiter*) of East Germany's State Security Service, its infamous *Stasi*?

These weeks in Erfurt and other seminars which I attended in Leipzig in 1992, and in Dresden in 1998 presented aspects of life in East Germany which challenged my childhood assumptions about evil communism and good democracy. Over time I rejected what the Germans call *Schwarz-weiß-Malerei*, the tendency to paint things in black and white extremes. Reality became more complicated and shaded into hues of gray.

During these years as I became a feminist, I came to wonder whether some of the portrayal of communism as unthinkably evil might result from the changes it had made in women's lives. I had been taught that communist states took babies from their families and reared them in daycare centers while mothers as well as fathers were forced to work. As I raised my own children and *sent* them to daycare so that I could pursue my teaching career, it occurred to me that this might have been a choice for women, rather than a punishment.

While I studied in Erfurt, my own daughters were three and seven years old; comparisons with my own life as a working mother confronted me at every turn. In Erfurt I was struck by the sight of mothers far younger than I, wheeling splendid baby carriages. Streetcars waited while bystanders or fellow-travelers helped them wheel their huge prams up and down stairs and held doors open. I had never encountered a society where there seemed to be so many young people; in fact 70% of the country's inhabitants had been born since the Second World War. In the seminar I learned of the generous incentives the socialist state provided for marriage and birth, including free pre- and post-natal care. The infant mortality rate here was lower than in the United States. I could only envy mothers such provisions as generous paid maternity leave and a paid monthly day off for housework. And why did the United States, "with liberty and justice for all" not celebrate International Women's Day on March eighth?

One of the most striking differences between West and East Germany was the extent to which East German women were able to combine paid work and family responsibilities. Over 91% of women aged fifteen to sixty were workers, students, or apprentices, and about the same percentage had at least one child. (Of West German women in the same age cohort, only 55% were in the labor force, and a third of those worked only part time.) As a mother and college professor, I wanted to know whether America might learn something from East

Germany, whether the social structure that made it possible to combine motherhood and paid employment could serve as a model for the US.

Unfortunately, in the decade since unification, East Germany's achievements in women's issues have been obliterated. Eighty-one per cent of East German women, surveyed in the summer of 1992 by the Institut für Demoskopie in Allensbach, said that their overall condition had worsened since unification. Post-unification changes have meant huge losses in earning power, daycare, and abortion rights. Today East German women struggle to find their footing in a society which has rolled back their hard won gains. *Kinder, Küche, Karriere* is becoming as outmoded as its predecessor, *Kinder, Kirche, Küche*.

Beginning in 1992, I decided to research the question of East German women, their achievements, and the limitations placed on them by the political turnaround of 1989 and 1990 which they call *die Wende*. A former student, Robert Jay Cook, offered to interview students in his English classes at the adult education school in East Berlin's Prenzlauer Berg. He widened the circle of interview subjects to include mothers, sisters, and friends of his students. With the help of one of them, Gisela Meise, I was able to make contact with other women in Berlin, Brandenburg, and Mecklenburg-Vorpommern who permitted me to interview them in the summer of 1998 and spring of 2000.

Some of these women realized that they were experiencing the same kind of re-writing of history that had occurred after the Nazis' defeat. Declaring itself an ally of the Soviet Union, the young socialist German Democratic Republic placed itself on the victors' side after World War II, which it portrayed as a class struggle between the capitalist imperialist Hitler regime and the workers and farmers of East Germany. Thus, perversely, Hitler's defeat could be interpreted as a kind of victory for the new people's republic. By the late 1990s, the history of the German Democratic Republic was undergoing a similar revision. Its achievements: high rates of education and literacy, low infant mortality, a distribution of wealth more nearly equal than that of the West, were being erased from the history books. Some East German women have already learned that history is written by the victors. That is why they want their stories told. They are proud of their careers and they are proud of their children. They told me that they were not forbidden to practice religion, nor coerced to go to work; they lost faith in organized churches through the war experience, and they entered the workforce because they wanted self-respect and independence, as well as money. While western capitalist interpretations of their present status emphasize their loss of income, they are more concerned with the loss of self, as they can no longer define themselves by education, training, and occupation.

Before the German Democratic Republic is relegated to the dustbin of history, we must take another look at what it might teach us. The negative image Americans have of communism certainly rests in part in the eye of the beholder: sociological studies of the former communist states are written by highly educated white professionals, mostly male, to whom everyday existence in the GDR inevitably must appear constrained, monotonous, shabby. But imagine the American viewer is instead a mother of three pre-school children, subsisting on minimum wage labor and food stamps in the garbage-strewn, crime ridden inner city. She might well esteem more highly the safety of Leipzig's streets, the absence of litter, the availability of cheap, reliable public transportation, accessible daycare, and monthly child support payments. Our point of view determines what we see.

The German Democratic Republic's record on women's issues merits special consideration in our appraisal of its achievements. Could its progress toward greater equality for women be one reason why western democracies were so frightened by communism? Could communism's rejection of Christianity simultaneously contribute to freeing women from the ancient yoke of patriarchy?

The answers to these questions will prove as multi-faceted and as difficult to categorize as the women who explored them in their interviews. None wished themselves back in what they laughingly called *die seligen Zeiten*, (the good old days) and most dismissed as sentimentality that feeling called *Ostalgie*, a neologism of the mid-nineties meaning a nostalgia for the East, more specifically, for East Germany. But their experiences made them insightful critics of much that characterizes western capitalist democracies, including our own.

To understand how women lived in East Germany and how they have coped with the transition to capitalism in the decade following its collapse, we must outline the political structure of the country and the legal framework surrounding women in the workplace. Religion or its absence, and education further defined their existence. Then we will move forward to consider how capitalism has left many of these women sidelined, pushed out of the paid labor force into early retirement or back into their homes. We will focus in turn on the situation of women pensioners, the plight of rural women, on the fresh start some women have made in the beauty and fashion industry, and the promising success of a new crop of women entrepreneurs. In each case I have interspersed statistical material gathered from a wide variety of sources with the life stories gained from interviews. It is one of the central tenets of feminist scholarship that we measure "realities" described to us against women's experience, and that is the method I have chosen to pursue here.

I have not considered East German literature and the arts because they have been exhaustively treated elsewhere, and they present a fictitious image of actual conditions, shaped, at times, by the censorship which existed within the GDR.

A word of explanation about the terms socialism and communism is in order here. In the title of this book, I have chosen to use communism because that is the term used in the West to describe the economic and political system we will explore: at the end of the Cold War, Americans speak of the collapse of communism. East Germans and Russians, however, name the system under which they lived socialism (e.g. the Union of Soviet *Socialist* Republics). East Germany described its own system as real, existing socialism, in contrast to communism, which meant the ideal, theoretically possible Marxism. One East German woman took me to task for using the word communism in the title, insisting that her country had never achieved that. Thus I use the word communism here to evoke its connotations in American parlance, while adopting the term socialism as used by the women who shared their life stories with me.

It is my hope that the experiences of these women under communism and now under capitalism can illuminate some common truths of women's existence. I invite the reader to ponder with me whether the negative image of communism presented to Americans during the Cold War era (and the speed with which its achievements have been buried since 1990) were based in part on the threat its modest successes for women posed to our own patriarchal capitalistic system.

Chapter One
The Political Background

For most of its forty years of existence, the German Democratic Republic was governed by the Socialist Unity Party, formed in 1949 in the union of the German Communist Party (KPD) and the Social Democratic Party (SPD). Avowedly Marxist-Leninist, this party, which will be referred to here by its German initials SED (Sozialistische Einheitspartei Deutschlands), encouraged the existence of smaller, but by no means independent parties, one for farmers, and one for labor unions (Freier Deutscher Gewerkschaftsbund) for example. An affiliate of the West German Christian Democratic Union (CDU), the party of Germany's longest-serving chancellor, (Helmut Kohl, in power from 1982 through 1998) was also allowed to function.

The purpose of all of these mass organizations was by no means to encourage free political debate, but rather to bring into the fold voters who might otherwise have been tempted into political opposition. The Democratic Women's League (Demokratischer Frauenbund Deutschlands) for instance, founded on March 8, 1947, sought to include women absent from the typical workplace: those on maternity leave, the elderly, or women in rural areas who might otherwise not have maintained any political ties. It preached allegiance to SED policies and helped propagate the positive view of mothers working outside the home. The DFD counted a million and a half members in 1988, but membership stagnated as its activities focused on residential areas, where it offered knitting and cooking courses that failed to attract younger working women (Kuhrig, 224). Official SED policies depicted the struggle for women's rights as part of the larger issue of workers' rights. Feminist activism was considered a distraction characteristic of capitalist societies, a way of diverting attention from the larger and more significant problem of workers' rights.

Socialist Unity Party membership was not obligatory, but was strongly encouraged for those who wished to rise to prominence or status. About 30% of its members were women; thus relatively few gained access to such benefits as foreign travel or preference in consideration for education or promotion which party membership could provide. Young people received an indoctrination into party allegiance through the Young Pioneers (for children ages seven through thirteen) and the Free German Youth (Freie deutsche Jugend, or FDJ) for those fourteen through twenty-five. The FDJ in particular, had representatives in every school and university class. It organized study groups and recycling efforts and advised on awarding scholarships and in career promotion. Those who refused to join the FDJ were unlikely to receive such perks as access to a university education. These youth organizations taught allegiance to the state, social responsibility, and a sense of community. They provided after school programs and summer camps for children of working parents.

In 1985 I visited an camp outside of Erfurt which housed 850 Young Pioneers and FDJ members in bungalows and tents. The uninsulated buildings, without window screens, were full of the clothing, belongings, and baggage of dozens of untidy teenagers. Showers were taken in groups, but not every day. The guests from the capitalist West, as we were called, were greeted by a youth chorus wearing the FDJ uniform of bright blue shirts and yellow scarves and singing a song about the horrors and injustices of the Vietnam War. "Do you see anyone smiling?" whispered a guest from Denmark. We didn't. Days were filled with activities such as sports, first-aid training, music, and work projects like helping with the cucumber harvest on a nearby collective farm; proceeds went to help the children of Nicaragua. True to its mission as a camp "for work and education," the place offered seminars in such topics as "Accusing Capitalism." As we ate lunch in the camp cafeteria, I mentally compared the organization to the Boy Scouts and Girl Scouts of America. While the political framework differed, the uniforms, the activities, the training for participation in one's country's affairs seemed more alike than different, but the FDJ was not segregated by gender.

Under the aegis of the Socialist Unity Party, government formed two distinct layers. The broadest, visible layer consisted of five hundred locally elected representatives to the People's Assembly (*Volkskammer*) which met in the People's Palace (*Palast der Republik*, known popularly as the *Volkspalast*) in Berlin. This modernistic building, whose copper colored windows reflect the surrounding cityscape, was constructed in the 1960s on the site of the former Hohenzollern city palace. News programming in the German Democratic Republic proudly featured its assembly chamber, where Chancellor Erich Honecker greeted Free German Youth delegates or visiting dignitaries. The building remained closed through most of the nineties, ostensibly because of asbestos contamination, but largely because of disagreement over what should become of its symbolic value. A plan to reconstruct the old city palace in its stead has spurred the creation of an organization to support keeping the Volkspalast where it is.

The less visible but far more powerful layer of government was the SED's party structure. At the bottom was the Party Congress which met every five years and elected the Central Committee. That organ in turn met every six months and elected the Politbüro, the locus of real power, and the Secretariat. In 1989 the Central Committee counted 148 male and sixteen female members and an additional seventy-seven male and ten female candidate members. The Politbüro had twenty-six male and two female members in 1989, all of them simultaneously in the Secretariat. Both of these smaller organs met frequently and held the reins of power. The specific responsibilities of these smaller bodies were unclear to outside observers, and their membership often overlapped. Furthermore, the fiction of collective political power obscured their workings. In the government of General Secretary Erich Honecker, head of the Secretariat since 1971, there were twenty-five male cabinet ministers and three women.

In general, the larger, less powerful bodies included more women. At the top echelons where real power was exercised, there were few, or none. At the lowest level, women comprised a third of the People's Assembly's five hundred members by 1983, but that legislature met for only a few days each year and held little real power. In contrast, at the Party Congresses held in 1976 and 1981, about one of every eight members elected to the Central Committee was female. In the Politbüro there were usually two or three candidates among the twenty-five-odd candidate and full members, but few attained full membership status. Inge Lange served as head of the women's department within the Secretariat from 1961 until 1989. She became a candidate member of the Politbüro in 1973 but never rose above this status, although she headed the ministry for women and youth created in 1986. The Council 1963 through the mid eighties its only female member was minister of of Ministers had two women members in the early sixties, but from education Margot Honecker, wife of the General Secretary and head of state Erich Honecker, in power from 1971 until the fateful fall of 1989. By and large policy was made for women, not by women.

One woman interviewed in 1994 commented on the change from communism to democracy. The Federal Republic of Germany, she said, was dominated by old men. Of course that was the case in the GDR too, she conceded, only then nobody thought we were living in a democracy.

Establishing the country's five-year economic plans was the primary task of the Central Committee and the Politbüro, although a GDR handbook for 1988 states triumphantly that six million workers had contributed over 650,000 suggestions for the country's five-year plans. The proclamation of a new five-year plan and festivities surrounding its fulfillment took place in the Volkspalast. The centrally planned economy attempted to determine five years in advance how many of every kind of appliance, housewares, or article of clothing the country would require. Supply and demand should not be allowed to govern prices. The result always fell shy of the intent, and services such as shoe repair or replacement parts such as tires or plumbing fixtures were in chronically short supply.

Waiting lists for telephones and automobiles grew longer than a decade. Party functionaries, public officials, and school directors might be allocated telephones, but ordinary people were not. After unification West Germans would complain that their new East German acquaintances simply dropped in to visit; after years of living without a telephone they didn't think of calling first. A family which finally received a new car immediately applied for another, knowing that by the time the waiting period expired, the old car would be defunct. Used cars were more expensive than new ones simply because there was no waiting period. Neither the Trabant, the GDR's Volkswagen, nor the more elegant Wartburg (named for the castle where Martin Luther translated the Bible) came with automatic transmission. The little *Trabbi,* as East Germans affectionately called the Trabant, looked like a cheap plastic box. Most women learned to perform their own car repairs, and Trabbis were so lightweight that they were easy to push when they broke down, as they often did. Housing was built with one parking space for every two apartments, in contrast to the US, where one apartment normally provides for two parking spaces. After unification everyone who could afford to do so bought a car, and parking became a serious problem. When ticket booths and metal barriers were installed to control access to parking lots, the barriers failed to rise to allow Trabbis to pass because the little cars didn't contain enough steel to activate the booth's metal detector.

Aside from luxuries such as cars, the centrally planned economy touched the lives of consumers in other ways. Factory workers ceased work at midday when components for the products they were manufacturing ran out. While schoolbooks were kept artificially cheap, some East German bestsellers could be purchased only in the West; they were out of print in the East because no one could predict how much paper would be needed to print adequate copies of the book. Of course at the same time, the allocation of paper functioned as a form of censorship.

One woman who understood the workings of the GDR's centrally planned economy and the political structure from the inside is Jutta Freiberg, a widowed pensioner interviewed in East Berlin in 1997. Her story provides insight into consumer economics, the question of censorship, and the effects of party membership.

Jutta Freiberg lived in Leipzig until 1960. Her oldest sister became a neurologist, a younger sister taught English, and their brother worked for the ministry of justice. Her mother stayed at home and raised four children, but felt inferior to women who worked outside the home, developing their full capacities in keeping with Marxist teachings. SED ideology depicted stay-at-home mothers as parasites, or as failing to contribute their due to society. Frau Freiberg studied French and English, hoping to become an English teacher, but she was persuaded to take up civics (*Staatsbürgerkunde*) instead. This process of persuasion, which the East Germans called "being steered" (*lenken*) was itself a link in the centrally planned economy. Based on predictions of how many textile workers or masons or diesel mechanics the country would require, students were directed toward those fields where more staffing would be needed, and trained in apprenticeships or further schooling. Most of the women interviewed bore this alteration in their plans with good grace, though several noted that one of the benefits of unification was the freedom to choose a path of study and a career. That freedom, of course, always carries the risk of future unemployment.

Jutta Freiberg taught civics for one year and then moved on to the government office which set prices for various commodities, where she worked for fifteen years. She had a college degree and was twenty-three years old when she began, and she became secretary for the office's Free German Youth chapter. In keeping with Marxist economic theory, the prices for necessities such as bread and butter were held stable; in the case of the German Democratic Republic these prices remained at the level where they were in 1958 when post-war rationing ended. A hundred grams (about a quarter pound) of cold cuts cost one mark, about thirty-five cents. Frau Freiberg's East Berlin apartment, measuring fifty-three square meters, cost eighty-five marks (around thirty dollars) a month. Workers such as kindergarten teachers and bus drivers earned six to eight hundred marks a month. For those who could afford them, high quality imported foodstuffs such as coffee, chocolate, champagne, and fresh fruit were sold in groceries labeled *Delikat.* Prices for imported commodities were set by the pricing office in cooperation with the SED's Council of Ministers. In those days, Frau Freiberg says, pineapples were only available in the Delikat stores, and cost the unthinkable price of ten marks apiece. Now they can be bought more cheaply in an ordinary supermarket, but the price of apples has risen to four marks a pound. Apples and tomatoes, she recalls, were much cheaper in the old state-run groceries called *Handels Organisationen* (trade organizations, abbreviated HO), but of course they were only available in harvest season.

Comparable to the Delikat shops for foodstuffs, *Exquisit* shops sold higher quality clothing and accessories. Unlike ordinary stores, they did not display prices in their shop windows, and people said if you had to ask how much things cost in the Exquisit shops, you couldn't afford to buy there. A man's suit which might cost two hundred marks (about seventy dollars) in a state-run clothing store would cost four times as much in an Exquisit shop, but the fabric would be first quality and the tailoring as well. Today, Frau Freiberg says, she never knows what quality she is buying, regardless of the price of wares.

A twenty-year-old television set might cost six thousand marks, or ten month's wages. In 1985 a washing machine, which few people would consider a luxury, cost the equivalent of six hundred dollars. Most people carried their laundry to large commercial laundromats, or washed it in the bathtub, if they had one. Appliances were cheaper in West Germany, but everyday necessities such as food and public transportation were far cheaper in the East. For the individual consumer, the results of this price structure were twofold. First, working families often had a great deal more disposable income than they could spend, since the range of consumer goods was limited, and opportunities for vacation travel were restricted to Soviet block countries where the range of goods offered for sale and the price of vacation travel were similarly low. Jutta Freiberg, for example, well paid in her government office, earned 1,650 marks (around $560) a month, and her expenses came to just three hundred marks; the remainder was disposable income. Second, there were relatively few visible signs of being rich or poor; therefore money did not serve as a measure of social status. Sometimes party loyalty rather than high earnings procured a larger apartment or a newer car.

Frau Freiberg enjoyed her work in the pricing office, she recalls. Once a month obligatory meetings (the *Parteilehrjahr*) were held for industrial workers, farmers, or employees where such things as government pricing policy were explained. She connected this part of her job to her training as a teacher, as she and her co-workers traveled to industrial cities like Schwedt and Dessau to explain how prices were set and why the prices of some consumer goods were so high. For every hundred marks paid for food, government subsidies accounted for an additional seventy-five marks of the cost. By 1980 subsidies became so costly that the stability of consumer prices could no longer be guaranteed. Now she realizes that the collapse of the German Democratic Republic can be attributed in large measure to its untenable price support system.

Nevertheless Frau Freiberg wants people to understand that at its worst the German Democratic Republic was never as heavily in debt as the Federal Republic of Germany is today. People understood that the high prices for luxury items such as cars meant that the average East German citizen enjoyed lower prices for everyday necessities. In the Federal Republic, in contrast, high prices profit only the manufacturers, never the society as a whole. And pineapples and other imported goods bring in high profits for the capitalist retailers, not for their third world producers.

Jutta Freiberg believes that the average worker in the German Democratic Republic was well educated and comprehended common economic problems. People read more then, she says, than today, when they only read tabloids like *Bild Zeitung*. It's true that they were obliged to attend political party seminars, but they got off work early to do so. Sometimes, she says, you have to force people to do what's good for them. Today no one talks about politics any more; they only talk about work and money. (She's right in asserting that people have lost interest in politics; the new word of the year in 1994 at the time of the federal election was *Politikverdrossenheit*, meaning feeling sick and tired of politics.)

Frau Freiberg's solid allegiance to the Socialist Unity Party undoubtedly figured into her personal life as well as her career. Her husband, who died a few years ago, worked for the Stasi, as East Germans called the state security service, in counter-intelligence against the Russian KGB. He was sixteen years older than Frau Freiberg; it was a second marriage for both. She thinks maybe people got divorced a little too easily in those days, because there were no problems attached. But housing was a problem. If there were children, the parent who received custody usually kept the family's apartment, but if the husband had received it through his employment, he held the stronger claim. After the divorce from her first husband, Jutta Freiberg had to go on sharing an apartment with him for two years. Fortunately by that time he lived mostly with his girlfriend. Alimony was paid only if there were small children. Frau Freiberg thinks the very idea of alimony is crazy. Nowadays people are unfaithful to each other but they don't get a divorce because of money.

In 1986 the Freibergs moved into a new building reserved for police and intelligence employees because it stands so close to a women's prison that prisoners might be able to make contact with residents of the apartment building. Nowadays most of the men who live here are unemployable because of their connection to the socialist regime (*Staatsnähe*, this obstacle is called). Some work as watchmen earning 7.50 DM (about four dollars) an hour. Women, Frau Freiberg says, have an easier time adjusting to the state of affairs today, because they can return to the traditional role of housewives. The men sit home as if they were in a cage. Some have taken to drink, or television. Men don't do a thing any more around the house; they want their wives to stay home. The distribution of labor that began in the GDR has gone backwards now. Her husband believed that women who just stay home get strange ideas; it's bad for the marriage.

Over time, the Freibergs' connection to the ruling elite isolated them from friends and neighbors. Today East Germans cite as one reason for the collapse of their country the alienation of the party elite from the masses of ordinary people. "Ossified" (*verkalkt*) is the word they use to describe the men in gray suits who drove in black Ladas through the East Berlin residential district called Pankow. Herr Freiberg's work imposed certain limits; he couldn't have contact with just anyone. If his wife saw him on the street she shouldn't speak to him for fear of exposing him. After his death she became very lonely. She thought about which old friends she might resume contact with. Those who work don't have any time. And she can't talk to someone who has nothing to talk about except shopping. It's not easy rebuilding a circle of friends at fifty. One day she visited a former neighbor in Berlin's Leipziger Straße. She went there for coffee at four o'clock and didn't leave until half-past nine. They talked about everything; it was as if a dam had broken. Like her, this neighbor only has contacts among her old friends; there are no new ones.

She says it's rubbish to claim that people didn't dare say anything in the old days. She always spoke freely about what she didn't like, and she didn't land in any dark cellar. There were debates then, even with the boss. Today people just swallow everything. Today who would dare argue with the boss? Her brother-in-law, for example, has to work at least one Sunday a month. When something goes wrong, he jumps. He knows he can't say anything if he wants to hold onto his job. There are others behind him just waiting for a chance at it. She finds that perverse.

Today people complain that workers in the GDR had to work in a brigade or a collective. But these brigades went to the theater together, or organized a garden party. The other side of the coin is that without being pushed, some people would never have gone to the theater. Today there's a different atmosphere among co-workers. Whatever anyone says is brought directly to the boss. In the old days there was always a company party; at least once a year everyone got together. You could eat and drink your fill. Older people miss that nowadays. Younger people don't know anything about it.

In the old days political discussions in the workplace were common. People always discussed West German television. East German news reports aired at seven-thirty and West news at quarter of nine. People heard both and thought things over. Today you only hear one side of events, and certain information doesn't come up at all. She's still a member of the PDS, the Party of Democratic Socialism, successor to the old SED, but there's no newspaper that reports objectively about her party. Even *Neues Deutschland* (which belongs to the PDS) is too party-oriented, not factual or impartial enough. *Der Spiegel* seems chiefly interested in the old GDR's state security apparatus, the *Staatssicherheitsdienst*, but even there it's an effort to shoot down certain people, not a matter of telling the truth. Soon the brain-washing will have gone so far that everyone will say they weren't allowed to travel in the old days, they weren't allowed to say anything, and the police were brutal. People who know better won't dare to say anything.

Even Frau Freiberg doesn't dare complain today about the kids who hang out in front of the elevator in her building and write on the walls. She knows they've beaten up a couple people already. In the old days kids were better occupied. She has a nephew in kindergarten and there they have a mattress that children are supposed to hit to take out their frustration. But they want to take out their frustration at home too; the tone of voice he uses to his parents scares her. She says the new emphasis on individualism has made children alienated and aggressive. They think that it's everyone for themselves: "If I can't make it on my own, who will help me?"

Today Jutta Freiberg lives modestly. She lost her job in November of 1989. Women of her age were considered too old to re-train. With her additional stigma of attachment to the socialist regime, she will probably never find meaningful work again. Party loyalists like her husband and herself participated in a supplemental pension fund apart from the state system. Over twenty such pension funds evolved during the existence of the socialist regime, and they rewarded workers such as teachers as well as party functionaries. Despite assurances to the contrary during unification negotiations, such funds have disappeared. Jutta Freiberg supplements her meager income by working as a cleaning woman.

The configuration of political parties in existence in 1989 shaped the process of unification and its aftermath. Since their forced union with the communists in 1949, the Social Democrats, West Germany's long-term opposition party, were banned from any independent existence and thus had no foothold in the East at the time of unification. By contrast, the Christian Democratic Union existed within the German Democratic Republic as a small but legitimate political party, charged with encouraging participation in the process and appealing to those who kept their faith. Founded after World War II in both East and West Germany, it aimed at restoring Christian principles, Protestant or Catholic, to the center of political life. The modest following it gained over the next decade in the East shrank as the party failed to accomplish anything against the socialist collectivization of agriculture. The party fulfilled its more modest task of publishing the Bible and religious materials, as well as an official newspaper, *Der Morgen*. The party's very existence, with its access to office space and publication facilities, gave Chancellor Helmut Kohl an enormous advantage in winning the East German vote in the 1992 election. Furthermore, he became identified with gaining acceptance for German unification in the US and the USSR. Of the major parties East or West, Kohl's Christian Democrats had the fewest women members.

The SED re-invented itself after 1989 as the Party of Democratic Socialism (PDS). Although initially rejected by the voters whose lives it had heretofore controlled, it inherited from the SED era the infra-structure that a political party needs to function: office space, full coffers, party functionaries, and publications, chief among them the newspaper *Neues Deutschland*, the major East German newspaper still printed today. The PDS entered the Bundestag despite failing to win 5% of the vote in the 1990 election because it won a larger share in Berlin, thus earning the right of representation in the national legislature. As disillusionment with unification grew, the party regained strength. By the end of the century each of the East's three major parties, PDS, SPD, and CDU, polled about a quarter of the vote in the new federal states, with smaller numbers counted for the Free Democratic Party and the Greens. The PDS now stands for environmentalism, peace, including withdrawal from NATO, limited support for political refugees, equitable pensions for East Germany's elderly citizens and those forced into early retirement by economic transformation, and introduction of the thirty-five hour work week. Several of its platform planks are intended to attract women voters: access to retraining programs based on the proportion of men and women unemployed, repeal of restrictions on abortion, and equal rights for all domestic partnerships, with an end to tax privileges for heterosexual marriage. It also emphasizes some issues such as gay and lesbian rights which never received widespread attention in the GDR.

In united Germany today only the PDS and the Greens (allied with the East German splinter parties which arose during the collapse of the GDR) have equal numbers of women and men as members. Between a fifth and a fourth of Christian Democrats are women; the allied Christian Socialist Union from Catholic Bavaria has only about 15% women in its membership. The Socialists (SPD), elected to power in 1998 under the chancellorship of Gerhard Schröder, are about 27% women. Overall, women have lost political clout in East Germany in the decade since unification.

The federal Bundestag elected in 1990 from united Germany counted more women members than any German national legislature since the advent of the Weimar Republic in 1919, when women won the right to vote. After the 1998 federal election, two out of sixteen cabinet posts were headed by women, and 30.1% of the Bundestag's members were women, the same percentage as in the parliament of the European Union.

The Social Democrats laid out a legislative program called Women and Careers (Frau und Beruf) in January 1999. This program would strengthen affirmative action in federal hiring, distribute educational and apprenticeship opportunities to promote women in careers with good future prospects, promote computer and Internet training courses for women, advocate for equal rights for same-sex couples, increase the numbers of women in commissions that advise politicians (from under 13% in 1997), and strengthen the authority of women's commissioners. Several of the program's other initiatives pertain to working women, and will be examined in more detail in the following chapter. In brief, the SPD proposes increasing support for women entrepreneurs, re-examining laws on sexual harassment, and expanding the concept of equal pay for equal work in the direction of comparable worth.

Women's commissioners (*Frauenbeauftragte*) have existed in some West German cities since the early eighties (in the western federal state of Hesse since 1994) and are also required in every government office with twenty or more employees. Since unification, they exist in the new federal states as well; however the office holders may be West Germans, and are not necessarily feminists. These offices disseminate information on a variety of women's issues: payments to stay-at-home mothers, child-rearing leave, dealing with sexual abuse and domestic violence, sexual harassment, same sex partnerships, and educational opportunities for women. Some offices also collect and support documentation of women's contributions to history and culture. Their purpose is to acquaint women with their rights and opportunities within the political and economic system of united Germany; they are not a focal point for those who wish to change it.

Since 1986, the Federal Republic of Germany has had a ministry of women's affairs and youth. Under the post-unification chancellorship of Helmut Kohl, Claudia Nolte, a thirty-something Christian Democrat from Brandenburg, held the office. After the 1998 election the Social Democrats named Christine Bergmann to the post. With the exception of the PDS and the Greens, political parties have rejected quotas for women. Christian Democrats and particularly the Catholic Christian Socialists, fought for and succeeded in repealing access to legal abortion. In the depressed state of united Germany's economy, both the Christian Democrats and the Social Democrats have focused their efforts on combating unemployment by returning women to housewifery and motherhood. The family norm, favored in the tax code and in the structure of the typical school day, consists of a wage-earning father and a mother who either works part-time or not for pay at all. Women's loss of political power and earning power, and their forced return to a traditional family role are interrelated developments which constitute major setbacks for women.

A study of women in politics conducted at Berlin's Technical University in 1997 surveyed women at all levels of government, from the European Union to the town, and concluded that women must be better qualified than men to succeed in politics. Women find their speeches are taken less seriously than those of men, and they must over-prepare before any presentation, not daring to speak impromptu as men often do. Women are handicapped by being closed out of the old-boy network, and find it difficult to strategize. They seldom nominate other women for higher posts, distrusting both their own abilities and those of their peers. Media treat women in politics differently from men, reporting their age, dress, and appearance before attending to what they have to say. It is worth noting here that Germany's publicly-owned media are a bastion of male dominance: the first woman head of a major broadcast network, *Sender Freies Berlin*, was elected in 1998. Women, but not men, are questioned about combining professional and family responsibilities. Because there are no training institutions for a career in politics, women find it difficult to learn to be more assertive and ambitious. East German women must first prove their allegiance to the democratic system of united Germany. While West German politicians freely discuss what's best for the East, East German politicians, especially women, are not expected to voice opinions about western affairs. Undoubtedly the German Democratic Republic's educational system, with its emphasis on conformity and selflessness rather than competitiveness, leadership, and creative thinking, will continue to hinder these women as they struggle upward in the political hierarchy.

A 1999 *Sozialreport* assessing East German attitudes toward democracy found considerable disillusionment and skepticism. The CDU and SPD both lost over 40% of their members in the East between 1991 and 1998; other parties lost smaller fractions of their membership (*Sozialreport 1999*, 366). The 1998 elections and the turnover in government which they produced increased awareness that voting in a multi-party system could create change, yet individual voters doubted their power to influence decisions (*Sozialreport 1999*, 338-39). Belief in that power weakened even further a year later with news of former chancellor Kohl's refusal to divulge the source of secret campaign contributions. The Kohl scandal confirmed many East Germans' suspicions that money wields greater political power than a few thousand voters. Another factor contributing to the decline in their faith in pluralistic democracy is that the West German parties dominate the national scene. The PDS, which held its first party congress in the West early in 2000, remains almost unknown there. It is interesting to note that while support for the CDU diminishes with increasing levels of education, support for the PDS is higher among those who are better educated (*Sozialreport 1999*, 362-63). Dissatisfaction with their political influence is higher among East Germans aged eighteen to twenty-four (the cohort trying to enter the workforce) and among those forty-five to fifty-nine, who are trying to keep a foothold in it. Forty-seven per cent of those with a college or university degree express dissatisfaction with their political influence (*Sozialreport 1999,* 47). One encouraging note is that East German voters express more satisfaction with their political influence at the local level; that is, close to home where they are more likely to know those in power, things can be accomplished.

The emerging pattern here is shaped by time and distance. In the wake of the Leipzig candlelight vigils and the demonstrations which brought about the collapse of the German Democratic Republic, East Germans believed their voices would be heard and their shouts could open other walls. In the intervening years, experience has shown them that the collapse of the German Democratic Republic also cost them things which they valued, such as secure employment and stable economic conditions. Their opposition to German involvement in NATO and in the Kosovo bombing, and their disagreement with European Union agricultural policies have shown them that their national government is only one structure, behind which stand others, more imposing and less penetrable. Some recognize themselves as resembling the man from the countryside who seeks entry in Kafka's parable "Before the Law." After waiting for years to enter the realm of the law, the peasant learns that the doorkeeper who appears to block his entrance is only the first of many such doorkeepers, guarding many entrances, each more formidable than the last.

Chapter Two
Women in the Workforce

In order to understand the situation of East German women in today's capitalist labor market, it is necessary to look backward to their status in the German Democratic Republic. Friedrich Engels in *Der Ursprung der Familie* assumed that women's emancipation would evolve from their participation in production as part of the paid labor force. True equality between the sexes would only become a reality when household labor had been transformed into a public industry. The German Democratic Republic's constitution of 1949, which guaranteed women equal pay for equal work, created the first condition necessary for women's emancipation. In 1952 the Council of Ministers required *Frauenförderpläne*, plans which projected the increased employment of women in all sectors of the economy. Further measures adopted in 1966 encouraged women to enter non-traditional occupations such as machinist, chemist, and engineer. Although many western critics disparage the achievements of the German Democratic Republic, it is worth noting that the United States passed an Equal Pay Act in 1963 during the civil rights movement, but has yet to ratify an equal rights amendment granting women the same rights guaranteed to East German women fifty years ago.

While West Germany solved the labor shortage by importing *Gastarbeiter* (guest workers) to support its post-war *Wirtschaftswunder* (economic miracle), East Germany brought women into the workforce in unprecedented numbers during the reconstruction period. Women's entry into the labor force was an economic as well as a political necessity. For every hundred men living in the Soviet zone of occupation in 1945, there were 135 women. One ninety-one year old widow living in East Berlin, responded to my question about women's transition into the workforce during and after World War II by saying, "Wir mußten einfach." (We simply had to). So women rolled up their sleeves, spat into their hands, and went to work clearing away rubble in the bombed-out cities. In the countryside they milked cows and threshed grain. Many had worked in factories or hospitals during the war; others had driven streetcars or "manned" anti-aircraft weapons. Most girls had been trained in the period of *Arbeitsdienst* (service work) mandated by the National Socialists.

In post-war America, women were pushed out of the workforce when men returned from the battle front. A new cult of domesticity urged them to become model housewives and mothers, buyers of floor wax and detergents and readers of women's magazines like *McCall's* and *Ladies Home Journal*. A similar trend prevailed in West Germany, delayed until the 1960s by post-war poverty and devastation. After the deprivations of defeat, West German women considered returning to unpaid household duties a luxury.

East Germany could afford no such return to domesticity. Unlike capitalist economies, which produced an abundance of consumer goods in the postwar boom, clothing, appliances, cleaning products, and household furnishings remained scarce in the new German Democratic Republic; there was no need to market them to avid housewives. In contrast to the Marshall Plan which channeled cash and humanitarian assistance into the West, the East had to cope with Russian occupation forces, who dismantled factories, railroads, and military installations and carried them off to the Soviet Union. Beyond the natural desire for revenge, the Soviet Union, with over six million war dead, had suffered more than the three Allies who ruled the West. Manpower as well as material goods were in critically short supply in both Germany and Russia. German soldiers imprisoned in Russia were not released until the mid-fifties.

Through the 1950s, a higher ratio of working-age women to men (124 to one hundred) prevailed in the East than in the West. Furthermore, the process of de-Nazification was carried out far more rigorously in the East than in the West; anyone with ties to the Nazi Party, even highly-trained essential workers, was sacked. The ensuing vacancies opened some new opportunities for women in positions such as school principals or village mayors. The collectivization of agriculture in the early fifties and the confiscation of real estate motivated many property owners (most of them men) to leave. Migration to the West before construction of the Berlin Wall reduced the country's population by 6.5% during the 1950s. Westward emigrants were chiefly well educated males whose loss harmed the fledgling socialist state. By 1960 the gender balance had been largely restored in the West (104 women per hundred men) but remained skewed in the East (112 women per hundred men). This emigration caused both a labor shortage and a population deficit, which could only be remedied by increasing women's participation in both production and reproduction.

The Socialist Unity Party recognized early on that special conditions would be necessary to keep women both producing and reproducing. A 1950 "Law for the Protection of Mothers and Children and the Rights of Women" established the mother as the center of the family, giving legal and financial assistance to single mothers, guaranteeing women job protection during pregnancy and offering incentives for large families. The law confirmed women's right to full employment, following the Marxist-Leninist tenet that women's liberation would occur only with their full participation in the workforce. The women's department within the Socialist Unity Party's Central Committee (headed by Inge Lange) attempted to reconcile motherhood rather than parenthood with employment, and discouraged women's demands for part-time work. Moreover, the new ideal of a fully employed woman was depicted as a rejection of the Nazis' ideal of motherhood. Beginning in 1952 women's committees formed inside labor unions and collective farms to discuss women's concerns and make recommendations to management about women's working conditions. By 1988 over five million women belonged to labor unions and comprised 53% of their membership.

Provisions incorporated into the civil code in 1965 specified that both parents should share in household labor and child-rearing. Relations between marriage partners were to be arranged so that women could combine their occupation with motherhood (Kuhrig, 235). A constitutional revision in 1980 made it clear that it was women's duty as well as their choice to work outside the home.

By the end of the 1980s, 78.1% of all East German women of working age were employed. Including students and apprentices, the proportion of women who worked reached 91.2%, and 87% of them had completed professional training. Twenty-seven per cent of working women were employed part-time, but 60% of part-timers worked twenty-five to thirty-two hours per week. Beyond the official policies of the Socialist Unity Party which encouraged women to seek employment, large numbers of war widows and divorced women had no other choice but to work. By 1989, 48.8% of the country's workers were women.

As it integrated women into the workforce, East Germany trained some of them for non-traditional occupations. In heavy industry or construction, women were trained as crane drivers or operators of threshing combines, giving them a visible part in the work which did not require great physical strength. A children's poem glorifying a woman crane driver demonstrates the state's attempt to surround such women with a positive image:

Die Kranführerin

In unserer Straße, sag' ich euch,
Da wird ein Haus gebaut.
Ihr glaubt es nicht, wie schnell das geht,
Ich habe zugeschaut!

Ein großer Kran schwenkt seine Last,
Befördert Block für Block.
Jetzt bringt er schon die nächste Wand
Hinauf zum fünften Stock.

Und wißt ihr, wer den Kran dort fährt?
Das ist ja eine Frau!
Sie hat ein rotes Kopftuch um,
Ich seh' es ganz genau!

(In our street, I'm telling you, there's a house being built.   You wouldn't believe how fast it goes–I've been watching. A big crane lifts up its cargo, carrying up block after block. Now it's bringing the next wall up to the sixth floor. Do you know who's driving the crane there? It's a woman! She's wearing a red kerchief, I can see it plainly.)

The German Democratic Republic encouraged women to study chemistry, physics, and engineering. Where large numbers of women entered an occupation, wages decreased, and after unification women in these non-traditional fields were hard hit by unemployment. One chemist who completed her doctorate at Leipzig's Karl Marx University just after the fall of the Berlin Wall, recalled that there were sixty-three students in her class, half women, half men. In physics there were fewer women, perhaps three out of ten. Today she knows many women chemists who can not find a job. Applications from women in chemistry are considered second class, she says. In the German Democratic Republic, that was absolutely not the case; many already signed an employment contract before finishing their studies.

Such efforts (which we call propaganda in a system we oppose, and public relations campaigns in a system we agree with) produced only modest results. In 1970 just 13.3% of construction workers were women, and by 1989 that figure had only risen to 17.2%. Nonetheless, four to five times as many women worked in such non-traditional trades in the East as was the case in West Germany. Ironically, as the Socialist Unity Party improved benefits for working mothers, employers increasingly preferred hiring men who would not lay claim to maternity leave or leave to care for sick children. As a result, girls were more frequently steered into traditional women's occupations in the late eighties, and the percentage of female apprentices in male trades declined. Between 1980 and 1989 the proportion of female apprentices in media, control, and regulatory technology declined from 23% to 12%, in electronics from 50% to 20%, and in the machinist trade from 45% to 31% (Braun, Jasper, and Schröter, 197). After unification, the employment of women in such sectors declined even further. East German agriculture and forestry, where the workforce was 45.8% female in 1970, experienced a decline to 37.4% in 1989 (*Frauenreport '90*, 66). Gradually mechanization replaced unskilled laborers; 60% of them were women (Braun, Jasper, and Schröter, 196).

Nevertheless, the majority of East German women worked in stereotypically female professions such as childcare, textiles and clothing manufacture, and clerical jobs; 92% of the workforce in social services was female, 83% in health services, 82% in chemical production, 72% in commerce, 71% in data processing, and 69% in postal jobs and telecommunications. To promote the hiring of women in postal services, a weight limit of ten kilograms (twenty-two pounds) was placed on packages so that women could lift them. In 1987, 60% of those finishing their schooling entered just sixteen of the 259 non-college occupations available. Teaching, where women comprised 77% of the workforce, nursing, and paramedical training were the most popular occupations requiring post-secondary education.

Between twenty-five and thirty of the country's nearly three hundred occupations were closed to or "not recommended" for women in protective legislation passed in 1973 (*Frauenreport '90*, 239). Besides excavation and high-rise construction, these included underground mining, working with gases or high pressure, or in places where women would be exposed to radiation, dust, infection, or required to lift or carry heavy loads. Skepticism is in order here. The risk of infection did not preclude women from becoming nurses or doctors. Women in agriculture, nursing, and those who worked with disabled children regularly lifted heavy burdens. Despite the occupations closed to women, they were more frequently exposed than men to health risks such as noise, heat, dust, and chemicals, particularly in chemical production, glass and ceramics industries, and in forestry and agriculture (*Frauenreport '90*, 72). Overall, prohibitions against women's employment in certain occupations usually protect them from higher pay, not from health risks.

In the white-collar professions women made some significant inroads. East German women held lower and mid-level management positions in sectors with many women employees such as commerce, services, light industry, the postal service and communications, and the lower echelons of the court system, all sectors where at least half the managers were women. In agriculture and forestry, one-fifth of managers were women, and in state-owned enterprises, where public policy could make the greatest impact, 31.5% of managers were women, an enviable record (*Frauenreport '90*, 94-95). Undoubtedly their presence made it easier to accommodate the needs of working mothers and to protect women from unfair treatment or harassment. Half of all judges were women, (as compared to 18% in the West) and their decisions affected custody suits and other matters concerning women. Nine per cent of East German university professors (albeit concentrated at the lower levels) were women, serving as role models for students.

Frauenförderpläne, affirmative action plans to promote women in industrial production, education, management, and commerce, set specific quotas for the employment of women in key areas, often granting them paid time off from work to re-train. According to most accounts, the system worked. Several women explained in their interviews that they owed their access to education, vocational training, or a better job to a manager's need to fill the quota set by these plans.

The wage gap persisted in East Germany, although to a lesser extent than in the West; it is difficult to find comparable statistics. Among East German women aged fifteen to twenty-five in 1988, 60% earned less than seven hundred marks per month. Among males with similar levels of training, only 27% earned less than that amount. West German statistics describe the opposite end of the wage spectrum: only 4% of women aged thirty to thirty-four earned over four thousand DM per month, while 22% of men in the same age bracket earned that much. Most East German women worked in the pink-collar ghetto where wages remained lower. Construction workers, for example, earned an average of 1,135 marks per month net in 1989, while workers in postal service and communications earned an average of 1,040 marks (*Frauenreport '90*, 87). To discourage class stratification, managers earned less than double the pay of their skilled workers; thus women's advancement in white-collar professions did not necessarily bring them higher earnings. Their lower wages were attributed to the fact that women worked only one-third as many overtime hours as men, were exempt from or seldom chose shifts for which a wage differential was paid, and were excluded "for health reasons" from some highly paid positions in high-rise construction and excavation.

Nevertheless, East German women had come closer to equal pay than either West German or American women. They earned about 83% of a man's average monthly pay, as compared to only two-thirds as much in the West, and around three-fourths of a man's salary in the United States. Overall, women whom I interviewed stressed equality and asserted that they had been paid fairly in comparison to men.

Women with two or more children received full-time pay for working a reduced week: forty hours instead of the standard forty-three and one-half hours, which prevailed since 1968. In addition they could make flex-time arrangements with their employers to accommodate family needs. Mothers received twenty-six weeks maternity leave at full pay (six weeks before and twenty weeks after birth), and a leave of up to one year (the baby year) for a first child or eighteen months for a second (or any subsequent child) paid at 90% of their net pay. Nursing mothers could claim two forty-five minute pauses a day to nurse their infants, who were usually cared for close to the workplace. Pregnant and nursing mothers were protected from nighttime or shift work, or from hazardous materials. Neither they nor women on maternity leave (including the baby year) could be fired. Those on maternity leave or the baby year could reclaim their previous job upon returning to work.

A basic leave of four to five work weeks was granted to care for sick children, depending on their number (*Frauenreport '90*, 80-81). Because sick leave, part-time work at full pay, and the monthly housework day were not available to fathers until 1986, the burden of household chores fell almost entirely on women, whose employers were obliged to accommodate their needs. While the leave time used by twenty- to thirty-year-old women did not, in fact surpass that claimed by older women or men, some employers viewed mothers of young children as an economic risk and made excuses not to hire them. Paradoxically the initiatives aimed at facilitating the employment of young mothers ultimately worked to their detriment, even though younger women tended to be better qualified than older workers (Braun, Jasper, and Schröter, 195).

The German Democratic Republic attempted to meet Engels' second condition for the emancipation of women: the transformation of household labor to a public industry. Care of infants and children took place in publicly funded institutions. Routine medical care was provided at workplaces or childcare facilities. Cooking and serving at least the main meal of the day was done in factories, cafeterias, and schools. Large-scale laundries washed clothing and linens. However, shortfalls in the production of clothing and preserved foods forced women to perform these chores—which should have been done by public industries—at home.

Beyond their full work week, East German women reported spending as much as forty hours per week on housework, a figure which remained constant for twenty-five years (Nickel 1993, 148). This time allotment seems inconceivable, but women insist it was accurate. To understand how a woman could devote forty hours a week to housekeeping, we must imagine family care in a socialist economy: carrying bed sheets by streetcar to the nearest large-scale laundry or retrieving them clean three weeks later, standing in line to buy whatever could be had, gardening and canning or preserving food, knitting, sewing, altering or repairing clothing, bartering for spare parts or building materials, or arranging for repairs of household goods. Despite this monumental investment of time and energy, the economic value of childcare and housework received only token recognition. The norm for defining work remained the male pattern of wage earning labor. Working women with a child or elder relative to care for, and women over forty received one day off per month, the *Haushaltstag*, for the purpose of doing household chores. The introduction of domestic appliances failed to relieve women of their household burdens; instead expectations for personal hygiene increased. Furthermore, draperies, upholstery, and clothing of higher quality required more time-consuming care. In addition, the high prices for clothing (which consumed about 10% of a family's monthly budget) meant that women often sewed or knitted children's garments, an unpaid contribution commonly regarded as a hobby or leisure pastime. The result, in East German parlance, was the *doppelte Last,* or *zweite Schicht,* (the double burden or second shift) for working women.

To a lesser extent, men's lives were also affected by scarce consumer goods as their time was taken up with repairs in the apartment or work in the garden or repairing the family car or bicycles, provided the family had such things. Men found more time for sports, social and political activity, and for furthering their education (*Frauenreport '90*, 130-36).

Critics have pointed out that the socialist state substituted its public patriarchy for the private patriarchal system prevalent in capitalist economies. Instead of pressuring fathers to assume equally the burdens of housework and childcare, "father state" took over daycare responsibilities, freed women from some cooking chores by providing hot meals in schools and workplaces, and placated women with the Haushaltstag, separate women's lounges in factories, and the celebration of International Women's Day on March eighth. No attempt was made to change the traditional female-male division of household labor. Men were most likely to help with shopping, washing dishes, or playing with children, helping them with sports or homework, but their estimate of what they contributed to household responsibilities surpassed the amount of work their wives attributed to them (*Frauenreport '90*, 128-129). Young women complained that progress made toward a fairer division of household labor regressed during the baby year as fathers simply took it for granted that mothers should carry the household burdens because they were at home (Kuhrig, 235). In fact shortages of consumer goods, which fell outside the framework of the planned economy and were compensated by individual unpaid labor, actually preserved the traditional female/male division of labor as women assumed responsibility for sewing, knitting, and canning food while men cobbled together house and vehicle repairs.

Barbara Teuber, who works at East Berlin's *Volkshochschule* in adult education, described a typical working woman's existence in the German Democratic Republic. After teaching German for ten years, she became a literature researcher at a museum in Frankfurt an der Oder, a mid-sized city on the Polish border. She lived there for twenty years before moving to Berlin in 1985 to work at the German-Soviet Friendship House. There she organized literary lectures and theater programs during the exciting Gorbachev era. She transferred to the state-owned publishing house *Volk und Welt*, wrote its history, and worked in its archives until the political turnaround occurred. She says that the socialist state promoted the arts as a showpiece of community; while the arts were supposed to glorify socialist conditions, they actually became very critical of the regime. The state sought something different from what ultimately resulted.

She agrees that women performed 80% of the housework in the German Democratic Republic, the same proportion as in the West, although West German women are far less likely to work outside the home. At least today services have improved. In the old days, she says, you had to plead with a cobbler to repair shoes; there was no incentive for him to work quickly. Today it's easier to take care of chores like getting the laundry done. Back then there were few fresh vegetables and few canned goods; you had to stand in line a long time to buy asparagus or strawberries. She waited in line for an hour to get strawberries and read to pass the time, but when she reached the head of the line the strawberries had sold out so she had nothing to take home to her children. Children wanted jeans made of cotton denim, not synthetic fabric, and mothers went to great lengths to get such things. Women's time was taken up with running around, standing in line, buying. The stores were full of cheap goods that nobody wanted.

Her first husband left the country in 1987 through trickery and became a West German citizen. She cites the second shift and men's resistance to change as one of the factors in the country's divorce rate, one of the highest in the world. She says women earned as much as men and were not willing to carry a man who took no part in housework. With respect to household chores she thinks women's equality in the German Democratic Republic was a fiction enshrined in law. Women in the workforce were irreplaceable. But it wasn't always pleasant to march off to the factory at the crack of dawn. Women had to work because men earned so little; two incomes were necessary to pay the cost of living.

Frau Teuber describes how East German women worked in collectives or teams. While working at a monotonous assembly line they could discuss their children or personal problems with co-workers; that's why single and divorced women didn't miss a partner so much. Today women don't share such common experiences, so they feel more need of a partner. For financial reasons as well, since the cost of living has risen, young women realize that if they can't find work they'll have to get married.

A study of the country's only women's magazine, *Für Dich* (published by the Central Committee's propaganda wing) found that housework largely disappeared from photographs of women (Dölling, 170-72). Most photos showed women working on assembly lines or in groups, demonstrating the value of their productive labor without portraying them as individuals. In contrast, where women did appear in positions of power, photos emphasized their attractiveness, complemented by stylish clothing and cosmetics, thus underscoring their womanliness. Most female workers performed traditional women's jobs and were shown working under the direction of men, not with them.

The burden of combining paid labor with motherhood and housework took a toll on women's health. While women's life expectancy surpassed that of men, and rose to an average of seventy-six years in 1987, these gains resulted chiefly from lower infant mortality and the decline of such infectious diseases as tuberculosis. Women suffered from several non-fatal health problems: sleep deficit, poor diet, and lack of physical exercise. East Germany never attained the level of consumption conspicuous in America, where less has become more: smoking less or eating less meat, for example, have become marks of status. In East Germany smoking was ubiquitous because the air quality was poor, particularly in winter when coal smoke as well as diesel exhaust fouled the air. Although only 18% of women (as compared to 41% of men) smoked, girls took up the habit as a symbol of their emancipation (*Frauenreport '90*, 154, 156). Meat products, usually fatty, heavily salted cold cuts, and cheeses were fairly easy to buy, while fresh fruits and vegetables could be found only in season, and only at the head of a long queue. Women often bought large quantities of farm produce when they could get it, and canned it for winter consumption, because frozen or preserved foods were scarce or of poor quality. Their diets included too much fat and too little fiber, although obesity was never as visible as it has become in the US. Very few women engaged in sports or structured physical exercise; neither workout rooms, sports clothing, nor exercise machines figured in the country's five-year economic plans. On the national level, trained athletes' success in Olympic sports received far more support and attention than fitness for the masses. Women preferred leisure activities that included their families, and these were often sedentary (*Frauenreport '90*, 155-58).

To learn more about the health of working women, I arranged to meet Dr. Christa Anders, a retired physician who now manages the Society for the Protection of Civil Rights and Human Dignity in Berlin. I was also curious about her own biography, and about the careers of East German women in medicine.

Dr. Anders was a tall, big-boned woman with a fondness for silver jewelry. She greeted me with a firm handshake which left no doubt that she could direct a clinic. Born in Leipzig in 1930, she decided relatively late to become a doctor. Growing up in wartime, she thought first of becoming a nurse. At the age of twenty she was working in a shoe factory and joined a youth club, a precursor of the FDJ. She studied Russian for three years in Halle at an *Arbeiter- und Bauernfakultät*, a postwar institute for adult education, and she joined the Socialist Unity Party. Because of her knowledge of Russian, and the significance of Party membership, she was chosen to study for six years at a medical institute in Leningrad (now St. Petersburg). Conditions were hard at first. A half-dozen students shared a room. Food was scant, but at least adequate. She took a three-month preparatory course in Russian, but found she still needed to translate texts laboriously for the first six months. Afterwards she could speak fluently. She met other students from Czechoslovakia, Bulgaria, and China, the largest group, and she emphasizes that the Russians treated them well, despite the carnage of the Second World War.

She finished her studies in 1960, interrupted briefly by marriage and the birth of her son. When she began to practice at Berlin's hospital, La Charité, she found that German medical students might have learned more theory and technique, but she had received excellent practical training in Russia, and gained more clinical experience. As she began her career, her country had only about 14,555 doctors, 70% of them women (Lützenkirchen, 73). The number of doctors per thousand inhabitants about tripled over the next thirty years.

Dr. Anders took her two children to a weekly daycare center in the hospital where she worked; she dropped them off on Monday morning and picked them up on Saturday afternoon. Because the center was at her workplace, she could stop in anytime to see them. After her divorce she had to give up working nights and weekends. It would have been unthinkable, she says, to stay at home with children, after her long medical training.

Technicians and industrial engineers earned more than doctors, probably because those professions were more predominantly male. The pay differential between doctors and nurses was far smaller than it is in capitalist economies; in the early sixties doctors earned about seven hundred marks, and by the late eighties 1,200 to 1,400 marks as compared to six or seven hundred marks for nurses. Male nurses were scarce; a few men trained as medics worked transporting patients.

Paying doctors a fixed salary meant that they had no incentive to recommend unnecessary treatments, as may happen in capitalist for-profit medical practices. Nor was there any need to curtail expensive medical procedures, as happens in the US within some health maintenance organizations. The choice of care depended solely on what was best for the patient, and what was available.

At first Dr. Anders worked in the cancer clinic at La Charité, a rather depressing job because the cancers were often diagnosed late and could not be cured. La Charité treated patients referred from clinics all over the country. Critical cases were handled at once, but there was a waiting period for routine operations, due to the shortage of doctors. Later she transferred to a general surgical practice in Friedrichshain. She says until the Wall was built West Berliners came there for treatment because they didn't need to pay.

Dr. Anders loved mathematics and collected medical statistics at La Charité in the days before computers. The German Democratic Republic created a cancer atlas to analyze cancer causes. Dr. Anders says Mecklenburg-Vorpommern had the highest rates, probably because of ground water pollution from the huge collective farms. Working with lead batteries was another recognized cause of cancer.

Health clinics were located at large factories, collective farms, or educational institutions, so that workers did not have to go far to receive medical care. In addition, these polyclinics were responsible for monitoring safety and working conditions in the workplace. Nearby residents could use these facilities as well; there were no firm rules. These facilities also tracked workers' health, and Dr. Anders recognizes that sometimes the medical system was abused. In construction, for instance, workers might get themselves certified sick because there was nothing to do at the building site. Workers in boring factory jobs might also feign sickness. Medical leave was paid at 90% of normal wages for up to six weeks.

The GDR led the world in consumption of beer and alcohol (*Frauenreport '90*, 155). In 1970 there were 515 deaths from alcoholism in Berlin, 370 men, the rest women. Alcoholism was a greater problem in rural areas, because of boredom, isolation, and the lack of leisure pursuits. Dr. Anders says that while doctors understood alcoholism as a disease, the general populace did not, and the problem was swept under the rug, like suicide. By the late eighties, people began to discuss these social problems more openly.

Between 1985 and 1990 Dr. Anders directed a rehabilitation facility for the mentally and physically handicapped in Köpenick. While social workers treated children, there was a shortage of trained people dedicated to caring for the most challenging cases. Often dissidents worked in such positions, because little specialized training was required, and their help was needed so badly that work documents were not always demanded. She admits that the facilities for the handicapped were better equipped in the West. In the East they offered disabled people handicrafts and as much instruction as practical.

In 1990 Dr. Anders was sixty years old and she was sent home. To open a private practice would have required a loan, and she felt she was too old to make the transition. She knows other doctors who have done so, but the pressure of coping with debt and practicing medicine nowadays destroys the professional satisfaction of working in health care. After a year of discontent at home, she became manager of the Society for the Protection of Civil Rights and Human Dignity.

Overall, Dr. Anders believes health care in the GDR was very good. She cites the low infant mortality rate, and notes that all children were routinely vaccinated against diseases such as polio, whooping cough, tetanus, and diphtheria. People carried vaccination certificates with them at all times. Preventive care was strongly emphasized. Experimental measures were tried to improve workers' health. Some factories instituted pauses for physical exercise, and some experimented with brief catnaps, which greatly improved workers' productivity. After all, the state had a vested interest in maintaining the health of its workers. Medical technology was augmented by purchases of special equipment from the West. Still the system suffered from certain inefficiencies. While easy access to polyclinics near the workplace or workers' homes made it easy to receive routine care, the system was somewhat redundant and made it difficult to track those who might be abusing it.

Some critics assert that the health care system was autocratic and dictatorial, for example in requiring infant vaccinations and well-baby weighings. Alternative treatments such as homeopathy were not available, and medical information about disabilities such as autism was difficult to obtain (Schäfer, 131). However, even critics agree that everyone could receive adequate care; paying for hospital treatment or prescription medicines was never an issue. Furthermore, the socialist system eliminated competition for patients, so that doctors cooperated willingly. Dr. Anders points out that health clinics made good use of expensive medical equipment, which doctors in private practice can ill afford.

We speak briefly about prostitution, which has become more visible in East Berlin than it was before unification. One person tells me that Linienstraße, where I am staying, was the old red light district. Another cites the Oranienburgerstraße or the area beside Monbijou Park. Another points out a tunnel beneath the street near one of the city's old Interhotels, formerly reserved for tourists from capitalist countries. She says that men used to wait there and lure women into prostitution by offering them lingerie or expensive consumer goods from the West. Dr. Anders agrees that prostitution did exist in the GDR and was tolerated despite being technically illegal; it drew in western tourists and hard currency. However, in contrast to today, prostitutes were not desperate for survival, nor were they addicted to drugs. Rather working women used prostitution to augment their incomes or obtain hard currency for luxury goods or to finance travel to the West. And she points out that prostitutes too were required to undergo regular health examinations.

The unification of East and West Germany fused the European country with the highest rate of women's paid employment with the country holding the record for the lowest rate of women's employment. In 1989, 91% of all East German women worked outside their homes, compared to 54% in the West. Of those who were employed, 27% in East Germany worked part-time, but 74% of West Germany's working women held only a part-time job. In contrast to the German Democratic Republic's early legislation establishing women's right to equal work and equal pay, West German law in effect from 1957 to 1977 tied a woman's employment to the consent of her husband, establishing the *Hausfrauenehe* as the ideal; a married woman was permitted to work outside the home only if her husband agreed and only if her employment did not alter household responsibilities. In cases of economic hardship, she was expected to work, but he was not required to help with the housework.

Today most West German working women follow the three phase model: education or vocational training and gaining some work experience is followed by childbirth and several years at home, then a return to work, often part time or in a less skilled position. A West German artist from Saarbrücken described the situation of two of her friends, both with a Ph. D. After the birth of their child, the husband continued his university teaching, while his wife could only find work as a secretary. The status of the husband as provider and the wife as secondary earner is reflected in tax law, which provides credits to a man whose wife stays at home, but not to a working woman with a house husband.

Conflict between the two systems was inevitable, and women were destined to become the victims. In mid 1991 the numbers of unemployed in the new federal states surpassed the one million mark. Aside from seasonal fluctuations, these numbers have not yet begun to decline. As late as 1998 more jobs were being eliminated than created in the East. Compared to the country's 9.7 million people working in 1989, there were only 6.4 million working in 1998; the workforce shrank by one-third in a decade. At the end of the twentieth century, Germany's unemployed numbered 4,047,000, about 1,335,000 of them in the East. The unemployment rate of 9.6% in the West is around half the 18.8% rate in East (*Sozialreport 1999*, 156).

Make-work programs called *Arbeitsbeschaffungsmaßnahmen* or ABM jobs were created soon after unification and increased briefly during Helmut Kohl's re-election campaign in 1998. Women's participation in such ABM programs is lower than what is warranted by their portion among the unemployed. These jobs typically last for a year or two, and then force their employees back out onto the job market. Nevertheless, they provide income and often the opportunity to learn new skills.

In the early nineties it was assumed that East German women would enjoy becoming full-time housewives, because they had never before had the opportunity to do so. ABM jobs were intended to bridge the gap while women made the transition from the labor market to unpaid household labor. In fact more recent studies emphasize their undiminished demand for paying work (sociologists labeled it "ununterbrochene Erwerbsneigung"); while a quarter of West German women are content to identify themselves as Hausfrau, only about 5% of East German women are willing to do so (Schröter 2000, 22).

The overall effect of a decade of unification has been to draw East German women's employment down toward West German levels, rather than to raise the rate of women's participation in the paid labor force in the West. Today only 73% of East German women work, and even fewer (59%) in the West (Versieux, 20). The impact of women's unemployment on a family's well-being differs sharply from East to West; while women's income made up 40% of the household budget in the East, it constituted only 18% in the West (*Stiefschwestern*, 103).

Women's unemployment is around 27% in the new federal states; however it is difficult to give accurate figures because many women work in ABM jobs, or in those paying 630 DM per month or less, which have only recently carried social insurance and been counted in statistics. Of the women working in East Germany a decade after unification, 57% had been unemployed at least once, a third of them for a year or more. Only about a third were still doing the same kind of work as they had performed before unification; women are far more likely than men to work beneath their educational qualifications, work part-time, or hold only a temporary job (*Sozialreport 1999*, 150). Women over forty-five when the Wall opened were considered not worth retraining and pushed into early retirement, where they disappear from the unemployment statistics; most will never work again. While East German women retired at sixty, those who were pushed into retirement prematurely now receive pensions based on lower lifetime earnings, an income deficit from which they will never recover.

The lack of opportunity for young people presents an even greater threat to social stability. In fall 1999, 140,000 young people were unable to find apprenticeships. Many equip themselves with both the high school diploma (*Abitur*) and apprenticeship training to maximize their employment chances. However, the lack of openings in the blue collar trades decreases their motivation to succeed in school and further dims their future prospects. Gender segregation is also on the increase in apprenticeships: 40% of those in the East were limited to male applicants in the mid-nineties, while only 30% were open to either gender (Braun, Jasper, and Schröter, 206). A 1995 survey revealed that 43.4% of young men, but fewer than one-tenth of young women in apprenticeships were satisfied with those positions and their future prospects (*Sozialreport 1995*, 161). Many older East Germans I spoke to deplored the rowdy youth who frighten them on the streets. I saw such groups in Dresden and Berlin, distinguished by their leather jackets and boots, boys with shaved heads and girls whose spiky hair had been dyed improbable shades of orange or purple. While their presence is not as dominant as in America's large cities, they do appear idle, disaffected, and prone to get into trouble.

Why have women been hardest hit by unemployment? First, they have become *Rationalisierungsopfer,* a neologism meaning they are victims of job losses due to better technology, consolidation, and other improvements. Women comprised a fourth of the workforce in the iron and steel industry and 82% in chemical production, where factories have been closed by West German environmental standards. Concern for the environment closed open bituminous coal mines, nuclear power plants (built on the Chernobyl model) and chemical factories in Bluna and Leuna. ABM jobs have employed some workers displaced from these sectors, but many of these positions involve heavy manual labor in environmental cleanup operations, and thus they go to men rather than women. In data processing, postal and communications services, and transportation, computerization has cost many women their jobs.

These losses become understandable when we consider the backward state of technology in the German Democratic Republic. At the seminar I attended in Erfurt in 1985, participants wanted to exchange addresses by distributing a list with our names and addresses. The Dr. Theodor Neubauer College of Education, we were told, had no photocopier, not even a mimeograph machine. That summer teachers were debating whether pocket calculators, which had just appeared on the market, should be introduced in high school mathematics classes. And when I applied for permission to visit Dresden for a weekend, I had to reserve a hotel room in advance (one way the Stasi kept track of foreign visitors). To do so, I went to the state-owned travel agency in Erfurt and filled out a form requesting a room in one of Dresden's Interhotels, reserved for foreign tourists. I had to return two weeks later, stand in line once again, and retrieve a post card confirming my reservation. Nothing could be accomplished by telephone. But I did try (unsuccessfully) to telephone family in the United States. At the city post and telephone office I waited in line at a ticket window, paid money and gave the number I wished to call, then sat and waited for an hour or two while my call failed to go through. Clerical workers at the College, the travel agency, and the post office were all women; today most of their work is done by telephones, computers, e-mail, and fax machines. The technological revolution which took place between 1980 and 1990 in the West occurred in the East within the first six months following unification in 1990.

This technological revolution leaves women further behind. While East Germans historically lagged behind the West, girls lag behind boys in computer skills developed through leisure activities, and in school training. Women become the users, men the developers of new technology (Bauermann, 17). New initiatives, some sponsored by women's centers and others arising from the SPD's Frau und Beruf program, attempt to help women catch up.

The transition from industrial production to a service economy, which occurred over thirty years in the West, took place in a decade in the East. In 1989 45% of East Germany's workforce worked in production, and the same percentage in services. By 1998 production had shrunk to a third of the workforce, while services grew to 63.2% (*Sozialreport 1999*, 137). Many of these new service jobs went to westerners, who had more experience in capitalistic forms of such businesses as banking, travel, advertising, and insurance. As manufacturing plants closed, their daycare centers and polyclinics shut down as well, and women working in these services joined the swelling ranks of the unemployed. Two-thirds of all East German jobs in agriculture and forestry disappeared. As men who once worked in production, forestry, or agriculture seek new jobs, their presence exerts pressure against women in previously female occupations. Men who lost jobs in the army, police, and state security units have replaced women as bank tellers and ticket agents, postal clerks and retail salespeople.

With unification, East Germany became part of the European Union. Thus cheaper imported manufactured goods, particularly small appliances and clothing, flood East German markets and have driven outdated, unprofitable factories out of production. Agriculture, which will be considered in a later chapter, was decimated by foreign competition and new European Union regulations.

Other professions have disappeared, or require complete rethinking of their practitioners.One young woman I met, for example, had trained as an *Orthoptistin*. She treated patients whose eyes were crossed or had difficulty focusing. West German techniques cure such problems with surgery. Psychologists who practiced group therapy aimed at returning the individual to responsible function within a group in the East have had to learn new techniques of individual psychoanalysis. Forty thousand teachers, about a fourth of the total number, lost their jobs within three years of unification. Most women teachers specialized in traditional female fields such as humanities and the social sciences, now considered tainted by Marxist-Leninist overtones.

Another factor in the high unemployment among East German women is that their chances of finding a new job are only one-fourth as good as those of their male co-workers, partly because new West German employers have brought their own hiring policies with them and view women with children as a heavy liability, a problem to be examined in greater detail in the next chapter. Stated briefly, it is more costly for an employer to hire women because those who become pregnant can now leave their jobs for up to three years while being partially compensated, and while their jobs are held open awaiting their return. The provision for leave with sick children is also often cited in interviews as a reason employers are reluctant to hire women. A 1991 census of women aged twenty-five through twenty-nine found that 80% of those in the East, but only 50% of those in the West had children (Cromm, 50-51). It's easy to guess which workers managers are more eager to hire.

Although the actual number of working women in West Germany has increased, most growth has occurred in part-time work; over the past twenty years, the number of part-time jobs has doubled, and 95% of these have been filled by women. The desire for part-time work in the East has increased slightly since unification because of cutbacks in daycare: 40% of married women with children under six would like part-time work, but the need to work full-time remains high among single mothers who depend on their own paycheck to support their children. In times of high unemployment, German public policy seems to drive women from the workplace, discouraging their competition with men. They are pushed into the reserve labor force (*die stille Reserve*) where some work in jobs paying 630 DM per month or less. Women comprise three-fourths of these 5.6 million employees, working, for example, as telemarketers, domestics, nannies, waitresses, or janitors. Employers favored these positions because they were not obliged to pay into the social security system for such workers. Of course the lack of contributions to their old age pensions will place these women at a disadvantage when they retire. As of April 1, 1999, even these positions require social security payments, and as a result employers have begun to eliminate them, throwing more women out of work.

Germany's affirmative action laws, mandated by constitutional amendment in late 1994, have no real teeth. Baden-Württemberg, Bavaria, and Thüringen have no affirmative action quotas for women in the civil service. Some states, such as Hesse, set a percentage of female employees as a target for certain offices, leaving it to department heads to decide how to attain the goal; this policy produced a miniscule increase of 0.4% women in Hesse's civil service in one year. In West Germany's institutions of government, women account for only 7% of administrators. They fare somewhat better in the East, where 11.2% of top government administrators and 13.4% in other administrative positions are women (Hosken, 72). However, rulings by the court of the European Union call into question the efficacy of affirmative action plans. In 1991 a man named Kalunke was passed over for the directorship of Bremen's landscaping office in favor of a woman with similar qualifications. The court ruled against Bremen's affirmative action policy, because it violates the principle of equal opportunity. A similar ruling in the fall of 1997 increased the likelihood that quotas for hiring women would be found in conflict with European Union regulations.

On the other hand, the European Union's court ruled in January 2000 that Germany's army must admit women; some 4,500 presently serve as nurses or musicians. (A few women did serve in the GDR's National People's Army as medics and technicians). A twenty-two-year-old woman from Hannover, Tanja Kreil, who was trained as an electrician, applied to the *Bundeswehr* as a weapons technician and appealed her rejection. By April nine hundred women from East Germany and Berlin had applied to the army, a choice with increased appeal in times of high unemployment. These women are less likely than West German women to feel intimidated by entering high-tech fields or male dominated occupations. The ensuing debate raises numerous questions; while women can now volunteer for the army, they are not required to serve, as men are. Problems of sexual harassment and the specter of women being raped in wartime will certainly become topics for discussion.

While the regulations governing equality in the civil service appear weak, there are even fewer teeth in laws governing private employers. Employers may state in advertising whether they seek male or female applicants, and age discrimination is not illegal. Applicants who can prove they were not hired because of their gender are entitled to compensation for the time and expense of applying for a job, but have no claim to the job itself, nor to punitive damages. Class action lawsuits have no precedent in German law.

Unification has further widened the gap between men's and women's earnings. While West German men (taking an average of both wage and salary earners) out-earned women by 900 DM per month in 1980, by 1994 men's earnings in united Germany were 1,600 DM higher than those of women. Comparisons of monthly incomes do not tell the whole story; we must also compare the numbers of women working at the various pay levels. In 1994 for example, about 31% of males earned over 4,000 DM per month net; only 3.2% of women earned that much. Overall, East Germans earn about three-fourths as much as workers in comparable occupations in the West (*Sozialreport 1999*, 177). East German women earn about three-fourths as much as East German men (down from 83% before unification) yet still come closer to equal pay than West German women. Women white-collar workers earn about 2,300 DM per month less than men, reflecting the fact that they seldom advance to the upper echelons of management.

A survey of Germany's 70,000 largest companies showed that only 6.3% of executives are women. Another source reports that only 0.7% of united Germany's 13.2 million working women occupy leadership positions (Hosken, 71). About 98.5% of managers, directors, or chiefs of staff are men, although 70% of the office workers or sales force they supervise is female. The SPD publication *Frau und Beruf* states that 6% of upper level managers are women.

The scarcity of women in decision-making and supervisory roles plays a role in other issues besides figuring how women's and men's earnings compare. It reduces the chances that working women will find role models for climbing the professional ladder. It reinforces a corporate ethic not attuned to the needs of mothers; indeed many women in the top echelons of West German management decide to relinquish the desire to have children. Women at the top may suffer from professional isolation, increasing the fear that becoming respected means sacrificing being liked.

Germany has no particular legal guarantees of equal pay for equal work. In August 1995 the constitutional court in Kassel rejected an equal pay lawsuit by ten women who worked at packing machines where men were also employed. The men's right to earn 500 DM more per month was upheld on grounds they could be called upon to do heavier physical work. Here again the fact that class action lawsuits are not legal in Germany denies women an important means of redressing such inequities in the courts.

The gender gap in income continues into unemployment because compensation there is also based on earnings; unemployed workers receive a maximum of 67% of their net earnings for one year, with longer-term payments of unemployment assistance amounting to a maximum of 57% of next pay, depending on total family income. The same gender gap extends into retirement, because pensions are also based on income.

Barbara Teuber is pessimistic about the possibility of reversing any of these setbacks through political activity. She joined the Social Democratic Party in 1990 and became a city councilor for the district of Prenzlauer Berg in East Berlin. She worked for the Party in the office of culture and education and was re-elected in 1992. Then the SPD lost ground in the next election, and she lost out to the Party's more conservative wing. Today, she says, women have withdrawn from politics. In the old days, all workers were obliged to attend Socialist Unity Party seminars; it was "the duty of the working class" to learn about and discuss topics that meant precious little to women. Nonetheless she learned a great deal from such seminars; she learned to think politically, and women today are better equipped to understand politics as a result, although she admits that she always thought something different from what the Socialist Unity Party intended. Today women don't believe they can change anything through political activity, she says. She didn't believe that in the old days either, but then you were forced into political activity. Nowadays women volunteer less in politics, because they were forced to do so before, and today such activity doesn't bring any advantages, either at work or in social position, she concludes.

Thus far most of the government programs and the sociological studies on women's unemployment in the aftermath of unification have focused on the loss of income and to a much lesser extent on the psychological impact of unemployment. Yet for men at least, Germany is a country where one's occupational title may appear in the telephone book and on the tombstone. Americans ask "What do you do for work?" Germans ask, "What are you professionally?" What does it mean for a working woman's identity if she can no longer identify herself through her occupation?

Linguistic change reflects another change underway in women's employment. In the German Democratic Republic, women identified themselves using the unadorned occupational titles *Techniker, Ingenieur, Chemiker* (technician, engineer, chemist). As women entered these occupations in the fifties and sixties, male terms simply extended to refer to them. Even though 96% of apprentices who completed training in sales were women, their official title remained *Verkäufer*–salesman (Kuhrig, 239). Women's occupational titles in the West typically end in the suffix –in: *Professorin, Ingenieurin*, etc., a practice now growing more common in the East. I asked several women how they felt about this change. Some, chiefly older women, had given it little thought, agreeing with the assumption I had made that East Germany's use of gender-neutral forms emphasized the worker, not her gender. Others countered that these forms were not gender-neutral, but rather exclusively masculine, and effaced women's work, making them invisible in the labor force. They recalled that the –in suffix was used in the GDR for traditionally female occupations such as daycare worker, seamstress, or nurse (*Erzieherin, Näherin, Krankenschwester*). Younger women often insist upon the female ending for their occupational titles, which they interpret as meaning that they can retain their identity as women even in a male-dominated workplace.

The unique nature of the East German workplace, where services such as daycare, medical care, dentistry, vacation lodgings, travel agents, beauty salons, and children's camp placements were provided, means that women who lost their jobs also lost access to a whole range of other amenities. Many women who lost their jobs also lost the friends or networks and peer support groups which their work teams had become. Perhaps because women's issues were not widely discussed in the GDR, such women rarely seek group solutions to their situation, tending instead to internalize their problems and make individual adaptations such as retraining, working beneath their qualifications, or accepting lower-paying jobs with unfavorable working conditions (Braun, Jasper, and Schröter, 208).

Other psychological factors make the search for a new job especially traumatic for women. For the first time, East German women are confronted with the importance of looks. In the German Democratic Republic, clothing styles were practical but unimaginative, good cosmetics high-priced and scarce, and physical improvements such as cosmetic surgery or cosmetic dentistry out of the reach of ordinary people. East German media did not glorify women's appearance or sexual attractiveness, but rather their social and familial accomplishments. Pornography and prostitution were illegal, and the country which controlled its borders and its media enforced these strictures completely. The commercial exploitation of nudity common since the mid-seventies in West German tabloids and magazines from *Bild* to *Spiegel* still surprises many East Germans. Nowadays in a culture which places a premium on body care and high fashion, many women feel themselves at a disadvantage, adding to the insecurities they may already feel about more important job qualifications such as training and experience.

Another novel and unpleasant experience for East German women is sexual harassment. Sexual harassment was virtually non-existent in the German Democratic Republic because men were not necessarily the dominant majority at work. A gender integrated workplace will not tolerate harassment, and women who are confident they belong there will not put up with it. Another reason for the absence of sexual harassment was that most working women were already wives and mothers; that is, the period of their greatest sexual availability or vulnerability did not coincide with the bulk of their time in the workplace. Today, on the other hand, working women are more apt to be unmarried or childless, thus presumably sexually available to men.

Harassment has increased dramatically for East German women because it functions as a means of keeping women out of places where men don't want them, especially workplaces. Furthermore, in the market economy pressure has increased for women to look attractive and to behave in a covertly sexual manner to increase sales or earn tips. Third, the lack of clarity about what constitutes sexual harassment and the prevalent male attitude that it needn't be taken seriously create an atmosphere where women become easy prey.

While Germany follows the US model of considering both quid pro quo and creating a hostile environment as components of harassment, it has no explicit legal definition. Thus many workers are unsure what sexual harassment means, and there is no well-articulated basis for legal action (Rastetter, 92). A West German study conducted in 1990 found that most men did not believe that suggestive jokes, whistling or staring at women or touching them "by chance" constituted harassment (*Deutscher Gewerkschaftsbund,* 10). Men's refusal to recognize sexual harassment explains why over 70% of women in the survey had been subjected to such behavior. Over a third of women surveyed had received unwelcome sexually explicit invitations, been groped, or shown pornographic pictures at work.

The 1990 survey determined that the typical harasser is about twenty years older than his victim; in one-fifth of the cases studied he is her boss. In more than half of the cases referenced in the survey women had been threatened with professional disadvantages if they refused sexual favors, evidence of quid pro quo which would clearly be prohibited under American law. It is useful to remind ourselves here that sexual harassment has nothing to do with erotic attraction and everything to do with power. It reinforces the image of males as self-confidant, dominant, and sexually potent, and forces women in turn to behave as passive and dependent (Rastetter, 98).

In today's united Germany offices for women's commissioners distribute pamphlets on sexual harassment, and the topic appears in women's newsletters. Standard advice for victims of sexual harassment includes complaining to one's supervisor, confiding in a friend, taking a self-defense course, learning a more assertive communication style, taking sick leave, or quitting. In other words, it is up to women to change. Legal action is not among the options suggested. Most victims try to ignore the harassment, avoid the offender, or laugh it off, although only a third of the women in the 1990 survey believed these tactics worked. Only 38% of them verbally confronted the offender and forbade him to continue, and just 27% defended themselves physically. The likelihood that the harasser will be punished for his actions is nil; only 14% of victims threatened to complain, and only 1% carried out any formal proceedings.

German women have no precedent for bringing sexual harassment cases to trial, and class action lawsuits, once again, are not legal. Germany's second law on gender equality, in force since 1994, does not specify complaint procedures or sanctions. The burden of proof rests with the victim, whose sworn testimony is not considered adequate, yet few victims of sexual harassment can produce witnesses (*Deutscher Gewerkschaftsbund,* 7). Women who do complain to their supervisors or pursue other channels may be branded as trouble-makers. Others may stifle their anger because of fear of losing their jobs. Sexual harassment frequently causes anxiety and depression. Its victims have difficulty concentrating on their work and lose enthusiasm for their jobs. By lowering their productivity, sexual harassment reduces women's chances for advancement. In times when jobs are scarce, sexual harassment is one more way of keeping women in their place, and out of the workplace.

The overall emphasis on the *differences* between men and women, gender-specific advertising for apprenticeships and job vacancies, the weight given to women's appearance, their exposure to sexual harassment, and the widening gender gap in earnings characterize the transition from communism to capitalism. These developments appear to confirm the Socialist Unity Party's view that western women's liberation movements pitting women against men, served capitalism as a way of distracting attention from the much larger struggle between the working class and its overlords. East German women today struggle against the forces that bring them into conflict with men and depict males, rather than the greed and social injustice of capitalism, as the enemy. "I'm no feminist," Barbara Teuber says, "but I'm a person who held her own in the working world and who claims the same right for other women. I don't think we can make it by working against men, but rather with men."

Chapter Three
Family Ties: Marriage and Children

From the promulgation of its marriage and family law in 1950, the German Democratic Republic defined families as mothers with children. In the aftermath of World War II, widows with children or mothers who had never married outnumbered intact two-parent families. Children born outside of marriage were guaranteed the same rights as children born within wedlock. Children were of the utmost economic and social importance, and they were scarce. Already during the pre-war years of the Hitler regime, the birthrate declined precipitously. The war brought further losses: fathers dead or imprisoned in the Soviet Union, mothers widowed, starving, some few desperate enough to turn to prostitution. Uncertain of their future under the new socialist regime, many who could afford to do so fled West. In its first decade, the country lost 6.5% of its population. During the forty years of its existence, 3.9 million of its inhabitants emigrated, most people of working age. As women responded to both the economic necessity and state policies calling them to work in the early 1950s, they decided to forego having children.

Increasing economic and political stability caused the birthrate to peak between 1960 and 1965 at 85.2 births for every thousand women of childbearing age (fifteen to forty-five) (*Frauenreport '90*, 25-26). The appearance of oral contraceptives available free of charge as part of national health insurance caused a downturn in the birthrate which Germans call *der Pillenknick* in the East as in the West. The country manufactured seven kinds of oral contraceptives, and around 40% of women of childbearing age used them, the highest rate in the world (Davidson, 9). Intrauterine devices were difficult to obtain, diaphragms and cervical caps impossible, but condoms could be bought easily (Schäfer, 132). At the age of sixteen, girls could obtain contraceptives without parental consent, and education and publicity urged them to control their own fertility.

In 1972 the German Democratic Republic legalized abortion, despite the decision's negative effect on the country's birthrate. Several factors contributed to this step. First, workers demanded access to abortion, and the state needed to keep women fully employed. Second, some contraceptives were suspected of being carcinogenic, and condoms were sometimes in short supply (von Ankum, 136-37). Third, abortion had become available in Poland. As many as seventy to eighty thousand women underwent illegal abortions yearly, and almost half of them required medical treatment afterwards (Ockel, 37). Sterility was a possible complication. The medical community had good reason to favor safe, legal abortion over the dangerous illegal practice. Another factor in the decision to permit abortion may have been the possibility of outdoing West Germany, where abortion did not become legal until 1976, and then only after considerable pressure was exerted by the feminist movement.

In 1970 the West German Bundestag discussed reform of paragraph 218, the country's law prohibiting abortion. The following year *Stern* magazine published "Ich habe abgetrieben," in which prominent women admitted having had abortions, although they could be punished with a fine or three years imprisonment. After legalization in 1976, West Germany permitted abortions only under certain conditions: rape, incest, danger to the health of the fetus or the mother, or if the woman could prove that the birth would endanger her emotional and social well-being. This fourth cause was cited in the two-thirds of the abortions that West Germany allowed (Ockel, 72).

In the German Democratic Republic the Socialist Unity Party's Inge Lange placed abortion on the agenda of the Secretariat of the Central Committee in December 1971. Before the Volkskammer legalized it in March of 1972, the issue was debated to a limited extent. The Catholic Church opposed it, and some voices expressed fears of a decline in public morality (Ockel, 37f).

In East Germany abortion during the first twelve weeks of pregnancy was treated as a simple medical procedure and fully covered by the usual public health insurance policies. Dr. Christa Anders, who had seen cases of botched illegal abortions in Leningrad in the fifties, believed legalization was a necessary step, although it was not widely discussed in the medical community. Dilation and curettage as an in-patient hospital procedure was the preferred method. No moral or ethical issues were connected with abortion, but doctors who opposed it on religious grounds were not obliged to perform the procedure. Abortion after the first trimester could be performed, subject to medical approval. Counseling was available on a voluntary basis; however little attention was given to the psychological effects of abortion. It was not widely discussed in public, and the numbers of abortions were not published in the GDR's statistical yearbooks. Not until 1989 did the women's magazine *Für Dich* publish an article about abortion (Funk 1993, 195).

In 1973 there were two abortions for every three live births (*Frauenreport '90*, 166). The abortion rate decreased from 33.7 per thousand women in 1972 to 21.4 in 1989 because of wider availability of other methods of birth control, greater acceptance of and government support for single mothers, and adequate sex education. On average there were about 74,000 abortions per year, or thirty-seven abortions for every hundred live births. Most abortions were sought by women aged twenty-five to twenty-nine, and most women in this age group were married. We can assume therefore that abortion was not widely used as a solution to teen pregnancy, but rather in cases where other birth control methods had failed. Sterilization was rarely performed, so women who already had as many children as they wished had no convenient way to end their risk of becoming pregnant. About a third of abortions were sought by women who already had at least one previous abortion, and most by women who already had at least the average number of children for their age (Funk 1993, 200). Some sociologists speculate that the ready availability of abortion meant that women rarely gave birth to unwanted children, and consequently there were fewer cases of child abuse or juvenile delinquency.

As was the case after the widespread introduction of birth control pills, a sharp decrease in births occurred following the legalization of abortion: compared to the 301,472 births in 1963, there were only 179,127 in 1974 (Childs, 256). The birthrate plummeted to 52.3 births per thousand women of childbearing age in 1975. This nadir in fertility in the East preceded by about ten years the lowest point in the West German birthrate, which occurred in 1985 (during the crisis over NATO's plan to station Pershing missiles in Germany), and was thus unrelated to abortion (Bucher, 11). In the GDR the number of deaths per year exceeded the number of births throughout the 1970s.

However, as a seminar leader in Erfurt pointed out in 1985, one of the advantages of a socialist state is its ability to engineer social policy to meet its goals. Accordingly in 1972 the Socialist Unity Party adopted a number of financial and social incentives to promote marriage and child-rearing as a counterweight to the legalization of abortion. Provisions such as paid maternity and child-rearing leave, free medical care, and childcare spaces, components of the SED's *Muttipolitik,* were increased at the IXth Party Congress in 1976 and again in 1984 and

1986 and achieved a modest success. By 1980 the birthrate per thousand women of childbearing age had risen to 67.4, substantially better, but still lower than the 70.1 births per thousand such women registered in 1970, before abortion became readily available.

The tendency to raise larger families in the countryside persisted. Nationwide, families became smaller, but over 90% of all women had children. Given that about the same percentage of women were employed, the country achieved a world record for combining motherhood with paid labor outside the home. Part of this success can be traced to economic and political security. Whereas 18% of women whose childbearing years coincided with National Socialism and war remained childless–this in an era before oral contraceptives and legal, safe abortion–only 10.5% of women whose childbearing years fell between 1951 and 1981 had no children. Most first births occurred when the mother was between twenty and twenty-five. Directors of technical colleges and universities were obligated to provide childcare, and to consider the needs of pregnant students, or those with young children. Students unable to find daycare received additional government subsidies of 125 marks a month for caring for their own children. The average mother's age at the birth of a second child was 26.3 years, and for a third child 29.3 years (*Frauenreport '90*, 27). While employers might bemoan the occurrence of pregnancy and child-rearing in the middle of an employee's training and early career development, women at these ages are resilient and healthy enough to cope easily with birth and the demands of a new infant. Two other aspects become apparent: women could space their children well, and they felt economically secure enough at a young age to start a family.

What were the financial benefits provided by the Socialist Unity Party's *Muttipolitik* which made it possible for couples to start a family? First, young couples who decided to marry received an interest-free loan whose amount increased through the years, finally reaching 7,000 marks, payable over thirty years. The loan was intended to fund purchases of furniture and housewares as the newlyweds set up housekeeping. Couples who had one child could cancel one thousand marks of this marriage loan, 1,500 for a second, and 2,500 for a third birth. This practice gave rise to a new German verb: *abkindern,* meaning to repay one's marriage loan by having children.

Housing became a second incentive to marry; by 1985, a fourth of all newly constructed apartments were destined for young married couples. A second 7,000-mark loan could be used to purchase, expand, or buy a share in a dwelling. Because housing, usually a rented apartment, was scarce, couples who did not take the legally binding step of marriage were often obliged to continue living with their parents. Housing remained a priority of the socialist economy throughout the existence of the GDR. Official policy decreed that every citizen should have a dwelling that was *sicher, trocken, warm* (secure, dry, and warm). However, the Second World War damaged or destroyed three-fourths of all dwellings in the territory that later became East Germany. Its socialist regime first devoted its resources to building new housing projects rather than modernizing the older dwellings in inner cities. By the end of the country's independent existence in 1989, 24% of its dwellings still had no indoor toilet, 18% had no shower or bath, and only 23% had central heat regulated within the building itself (*Frauenreport '90*, 126).

In Erfurt in 1985 I visited a construction site where new apartment houses were being built of pre-fabricated concrete slabs, each complete with pre-installed windows, doors, and openings for plumbing fixtures. Electrical wiring and pipes ran along interior walls rather than in channels within the concrete. Heat came from centrally located (and centrally regulated) heating plants that burned sulphurous, polluting soft coal mined in Saxony and Saxon-Anhalt. Our seminar leaders explained that such multiple-story apartment buildings had three disadvantages: the concrete slabs tended to shift or crack at the corners where they were fitted together, all the apartments looked alike, and the buildings could not be easily demolished, a drawback which has only recently become crucial. Building materials were in such chronically short supply that homeowners had to search, stand in line, and barter for paint, electrical hardware, and plumbing supplies, and work at construction sites often halted at midday because materials had run out. In fact I returned twice to the construction site in Erfurt and never saw the crane at work.

Aware of the adverse social effects of monotonous, anonymous public housing projects, the government's social engineers began in the seventies to include community houses and social meeting places. Satellite cities like those surrounding Erfurt's old center encompassed shops, cafes, and services such as hairdressers and laundromats. All were accessible by streetcar. In America such public housing projects are often defaced with graffiti and trash and endangered by the presence of thugs and drug dealers. Such problems did not exist in the German Democratic Republic because of strong social controls against juvenile delinquency and theft, and a police and border control system that succeeded in blocking the influx of drugs.

One result was that women could move freely in their cities at night, traveling by streetcar or on foot. Crime statistics for the German Democratic Republic in 1989 look quite harmless for a country of 16.5 million inhabitants: seventy-seven female murder victims, 658 female victims of reported rapes, 211 assault cases, 435 incidents of forced sexual activity, and 4,202 cases of intentional bodily harm, chiefly domestic violence (*Frauenreport '90*, 197-98). In contrast, America's "Take Back the Night" rallies remind us of how far from safety women live in the United States. Since unification, this sense of security at night has diminished: today two-thirds of East Germans say they fear being out on city streets at night. Many, particularly older women, lament that the disappearance of Young Pioneers and Free German Youth groups has increased juvenile delinquency because young people have nowhere to go and nothing to do. More radical political groups, the glorification of male power and strength in cultural offerings, and the pornography wave have caused increases in violence against women in the last decade.

Usually families lived for decades in the same apartment, paying stable rents that were held down through the use of government subsidies. On average families paid less than 10% of their monthly expenses in rent (*Frauenreport '90*, 120). Because of long waiting periods to obtain a larger apartment, children often shared bedrooms. Homelessness was virtually unknown. However, eviction for non-payment of rent was so unlikely that some people simply stopped paying. Funds for renovation or remodeling seldom appeared, and older buildings became seriously dilapidated. Only in the eighties did the country begin rescuing its inner cities, where many elderly residents clung to the homes they had occupied since the war. By 1989 most families had a washing machine, two-thirds had television (at least black and white) but only 17% had a telephone, and only half of all households had a car.

The country had little private housing. Today only two million households in East Germany own their own homes, as compared to fifteen million in the West. A homeowner who was a political dissident told me that his family was forced to live elsewhere, rent the house they owned, and turn over the proceeds to the state. Others explained that home ownership brought disadvantages: building materials and repair components were difficult to obtain, and it was simply cheaper to live in a publicly owned apartment. Newspapers contained no real estate advertising. Professions such as real estate broker, appraiser, or housing inspector were virtually unknown. Most people received newer or larger apartments, or at least access to a waiting list, through the workplace or cities and towns. Given that extra pay (a feature of competitive capitalist economies) was seldom offered for extra work, housing provided an effective incentive to increase production. Loyal party functionaries were also rewarded with better apartments, as were newlyweds.

Couples married young: the average age for a woman at first marriage was twenty-two and for a man twenty-four. West German cynics said that East Germans married young in order to get their own apartment. East Germans said they married young because their economic future was secure enough (with employment and housing provided) to start a family. Colleges and universities created housing for married students and daycare centers for their children. Over the years, the ages of men and women who entered a first marriage steadily increased. As an illustration, in 1970, 43.1% of all twenty-year-old women and 80.5% of twenty-four-year-old women were married. By 1988 these figures had declined to 18.2% of twenty-year-olds and 60% of twenty-four-year olds.

Reasons cited by both sexes for wanting to marry included love, marriage as a tradition, and the possibility of obtaining an apartment (*Frauenreport '90*, 105). It is significant that the desire for financial or material security, and the desire for children do not appear here. Over half of young couples would have preferred to live together in a trial marriage before the wedding ceremony, but the lack of available housing prevented them from doing so. Communal living arrangements or same-sex couples living together were virtually unknown: the 1991 census found that only 1.6% of multi-person households were not a traditional family, meaning parents and children, or married childless couples (Cromm, 47).

In 1992 I visited a young couple in Neubrandenburg who were twenty-two-year-old students at the college of education founded by Margot Honecker. They lived on the sixth floor of a fairly new building on Juri Gagarin Ring, named for the first Soviet cosmonaut, who orbited the earth in 1961. They shared a job in the summertime, earning about a thousand marks a month apiece working as waiters on a tourist boat that sailed the Tollensersee. The money they received as tips, as much as sixty marks a day, added to their good fortune and enabled them to afford an ancient Opel sedan. In fact they felt fortunate to have kept their job, since two other lake boats had been forced out of operations because their toilets flushed directly into the lake, no longer permissible under tougher environmental laws.

As we huffed and puffed up the stairs, my host explained that buildings were not required to have elevators unless they were higher than six stories. He and his wife occupied a tiny, cramped apartment that was immaculate and carefully furnished. While they fixed platters of bread, cheese, and cold cuts in their miniscule cubbyhole of a kitchen, I sat in the living room. The bathroom contained an automatic washer, and they had acquired a stereo system and a television, tuned to the "Feuerstein" program ("The Flintstones"). I asked where their bedroom was, and they pointed laughingly to the sofa I was sitting on, which unfolded to transform the living room into sleeping quarters.

They considered themselves fortunate and well provided for, but for many such couples, close living quarters, forty-three hour work weeks, and the struggles of housekeeping led to friction and ultimately divorce. When I asked in Erfurt about the divorce rate, the seminar leader who was prepared to respond literally beckoned me into a wooded area out of hearing of the rest of the group. Cautiously avoiding statistics, he told me that it was higher than anyone wanted to admit; perhaps as many as a third, or even a half of all marriages ended in divorce.

Why did so many marriages fail? Marxist sociologists liked to attribute the high incidence of divorce to the complete emancipation of women, whose economic well-being was ensured, with or without a husband. No-fault divorce, routine and simple, was the norm. Other critics have pointed out that by providing daycare, child support payments, and the monthly housework day for women, "father state" came to replace a husband who might have helped with these responsibilities. In this way husbands (though not lovers) became superfluous. Statistics bear out such claims. The 1990 *Frauenreport* finds that between 1977 and 1982 as daycare space became adequate and as single mothers received leave from work to care for sick children, the number of marriages declined. Sociologists have pointed out that whereas women in the West had to accept an unsatisfactory marriage or partnership for sake of economic stability for their children, in the East the socialist state played role of provider, and women had to accept dependency on government support for their children. Ostensibly, marriage brought fewer benefits to women than to men: divorced women were less likely than divorced men to enter a second marriage; 69% of divorces were sought by women. Other analysts of the country's high divorce rate pointed to the young age at which couples married as a cause of divorce: 65% of marriages contracted when the bride was between eighteen and twenty-three lasted less than three years. The *Frauenreport* cites as reasons for the failure of young marriages the confluence of heavy demands on women: career, childcare, and housework, young brides' immaturity and unrealistic expectations of the relationship, and marrying primarily to live independently of one's parents. No one, it is interesting to note, attributes the divorce rate to the absence of religion or religious teaching. Nor do people mention that access to contraceptives and abortion freed women from remaining in marriage as a way to care for children. Perhaps these two conditions had become so ordinary as to seem not worth mentioning.

Other observers have pointed out that sex lost its spontaneity and joy in the GDR. Where everything was planned for and no risks attached to sex, the allure of its dangers disappeared. Erotic expression in film, literature, and visual arts was taboo, sexy lingerie unavailable, and sexual manuals or videos became available only after unification, when Beate Uhse's famous sex shops opened in the East. Thus lack of sexual pleasure in marriage may have contributed to the high divorce rate (Sieg, 114). Another source remarks on the sexual sparkle in the workplace, which she attributes to the lack of prostitution in the GDR; that is, men sought sexual companionship among the women they worked with every day. In a setting free of sexual harassment, women could repulse or encourage flirtation as they chose (Kebir, 30).

Another factor in the country's alarmingly high divorce rate – and its high suicide rate–was the unique function of families. Life under a totalitarian regime forced its citizens to hide their true beliefs and emotions in the company of people they did not know well. The family compensated increasingly for the lack of credible social or cultural values and meaningful activities. The family became a protective cocoon (*Nische*) whose members sought trust and security within. "Family became–in contrast to the official political view–a sort of counter-world to society" (*Frauenreport '90*, 115). Ironically, the family became the counterweight to the function Marx had envisaged for it as the foundation of the socialist state. As a result, people placed a high value on a private circle of family and friends with whom they could speak freely, safe from the informants of the infamous State Security Service (whose files now encompass 125 miles of printed documents). Within marriage, women held high expectations of intimacy, equality, and family harmony, expectations fed in part by propagandistic images of perfect working mothers, yet not always met in the drudgery and humdrum of everyday life under socialism. For some, disappointment led to divorce.

The stress of functioning within two conflicting circles, public and private, led to a high rate of suicide, as well as divorce. At their peak in 1980, suicides reached 5,500 per year for men, and 3,300 for women. Suicides increased in the first years after unification as people lost their jobs, faced decisions about moving, and found themselves pilloried in the media for loyal service as SED party functionaries, police, or judges. Today's rate has fallen by around two-thirds, to 3,040.

Domestic violence, like suicide, received little public attention, although it has been estimated on the basis of interviews and police statistics that every fifth to seventh woman was harmed in her home (Kischke, 5). About the same rate prevailed in the West. Beatings may have been less violent in the East where men tried not to leave visible injuries because the issue was so taboo. Women might seek help and support within their work collective, and the batterer might be punished by a neighborhood conflict commission, but there were no therapy groups or women's shelters. The absence of formal solutions left women feeling helpless, bereft, and ashamed. In extreme cases the police might intervene and the relationship end in divorce. However, couples who divorced might have to continue living together, making it difficult for women to escape their batterers.

Several unique factors influenced the climate of domestic violence in the GDR. First, while women's work and financial independence changed their traditional role, men's roles as providers and wage earners weakened without any new role model appearing to replace the old. Sexual violence against women was one way men could reassert their dominance and control. Second, the stress of overwork, women's double burden, and limited housing exacerbated domestic disputes. Third, children were not taught conflict resolution or safe ways of acting out violent feelings. And finally, the family's role as the bastion of privacy secure from Stasi surveillance also reinforced the taboo, so that women were reluctant to reveal domestic violence outside the home (Igney, 56-59).

After unification, domestic violence was treated more openly, and hotlines and emergency shelters were established. The appearance or coming out of domestic violence has caused some observers to assume it arose from post-unification stress and unemployment, when in fact it existed beneath the surface for years. Today, however, unemployment has made many women more dependent on the men who abuse them. Recent estimates suggest that as many as one-third of all women are victims of domestic violence; 50,000 women each year seek shelter in Germany's 453 shelters. Although crime statistics do not track domestic violence as a separate category, estimates of its cost to Germany run as high as twenty-nine billion DM (about $15 billion), including legal costs, punishing batterers, and shelter, therapy, and medical treatment for their victims (Schindler 2000, 7).

East German women whom I interviewed agreed that divorce brought a woman few advantages. Alimony was paid only to support children under the age of eighteen, and usually children remained with their mother who covered most of their costs, such as food and housing. One great disadvantage was that divorced couples might need to continue living together: the centrally planned economy created housing for newlyweds, but not for those who divorced. Women who received custody of children usually retained rights to the family's apartment. If the husband held rights to it through his workplace, however, he could not easily move elsewhere.

These women all agreed that the central cause of divorce was that most men did not develop beyond their traditional role as wage earners and come to share the unpaid labor usually performed by women. Those who did help with household tasks were most likely to be involved in shopping and caring for their children. Meanwhile children of single mothers often became self-reliant and mature, giving their mothers the companionship they might otherwise have sought in a man. By the eighties, the picture brightened somewhat as such children matured: these boys grew into men who had learned to cook and clean. Working women met friends and new acquaintances at work, where the collective system fostered interpersonal relationships. They participated in company parties and holiday events and attended plays and concerts with their co-workers, so that single people did not feel out of place.

One result of the high divorce rate which has thus far drawn little attention was that over time East German society uncoupled the concept of marriage from that of having children. Motherhood, rather than marriage or shared parenting, was the goal of the socialist state; incentives such as leave to care for sick children and a shorter work week for mothers were not intended for fathers, who received little encouragement to become active partners in caring for their offspring. The percentage of births to unmarried mothers stood at 13.1 in 1955, a phenomenon created by the chaos and dislocation following the war. The rate fell to 9.8% of all births ten years later, and then began to rise; the fraction of births to unmarried mothers surpassed one-half in 1984, compared to 10% in West Germany and 27% in the US (Cromm, 41). The statistic stands out more sharply when limited to firstborns: 52.7% of mothers giving birth to a first child in 1989 were unmarried

(*Frauenreport '90*, 28). The 1990 *Frauenreport* cites the drawbacks facing single-parent households: poor home furnishings, less vacation travel, and little savings, but it is striking that homelessness, abuse, and true poverty do not figure in this list.

The high proportion of births to unmarried women raises the question whether children whose mothers care for them well and can support them financially need fathers. Fathers headed only 1% of the country's single parent households, estimated at 340,000 in 1989.

One West German sociologist has gone so far as to assert that the GDR became a matrilineal society. He points out that the presence of a male did not determine what constituted a family; the couple's attachment remained open even after they had children. About 80% of single mothers later married; in fact over a third of the women who entered a first marriage in 1991-92 already had children (Cromm, 33). The socialist state's political analysts declared that single motherhood demonstrated women's economic and social independence of men and proved that socialism ensured the secure future of all families.

It is interesting to contrast American attitudes toward teen-age pregnancy and unwed mothers with those prevalent in East Germany. Neither East, West, nor today's united Germany has a teen pregnancy problem, because sex education is widespread and contraceptives are available to females sixteen and older, without parental notification. Obviously easy access to contraceptives also keeps the abortion rate low. Another factor appears to be the relative ease with which unmarried couples can now live together in the East as well as West; many choose not to marry until they have children, and others do not marry then either. Unplanned sexual encounters and unprotected intercourse would appear to be rarer in Germany than in the US. While unmarried households with children are economically feasible in the United States, they are subject to stronger social criticism. (In 1995 55% of unmarried East German couples had children, as compared to only 19% of unmarried couples in the West.) And in Germany all mothers receive child support payments, regardless of income or marital status, so there is no particular image of a welfare mother having babies to increase her monthly allotment. Another factor preventing a negative image for unmarried mothers is Germany's need for a higher birthrate to sustain a stable population.

In the German Democratic Republic, all mothers, married or not, received a thousand marks per baby, issued in seven installments, collected at free pre- and post-natal medical checkups. Additional supplements were paid for breast-feeding. The birthrate slowly began to rise during the 1980s; by the end of the GDR's existence, it reached an average of 2.8 children per woman. Better yet, East Germany had one of the lowest infant mortality rates in the world, lower than rates in West Germany or the United States, where pre- and post-natal care is not free and easily accessible to all mothers.

Within the state-run economy, attention was given to producing cheap, attractive clothing, shoes, and baby carriages, their prices held down by government subsidies, although disposable diapers (as well as many other paper products) were not widely available.

Mothers received six weeks maternity leave before childbirth, plus twenty weeks afterward, paid from a social insurance fund at a rate equal to their average net monthly earnings. Contrast this policy to the American practice of granting six weeks of paid leave, which mothers may take either before or after childbirth. Mothers were entitled to a full year of leave for a first child, and for a second or any subsequent child, eighteen months, provided they cared for the child at home. The mother's husband (after 1986) or the child's grandmother could utilize this year of leave in the mother's stead. The "baby year" was paid, eventually at a rate equaling 90% of normal wages. Organizations such as the Demokratischer Frauenbund attempted to keep stay-at-home mothers interested in politics and committed to socialism. As women's maternity leaves expired, transitional programs helped them adjust to returning to their jobs, which were held until their return.

Beginning in 1976, mothers were paid for staying home when their children were sick: up to four weeks with one child, six weeks if they had more children. Women fought for the possibility that men stay home with sick children, a prerogative at first reserved for single fathers. By the mid-eighties a father could take a mother's place and claim the monthly housework day, sick leave, or baby year, although few did so. Two reasons are commonly given to explain why so few men used these childcare arrangements: they earned more, and payments for the baby year were geared to wages or salaries. It simply made better sense for the partner who earned more to continue working. Second, employers assumed that childcare was a woman's responsibility and made allowances. Mothers of young children, for example, were given jobs closer to home and excused from overtime or late shift work. Institutions where many women worked were regularly over-staffed to allow for mothers who had gone home temporarily to care for children. Single mothers, pregnant women, those on maternity leave, and mothers of young children could not be fired. Clearly this was serious pro-family social policy.

Today East German women freely admit that the system was abused; 11.5 million workdays were lost due to baby leave and sick leave in 1989 (Dahn, 161). The matter was further complicated by the lack of telephones: women staying home with a sick child could not easily notify the workplace of their absence, nor could brigade leaders telephone their homes to check their whereabouts. Given this state of affairs, cheating was easy. For some women, the baby year became a way of seceding from employment that was boring, laborious, or politically distasteful.

Monthly child support payments allotted to all mothers, whether or not they were in paid employment, reached 95 marks for a first child, 145 for a second, and 195 for a third child, extended through tenth grade, regardless of family income. Mothers of children over the age of twelve and those from lower income families received higher monthly allowances. It is difficult to give accurate values for East German currency. In 1985 Frankfurt banks offered fourteen East German marks for one West. Street handlers in the German Democratic Republic offered four to one. Officially, the East German government insisted than one East mark equaled one West, about thirty-four cents in 1985. Average monthly net wages for occupations such as kindergarten teacher or auto mechanic averaged six to eight hundred marks.

Eventually these components of the Socialist Unity Party's Muttipolitik, baby leave, sick leave, and child support, achieved some success. In 1989 the country counted 198,922 new babies, but deaths outnumbered births, and the country's population continued to decline.

In order to retain the 90% of female workers who had at least one child, the socialist state succeeded in creating adequate daycare space by the mid 1970s. By 1989, 80% of children aged three or under were in daycare (as compared to 52% of West German children aged four and under). Typically those who were not in daycare were infants home with mothers taking advantage of the baby year. Daycare centers subsidized by the government were open wherever women worked: in factories, hospitals, and collective farms. Employers were required to assist in the creation and maintenance of these facilities. Weekly daycare centers for parents working away from home stayed open around the clock. Infants could be placed in daycare as soon as their mothers needed to return to work, and were available for night workers.

Daycare workers had the same responsibilities as parents; they took sick children to the doctor and fetched and administered prescription medicine. Mothers whom I interviewed maintained that daycare centers created education plans, did handicrafts for the holidays, and taught pre-school skills such as numbers, the alphabet, and names of shapes and colors. Parents' advisory groups supported their work, and exercised control over the centers. Their cost, less thirty-five Pfennig a day, included three meals and milk; most children ate the hot noonday meal at the daycare center.

Care for children of working mothers extended well beyond pre-school accommodations. Ninety-five per cent of three- to six-year-olds attended kindergarten, which was considered part of the educational system and thus a state (rather than private) responsibility. Eighty-one per cent of those in the first four grades of the polytechnic school attended the *Schulhort*, an after-school program of sports, supervised homework, and extra-curricular activities (Drauschke and Stolzenburg, 104). Since school children had eighteen weeks of vacation a year, and parents only four or five, factories and other employers also funded summer camps like the one I visited outside Erfurt in 1985. Parents paid a token amount, four marks a week, for children to attend.

Opinions differ about the overall quality of care, in particular whether the centers provided educational development, or merely custodial care. Many East Germans viewed the extensive daycare system as a mixed blessing: it removed young children from the family sphere for long hours each day, socializing them according to the political views of the Socialist Unity Party. Some mothers regretted or resented not being able to spend more time with children over eighteen months who were placed in daycare. Others protested the presence of toy weapons in the daycare facilities, and propagandistic teachings about the National People's Army.

The daycare center I visited in Erfurt in 1985 appeared to be a clean, cheerful, orderly facility. What struck me at once was that I had never before seen so many blond, blue-eyed children gathered together! East Germany did not permit open immigration, and most children came from homogenous Germanic stock. Aspects of multi-cultural society appeared in maps of the Soviet Union and pictures of the native costumes of some of its republics. Groups of children as large as fifteen to twenty were supervised by a single woman, but disobedience and disruptions were rare, probably because the entire society enforced adherence to norms of group behavior with little encouragement for individuality. Children drew pictures of tanks and guns and played with toy weapons. I was told that they were not allowed to pretend to shoot anyone, and that the military toys were supposed to foster identification with their fathers, some of whom were in the National People's Army.

The teachers, all young women, seemed caring and patient, and the children's lunch smelled appetizing.

Later I had the good fortune to meet many women who had placed their children in daycare, and others who had experienced it themselves. All unanimously concurred that such facilities had cared well for their children, and that children develop best through good daycare and a good home life.

One of these women was Susanne W., who spoke freely about the integration of work and family life which became commonplace in the GDR. Frau W. was born around the time Hitler came to power. War's end found her living with her mother and brother in the central German area known as the Harz region. After losing their father in the war, the family became desperately poor; Frau W. remembers helping her mother earn some money as a seamstress. The family viewed their misery and the devastation which surrounded them as the inescapable outgrowth of the militaristic capitalism that had caused the war.

Susanne W. enjoyed studying math and physics, but left secondary school after one year when her mother became ill. She became a vocational teacher in a company training school attached to an electronics factory where switches, fuses, and circuit breakers were manufactured. To help fulfill the economic five-year plan, she worked without pay alongside her students, operating a drill press and a cutter. "We were inspired by the idea of creating a better world," she says. For three years she taught history, economics, and German there. Some of her students were truckers with a six or seventh grade education who already earned nine hundred marks a month; as a twenty-two-year-old she had to teach them elementary school subjects like German and mathematics to prepare them for a vocational degree. Women worked on the assembly line, but their supervisors and team leaders were almost all men, she recalls. She also taught a special training course to qualify these women to begin preparing for their master tradesmen's certificates. As a single woman she could invest all of her time in her career. She worked without pay on the assembly line to become familiar with her students' working conditions. She taught a course for older men who had worked as engineers immediately after the War, without the necessary credentials. In two and a half years they were prepared for the engineering examination. While Frau W. taught political economy of capitalism, her students had experienced it, for they had done piecework before and after the war. Coming from different directions, the young woman and her older students learned to appreciate each other.

After three years teaching at the factory's training school, Susanne W. applied to a engineering school whose director had a continuing education quota to fill, and was pleased to accept a young unmarried woman. She had always wanted to further her education so that she would be able to support a family more easily than her mother had. Thus in 1960 she began a distance-learning course (*Fernstudium*) in Leipzig lasting eleven semesters. I had often heard of such courses, but Susanne W.'s description first clarified what they entailed. In a two-week period, all the lectures for an entire semester were given at the university and reading lists were handed out. Every two weeks the distance-learning students in Berlin met in rooms belonging to the Humboldt University or elsewhere. In their study collective everyone was responsible for the group's success; she learned to carry a postcard with her so that any absent student could be sent a message with tips for the next group study session. During her distance-learning course, which consumed about fourteen hours a week, Susanne W.'s teaching schedule was shortened by two or three hours and she got a brief respite to prepare major exams and to write her thesis.

At twenty-five she became a teacher at the engineering school. Although her students were all men, she never experienced sexual harassment. "There was a certain boundary there," she says. "No one ever patted me on the behind." In her labor union she started a women's committee, served as treasurer, and organized bowling parties and theater evenings.

Around this time she met her husband. Their son was born at the end of her fourth year in the distance-learning course. She was given six weeks leave before and six weeks after childbirth; the day itself was not counted, since a woman had labored enough on that day. A "borrowed grandmother" or nanny cared for her son for the first year and a half. Not until the birth of their daughter two years later did the couple get a larger apartment and daycare space. Frau W. explains that in East German culture people focused not only on the nuclear family but also on a larger circle of friends and co-workers. It was perfectly natural that when anyone moved, the whole work brigade showed up to help out. The collective or work brigade formed the basis of one's circle of friends.

After the couple divorced in 1978 her ex-husband continued living on the same street, and the children could go to him at any time. He contributed to their support until they became self-sufficient, but Frau W. was responsible for feeding and clothing them. She tells all this without regret or bitterness; she explains that the whole social structure made it possible to care for children well. She quotes a study of single-parent households in the GDR: such families often made do for a long time with their first set of furniture, their closets were not overly full, and they traveled less than other families. Frau W. herself loves the Russian language and culture, yet never traveled to the Soviet Union. Nonetheless her existence as a single mother was by no means precarious. Such women were treated well, even preferentially in the workplace. In contrast to today, a single mother would be the last one to be fired. Whether children turn out well or not is a matter of organization, she thinks. "A working mother is more valuable to her children," Frau W. asserted, "not only financially, but because her horizon is wider; she has a circle of friends and acquaintances that constantly enriches her." Her son's favorite sport was rowing, and her daughter took accordion lessons and ballet. Such instruction was reasonably priced and within her reach. "My children wouldn't have become the people they are today if I hadn't worked," she says.

Frau W. emphasized that for the most part single women, whether widows or divorced women like herself, were treated with dignity and respect in the GDR. Working women were addressed as "Frau," whether married or not. (Frau originally meant "Mrs."; in the past ten or fifteen years its usage has extended to unmarried women as well.) Her daughter, who began teaching at the age of twenty, was already addressed as "Frau W."

Yet Susanne W. admits the German Democratic Republic's forty-year existence did not succeed in completely eradicating the patriarchal notion of devaluing unmarried women. Because she did not marry until twenty-nine, some people asked whether she hadn't found the right man yet. And once at her son's prom a waitress refused to bring her a drink because she was there alone; today she wouldn't stand for such a thing. Her best friend, unmarried, had a baby at thirty-one and had to swallow some hurtful remarks. Women are much worse about making such negative comments, she thinks. Such attitudes are a matter of development. She mentions a West German cousin, a father of three, who asked when her daughter would be getting married. Speaking of his own daughter he said, "She's a little young, but at least she's off the street." To Frau W. that expression suggested prostitution, but he meant that the girl was married: *unter die Haube gekommen*. (The German idiom literally means that the bride has been brought underneath the wedding canopy, but it suggests that she is taken care of or has become a "covered woman" in the historical sense of the phrase.)

Susanne W. joined the Socialist Unity Party at the age of nineteen. Even then she wanted to belong to those who were working to build a better society. Still, it irked her that she had to attend the monthly Party seminars, which always presented the same old political and economic themes. She had earned a degree in the field and taught history, but she was told that such people should attend to enrich others through their knowledge. On the other hand she had nothing against her children's education in the Young Pioneers and Free German Youth because there they learned discipline and working as a group.

After a total of ten years in adult education, Susanne W. became a tenured instructor working in various areas of higher education, and she threw herself into the work heart and soul. When the political turnaround came, Frau W. was simply aghast. She could see it coming: "How long can things go on this way, running around just to buy a zipper?" people asked themselves. "I'm not one of those who called out 'Helmut, Helmut' she says, "but I'm not one of those who threw eggs either. . . I just didn't go [to the historic festivities associated with the opening of the Berlin Wall.] I just stayed home. I still don't feel any relationship to this government."

This government has brought sweeping changes to women's lives; East German women have lost ground on the family side of the compromise which enabled them to combine work and families. In the decades to come, it is younger women who will feel these changes most acutely as they postpone marriage and children to follow a career.

In 1998 I met two younger women in Berlin. Elke Goltz and her friend Sabine were born in the late sixties, and their conversation helped me understand the span of women's choices before and after the Wende. Sabine, born in 1968, went to a daycare center while her parents worked. Her father did dishes and washed the family's laundry in the bathtub. People often carried bedding and large items to commercial laundries, transporting heavy articles by streetcar and returning to pick up laundered items weeks later. While washing machines were fairly common, some had no spin cycles, and in any case there was little space to hang laundry to dry in the apartment. Sabine's mother did the cooking, but her husband roasted the Christmas goose, wallpapered, and repaired the family car, a difficult task in an economy where spare parts had to be obtained through a complex barter network. Elke's family didn't own a car. Her father washed and ironed, cleaned windows, and did the cooking, in contrast to her grandparents, who divided household chores along traditional gender lines. Children helped with the yard and garden work. Sabine's mother rejected the official socialist party slogan "We help Mommy," which suggested that housework was women's work first and foremost. "It was our household," she says.

Sabine became a teacher for the first four grades in 1988. After unification, she was transferred to a school for the first six grades and taught music there. After four years as a successful teacher, she left education in order to study rehabilitation pedagogy. During her holidays Sabine volunteered to work with the disabled in Japan in Mina Mata, an area whose inhabitants suffer the effects of lead and mercury poisoning from eating contaminated fish. There she taught German and English in a school for the blind. She recently completed her dissertation on mainstreaming in Japanese schools.

I ask about sexism or discrimination. Sabine says she hasn't observed sex discrimination in schools, though there may have been fewer girls studying mathematics. However, she had only female classmates when she studied to become an elementary teacher before unification. Elke encountered male classmates training to teach math and geography in the polytechnic school. Thus sex stereotyping did occur, based both on the age of children to be taught, and the academic speciality. But men made coffee when women celebrated International Women's Day every March eighth.

The conversation turns to women in the workforce. Elke Goltz is finishing her doctorate at Potsdam University where she works as a teaching assistant in statistics. Her doctoral research focuses on the Brandenburg countryside and how it has changed since unification. She conducts surveys and gathers statistics to ascertain the effects of emigration, the collapse of industry, and transformations in agriculture on rural communities. She thinks that West German women see work as a social setting of secondary importance, or work to become independent of a man's financial support, while East German women view it as both a livelihood and self-fulfilment.

I ask how each of these women judges the overall effects of the collapse of the GDR on their own lives. Sabine finds it largely positive, for it has given her the freedom to travel. She defines her identity independently of her conflicted homeland. On the negative side of the ledger, daycare has nearly disappeared, and she finds the West German educational system that was imposed on her country out of date. Elke concurs in criticizing the West German educational system, which refused to recognize her degree, obliging her to study two more years. East Germans who had taught for thirty years had to present a model lesson and undergo an examination to attain permanent civil servant status, a humiliating experience. She too rebels at the idea that West Germany's laws were simply superimposed on the GDR, with little attempt to retain its good features. Although she has greater opportunities today, risks have increased as well; for example she wonders about her chances of employment once her degree is finished.

For many young East German women, employment takes precedence over the desire to have a family, as they struggle first to establish themselves in a profession before considering marriage. Even more remote is the likelihood of having children, given the cost and scarcity of daycare, and the restrictions on abortion, which make it impossible for women to control their own fertility as they could in the German Democratic Republic.

I was struck by the vehemence of older East German women, long past childbearing age themselves, who denounced the banning of abortion in 1993. Frau W. decried as "inhumane, impossible," the ban, which completely disregards the life of the woman seeking an abortion. The older women I met at a roundtable discussion concurred. "Today the state wants to protect an unborn life," one woman commented bitterly, "but when the child is born, no one gives a damn about it." ("Wenn das Kind geboren wird, kümmert sich kein Schwein darum.")

In 1990 the abortion issue figured in the campaign for hasty economic union waged by Helmut Kohl's Christian Democrats, and was crucial enough to be addressed in agreements governing German unification. Until December 31, 1992, both states retained their own abortion laws. Legislators from the Christian Democrats and Christian Socialists, among them Family Minister Caudia Nolte and over thirty other women, sought a ruling on the legality of abortion from the Constitutional Court. On May 28, 1993 the Constitutional Court ruled that abortion within the first trimester is illegal, but will not be criminally prosecuted. The 300-page ruling made it clear that the fetus's right to life takes precedence over the woman's right to self-determination. Abortion remains legal only in cases of rape or incest, or of health risks to the woman or fetus. Abortions outside these legal parameters cannot be paid for by national health insurance.

On May 29, 1994 the Bundestag approved new draft legislation eroding even further women's already limited abortion rights. By a narrow majority of 264 to 260, Helmut Kohl's governing coalition (Christian Democrats, Christian Socialists, and Free Democrats) voted that women and their doctors remain free from criminal prosecution in abortion cases *only* if women attend mandatory counseling from recognized social agencies. Both counselors and doctors performing abortions are obliged to encourage the women to carry through pregnancies to term. Of the country's 1,690 family planning centers authorized to provide such counseling in 1999, 264 were administered by the Catholic Church, and 255 by the Lutheran Church (Festraëts, 23). Because counseling centers receive 90% of their funding from the federal states, political parties can limit funding to curtail women's access to non-religious counseling. For example in East Berlin in the early 1990s there were three Protestant, three Catholic, and only one non-religious counseling center (Funk 1993, 200). Germany's largest state, Bavaria, which is largely Catholic, provided only three non-religious counseling centers from a total of forty. Thus although compliance with the law can protect a woman from prosecution, she may still face considerable obstacles, expense, and humiliation in seeking an abortion.

At first Catholic priests provided counseling, but after lengthy debate ceased doing so in late 1999. While the Catholic Church was eager to counsel against abortion, this service made it legally possible for women to obtain one. The dispute between the Vatican (opposed to any Church participation in abortion counseling) and Germany's Catholics led by the progressive bishop of Mainz, Karl Lehmann, continued through 1998-99 and focused debate on abortion as a moral issue, rather than a woman's private choice.

The issue of late-term abortions surfaced in the media in 1999; about 800 a year are performed in Germany, chiefly because of severe malformation of the fetus. Groups of disabled people lobbied against allowing such procedures, and compared them to Hitler's annihilation of the mentally and physically handicapped.

Doctors can be prosecuted for performing abortions on women who have not undergone mandatory counseling, and are prohibited from deriving more than 20% of their income from abortion. This ruling makes it impractical for doctors or clinics to specialize in safe, efficient abortion procedures, since they are forced to limit this sector of their medical practice. As a result of increasing restrictions, the number of abortions fell by around two-thirds during the first decade of unification. In the East, there are about 2.8 abortions per hundred live births (*Sozialreport 1999*, 116-17). Most are sought by women who already have one or two children. The rate remains lower in the West, where most abortions are sought by single women.

Since the federal states have considerable jurisdiction over restrictions on abortion, the ease of obtaining the practice differs from place to place, and contributes to the "them versus us" divisiveness between East and West. In predominantly Catholic Bavaria, for example, outpatient abortions are prohibited, making the procedure more expensive and more difficult to obtain than in the new eastern states. Bavaria has also erected barriers to the distribution of the morning-after pill mifepristone (RU-486, *die Pille danach)*, which is now available as an alternative to surgical abortion, but subject to the same requirement for counseling. Manufactured by a German pharmaceutical company, the drug became available in France in the late 1980s. It was reportedly also tested in 1989 in an East German clinic at the University of Jena, but political and religious opposition blocked its introduction in Germany for another decade. Cardinal Joachim Meisner of Cologne, speaking in early December 1999, compared mifepristone to Cyclon-B, used in Nazi gas chambers, saying that it would be an unspeakable tragedy if Germany's chemical industry again produced a deadly instrument capable of destroying a legally limited group of human beings. However, both his Catholic and Protestant brethren felt this analogy went too far.

Until age of eighteen, a woman needs the permission of her parents for an abortion, yet younger women may have the greatest difficulty coping with raising a child. Furthermore, outlawing abortion increases the burden on poor, single women, who may lack both the financial means to raise a child and the 600-800 DM cost of an abortion. Of course young and poor women are also least able to travel to one of Germany's neighboring countries like Holland where abortion is cheaper or more easily available. Restrictions on abortion have given rise to *Schwangerschaftsabbruchtourismus* (abortion tourism, an ironic expression if there ever was one).

Today attitudes toward abortion divide East and West; a 1996 survey reported that while two-thirds of East German women and men believe abortion should be possible if a woman wants it, only about a third of West Germans agree (Schröter 1997, 24). East German women react with anger to today's depiction of abortion as an ethical or moral problem. Some say that after unification there was a wave of child murders because women who wanted to terminate their pregnancies but could not carried babies to term, then despaired and killed them. They are furious that women's lives and their right to determine their own fertility now appear of lesser value than an unborn fetus. These women detect the influence of the Catholic Church in the abortion decision, especially in Bavaria. They resent what they see as the church's plan to re-Christianize East Germany. At the same time they recognize that opposition to abortion is often grounded in the desire to preserve Germanity, and to bolster the country's birthrate.

Reacting to the federal court's debate on abortion, reporters in the January/February 1993 issue of *Emma* connected rising opposition to abortion with hatred of foreigners. An article entitled "*Getrennt marschieren, vereint schlagen*" identified several right-to-lifers (*Lebensschützer*) as former Nazis, who believe that German women should bear German children. Part of Germans' angst about foreigners is grounded in the fact that they have a higher birthrate. The nervousness about Germans becoming a *Mischvolk* can be traced from Hitler to Günter Grass's 1980 novel, *Headbirths, Or the Germans are Dying Out*.

Thinking along the same lines, the Institute of German Business in Cologne published in late 1993 a study of the economic effects of Germany's declining birthrate and the rise in immigration which has historically compensated for a too-small labor force. According to the Institute, immigration could be reduced by utilizing the domestic female work potential through family-oriented working hours and better coordination between work schedules and daycare and school times. This study identifies the same hard choices as the *Emma* article: either Germany must accept larger numbers of immigrants, or succeed in keeping women employed part-time while encouraging motherhood. In 2000 a Christian Democratic candidate for minister-president of Northrhine-Westphalia campaigned under the slogan "Kinder statt Inder" ("Children instead of Indians"), suggesting that a higher birthrate would make unnecessary the SPD's loosening of immigration restrictions to encourage computer specialists to come to Germany. To compensate for its persistently low birthrate, Germany liberalized its citizenship laws in 1999, so that children whose parents have lived in the country for at least eight years can more easily become citizens.

Beyond the outlawing of abortion, a second target of East German women's anger is the depiction of daycare as harmful to children, which they consider another means of discrediting working mothers and coercing them to return to housewifery. A new negative epithet, *Rabenmütter* (raven mothers, or more accurately "monster-mothers") has been coined to describe East German mothers who placed their children in daycare and went to work. Some West German media portray GDR daycare as storage for children (*Aufbewahrungsstätte*) without educational value. Other critics emphasize the socio-political indoctrination in daycare and after school programs, and object that a highly-structured schedule left children too little opportunity to develop their creativity. Defenders of the East German childcare system counter that raising children without siblings exclusively in a home environment deprives them of socialization and the opportunity to learn group interaction skills and consideration for others.

While some older women I interviewed had been reared by stay-at-home mothers, this was seldom true of women born after 1960. Nearly all placed their own children in daycare, because they wanted to work, and because the socialist regime created a negative image of women who stayed at home. Mothers explained that daycare offered structured play, exercise, outings, and equipment far beyond what individuals could provide for their children. Young adults whom I questioned generally reinforced the positive impressions I had received in Erfurt.

It is important to recognize that the negative portrayal of daycare is one way of driving working mothers back into the kitchen. In the 1950s American media also depicted daycare as harmful to children, and working mothers as selfish and undutiful. In this way daycare remained a private responsibility, rather than being considered part of early childhood education, and therefore a governmental responsibility. These images served the country's need to persuade women who had gone to work during the Second World War to return to their homes and leave jobs open for returning soldiers.

East German sociologist Ursula Schröter asserts that turn of the century questions about the effects of daycare and kindergarten on children really focus not on the quality of care, but on the stability of the traditional gender-based division of labor (Schröter 1997, 45). In other words, some Germans oppose daycare because it challenges the historical assumption that women's work consists primarily of caring for their children. She also points out that surveys show that East German children brought up in daycare had more positive attitudes toward their parents than West German children; they said their parents were tolerant, supported them better, and punished or embarrassed them less. Moreover, women who were imperfect mothers benefited from support and guidance supplied by daycare workers and the companionship of other mothers (Schröter 1999, 143).

Today the childcare issue has become a critical factor in women's unemployment. While the GDR provided daycare spaces for 80% of two- and three-year-olds, West Germany had space for only 1.6% of children in this age group. Three per cent of the GDR's daycare spaces were provided by church-related organizations, 15% by workplaces such as factories and collective farms, and 82% by government entities (*Stiefschwestern*, 103). Many have closed as these offices and workplaces ceased to exist. As a result, women must travel further from home or work to find suitable daycare. Virtually all daycare workers were women, who now swell the ranks of the unemployed.

Those centers that remain open have increased their prices to 250 to 300 DM per month. In January 1996, Germany increased payments to stay-at-home mothers to 600 DM per month (*Erziehungsgeld*). The monthly child support payments known as *Kindergeld* (paid also to mothers who work outside the home) increased in 2000 to 270 DM for each of the first two children, 300 for a third child, and 350 for each additional child. All told, these payments are a better bargain than paying women unemployment compensation. This manipulation of social policy works against women who want to return to work: a woman whose children are not enrolled in daycare is considered unable to work and thus not eligible for work referrals, nor for unemployment compensation. Given the impracticality of paying out 250-300 DM per month for childcare while forfeiting 600 DM per month in compensation for staying at home with a child under the age of three, it is understandable that women lack the incentive to go job-hunting. And if they are not actively job-hunting, they conveniently disappear from the unemployment statistics.

Single mothers (who constituted 30% of women with children at the time of unification) have been particularly hard hit by the lack of daycare and the risks of being an employed mother. The percentage of births to single mothers has begun to decline. Today three-fourths of single mothers in united Germany live below the poverty line.

Fundamental differences in attitudes toward working mothers divide East and West. In March 1993 Schering pharmaceuticals, a large manufacturer of birth control pills, published a survey of around four thousand women entitled *Frauen in Deutschland: Lebensverhältnisse, Lebensstile und Zukunftserwartungen.* Perhaps as a reflection of better childcare facilities in the East, 73% of those interviewed there believed women were happier for having children; only 55% of western women agreed with them. These numbers show a significant decline for East Germans; in 1990, 90% of women and 85% of men aged eighteen to sixty in the GDR agreed that children were very important or important in their lives (*Frauenreport '90*, 116). In Schering's study of women in united Germany, younger respondents were less likely to believe that children enrich a women's life, a finding suggesting that Germany's birthrate will continue to decrease. While only 44% of East German women in the 1993 study felt they must choose between employment and family life, 57% of West German women thought this was a necessary choice, and that it is bad for a child if a mother goes out to work. A 1996 survey found that 73% of East German women and 62% of East German men agreed with the statement that "A working woman is a better mother," and these percentages grew between 1992 and 1996, even as conditions for working mothers worsened (Schröter 1999, 139). The percentages of West German women (45%) and men (28%) who agreed with the statement were far lower and increased only slightly between 1992 and 1996. As Schröter points out, the problem lies in the fact that it is chiefly West German men with their negative opinions who shape future childcare and employment policies.

By the end of the century the scarcity of daycare in the West was becoming the norm nationwide. Perhaps as a result of its increasing rarity, attitudes toward daycare were becoming less favorable. In a 1997 statistical study, half of the East Germans surveyed–and three-fourths of West Germans–agreed with the statement that children suffer when their mothers go to work ("Datenreport 97"). West German kindergartens had space for only about one-fifth of the children between three and six years of age, and fewer than 10% of West Germany's working women have children under six. In August 1996 Helmut Kohl's government promised adequate kindergarten space for all children, a promise which has not been entirely fulfilled. In some quarters, the declining birthrate has become an excuse for downplaying the need for kindergartens and saving public funds.

One-fourth of West Germany's career women have no children at all (Versieux, 20). West German schools begin at different hours on different days, and the school day ends in the early afternoon, meaning that they do not cover daycare needs, even for school-aged children. Only 22% of West German women with children under fifteen worked in the days before unification, and many of those were single mothers who depended on earned income. The comparable figure for East Germany was about three times as high: 68% of all working women had children under eighteen; women with children who were not working were typically those taking advantage of the baby year.

Despite the loss of the monthly housework day and the shortening of their maternity leave, East German mothers want to work. In a poll conducted in November 1991, only 13% of mothers of two or more children would opt to stay at home to raise children. More recently, mothers were questioned about the length of maternity leave, which has shrunk from the twenty weeks granted in the GDR to fourteen. Only 10.5% of East German working mothers (compared to 42.8% in the West) would prefer a longer break from work.

Women's pessimism about their chances for combining family and employment caused drastic changes in demographics in the aftermath of reunification. Faced with uncertain job prospects, East Germans are postponing marriage and children, or foregoing them altogether. Traditionally, West German couples married about two years later than East Germans; women at an average age of 25.2 years and men at 27.9 years. Since reunification, East German couples have waited about four years longer to marry, surpassing West Germans' ages at the time of a first marriage. The average age for a woman's first marriage in 1990 was 28.4 in the West and 27.3 in the East; for men, the average age was 31.4 years in the West and 30 years in the East. In the first year of German unity, the average age at first marriage for both sexes in East Germany rose by two full years! In America, by contrast, it took about twenty years for the age at first marriage to rise by four points; in 1992 the average marrying age for American women was 24.4 years, and 26.5 years for men. Between 1988 and 1992, the number of East German marriages fell from 130,989 in 1989 to only 53,000 in 1991, a drop of 60%, and the rate continued as low through 1993. The divorce rate dropped by a stunning 81%. The drop can be attributed to financial pressures that keep couples together, and secondarily to the imposition of tougher West German divorce laws, which require that couples live apart for a year before divorcing.

As market forces provide more suitable housing, East German couples have adopted the West German preference for living together before marriage: 80% of them now try out the relationship this way before they wed. While West German couples usually postpone marriage until completing an education and finding a job, East Germans are still more apt to marry, even if a young wife has not yet begun work (Vaskovics, 87). Eventually, freer choices about housing and living together may enable young couples to avoid divorce.

Births, as well as the numbers of marriages and divorces, dropped precipitously after the political turnaround. In the first three years after unification, the East German birthrate dropped by 60%. There were 198,913 live births in the country in 1990; by 1992 the country registered only 87,030, and by 1993 that number had plummeted to 79,926, a level comparable to the end of the Second World War. This trend has even gained a name: *der Wendeknick*, analogous to der Pillenknick of the sixties and seventies. Instantly East Germany attained the lowest birthrate in the world, an average of just 0.8 children per woman, as compared to the 2.1 children needed to hold the population steady. The Wendeknick bottomed out in 1997 and began a slow upward climb, with 102,882 births in the new federal states in 1998. Depopulation resulted not only from the low birthrate, but also from the emigration of about a million East Germans who moved West, among them 120,000 women of childbearing age. The effect of their loss will ripple through successive generations (Bucher, 16).

The separation of marriage from motherhood continues and has increased slightly in the East. In 1990 35% of all births were to single mothers, 41% in 1993, and 47.1% in 1998 (*Sozialreport 1999*, 115-16). In contrast, the West German rate of births to single mothers (10.4% in 1990 compared to 12.3% in 1998) has risen scarcely at all. A fourth of East German children under eighteen live with a mother who is single, divorced, or separated, and this proportion will continue to increase.

Germany responded to the threat of population decreases not only by outlawing abortion, but by increasing incentives for childbearing in early 1995. Women receive ten fully paid pre- and post-natal doctor's examinations. They receive six weeks off before childbirth and must remain out of work eight weeks after childbirth. They can take an additional four months maternity leave (*Mütterschaftsurlaub*) at a reduced salary; 93% of mothers do take a full six months after birth. Working women are entitled to a child-rearing leave of up to three years, during which their job remains guaranteed. All parents, regardless of employment or income, receive monthly child support payments until their child reaches eighteen (or twenty-seven, if still a student). Generous income tax exemptions also reward husbands who support a stay-at-home wife. The same tax deduction does not benefit working women whose husbands stay home to look after children, nor does it benefit single mothers whose children are in daycare.

Germany pays up to 600 DM per month for the first six months of child-rearing leave to whichever parent (or grandparent) leaves work to remain home with a new baby. Payments for the remaining thirty months are based on income. In 1999 the Social Democrats debated permitting both parents to work part-time while sharing the leave. Part-time work permitted under this scheme would increase from nineteen to thirty hours per week. While men may also use child-rearing leave to take care of their children, only 2-3% of parents on child-rearing leave are men. As was the case in the GDR, men earn more than women and therefore are reluctant to stay home. Of course those who do so are often the victims of negative stereotyping.

Germany's maternity and child-rearing policies are grounded in economic necessity. Today one-third of united Germany's twenty-seven million marriages are childless, and the number of childless women has doubled in the last twenty years (Drauschke and Stolzenburg, 102). The new federal states have lost around 10% of their pre-unification population (Bucher, 19). The loss of 2.1 million Germans by 2025, predicted by United Nations demographers and likely to continue or worsen in future decades, could seriously unbalance the country's national pension and social security system. Already Germany has a disproportionately high number of older inhabitants (16.4% are sixty-four or older), who require pensions and medical care.

The Social Democrats have responded to this demographic time bomb with *Frau und Beruf,* incentives for combining motherhood and paid employment. It is interesting to compare the SPD's program to the Socialist Unity Party's Muttipolitik. The latter offered mothers full pay for one year, as compared to partial pay for three years. Both guarantee that women can return to their job at the end of their leave; however this is not always the case today. Mothers returning to work today may have difficulty finding affordable daycare, a problem the GDR solved thirty years ago. Other aspects of the Frau und Beruf program—i.e. creating all-day schools and making workplaces more family-friendly—suggest that united Germany in 2000 aims to achieve goals which the GDR reached twenty-five years ago.

A survey of 352 East and 1,455 West German couples conducted between 1991 and 1994 suggests that depopulation will continue in the East. While 88% of West German couples who married in the early 1990s wanted two children, a fifth of East German couples wanted only one. The easterners were also less specific about when they would like children, due to insecurity about income and housing (Vaskovics, 90ff). The survey showed that the incomes of young East German parents did not decrease after the birth of a first child, but West German household income declined by about a thousand marks a month, presumably because the new mother left work. These findings suggest that young East German mothers are less willing than their stepsisters in the West to give up work to stay at home with a new baby. In particular, highly educated women are less likely to have children, and far less likely to stay home with them until they start school. Sociologists therefore also ponder the long-term implications of less educated women having more children (Drauschke and Stolzenburg, 102).

Given Germany's population woes and its surplus labor market, it is more economical to pay women a subsistence wage to stay home with young children than to pay them unemployment compensation. Consider how that system functions to drive women out of the labor force. Imagine a doctor's assistant who marries at the age of twenty-nine (the present average) and bears a child at the age of thirty-one. If she compares the government subsidy for staying home with a young child to her earnings for part-time work, minus the cost of daycare, she may discover that it doesn't pay to return to work for the next three years. If she returns to work but later loses her job, she can collect unemployment compensation only by proving (because of the subsidy paid to stay-at-home mothers) that her child is enrolled in daycare. Of course, if she's not working, she probably can't afford daycare. By the time her child has settled into school, she is thirty-seven, and has been out of her profession for about seven years. During that period, technology will have changed the workplace. Furthermore, she may no longer offer the docile compliance and attractiveness expected of female assistants in service industries. She may work part-time, juggling limited daycare with parenting responsibilities. Employers and employment agencies can specify whether they prefer male or female applicants, so she can compete in the labor force only with other women who have similar skills.

Sociologists have concluded that in times of economic transition, families provide security and stability. On the other hand, reliance on the family as the foundation of personal happiness sometimes stresses the family unduly (*Sozialreport 1999*, 284). This dual nature of family life also prevailed in the GDR, as we determined earlier. While expectations of harmonious and satisfying partnership appear to be met today for most German couples, their anticipation of satisfaction derived from raising children has declined. In 1998 about a third of adults of child-bearing age expected conditions for living with children to worsen (*Sozialreport 1999*, 291-92). Three-fourths of East German women and men surveyed in 1998 believed that conditions for combining work and motherhood have worsened since unification.

Women whom I interviewed repeatedly confirmed that decisions about having children are tied to income. In 1998 I visited again with the young married couple from Neubrandenburg and met their four-year-old daughter. When I asked about plans to have a second child, the young wife replied, "You know, it's so terribly expensive to have another child." Frau W. too confirmed that her son and daughter-in-law have given up hope of having a second child. After their daughter was born Frau W.'s daughter-in-law returned from maternity leave in December 1991 only to be fired. A licensed engineer, she took a re-training course in industrial sales and management and was to be hired on the first of February 1993, but learned the day before that she had no job. After a long search she found a good job, but became unemployed again twice. She's working now, but the fear of becoming unemployed forced her to resign herself to having just one child.

Women who become pregnant while working risk their jobs. *Spiegel* reports that half of the 10,000 young unemployed East German mothers surveyed lost their jobs during pregnancy; three out of ten were fired during child-rearing leave, one-fourth were forced to shorten it. Others returned briefly to work and were then fired, legally. Some were offered 10,000 DM as a settlement to quit without the mandatory period of notice ("Hemmnis Mutter"). Another source reported that over 40% of new mothers who returned to work in West Germany were assigned jobs beneath their level of skills and experience, a demotion which may drive them out of the workplace again.

In October 1992 the Federal Labor Court ruled that an employer may never ask a woman if she is pregnant. In practice, however, the question is so often posed that women in job training courses are taught how to handle it. Applicants know that they need not answer truthfully because the question is illegal. Increasing numbers of women seeking to become more employable have taken the extreme step of sterilization, the ultimate proof that they believe it is no longer possible to combine work and family.

As high unemployment continued through the nineties, East German women felt more acutely the fundamental clash between their own desires and public policy. What was originally framed as an economic problem has proven to be a psychological and sociological problem as well. Responding in 1991 to a survey by the Institut für Arbeitsmarkt und Berufsforschung, East German women chiefly named non-economic motives for working: "I enjoy working with other people" ("ich bin gerne im Beruf mit anderen Menschen zusammen": 81%); "I enjoy professional activity" ("berufliche Tätigkeit macht mir Freude": 75%), and "It's just natural for me to work" ("für mich ist es selbstverständlich zu arbeiten": 72%). Those who have been forced out of the job market find that full-time housewifery offers no independent income, little contact with peers, little experience of success, and poor self-esteem. While the Christian Democrats' political coalition which was voted out of office in 1998 seemed intent on coercing them into part-time work and a full-time commitment to raising the country's birthrate, they are only slightly more optimistic that the Social Democrats will restore some of the support for working mothers provided by the German Democratic Republic.

Chapter Four
Schooling for Socialism: From "I" to "We"

From its beginnings, the German Democratic Republic viewed education as an instrument for replacing the capitalist fascist Hitler regime with a new egalitarian socialist society. Schools in the Soviet zone of occupation re-opened in October of 1945, a Herculean effort, given that many school buildings had been damaged, teachers killed or displaced, and that the region was forced to cope with the influx of ethnic Germans dispelled from the territories east of the Oder and Neiße rivers which had been apportioned to Poland. Experienced teachers who had sworn the mandatory oath of loyalty to the National Socialists were sacked, and 15,000 new teachers, young and hastily trained, entered the classroom in that first year. Twenty years later, 93% of the country's teachers had been trained since World War II (Childs, 169). The replacement of such a large portion of the teaching profession gave the German Democratic Republic an opportunity to start anew. Control over the educational system was centralized at the national level, creating a uniform curriculum that was to be free of militaristic, racist, religious, or imperialist teachings. Achievements of the peasants and working class were highlighted in history, literature, and the social sciences. Special adult education courses in existence from 1945-1969 (*Arbeiter- und Bauern-Fakultäten*) were offered for workers, former soldiers, and returning political prisoners.

The philosophy of education promulgated with the new state established three goals for its schools: they were to eliminate the barriers between city residents and rural people, overturn the traditional class structure, and equalize the education of girls and boys. In keeping with these goals, children of farmers and workers received preference in access to higher education, while the offspring of white-collar professionals, the landed aristocracy, enemies of the socialist state, and some adherents of organized religion, were sent into apprenticeships and factories. Schoolbooks and materials were free for all pupils, in contrast to the West, where the costs of such items as uniforms and school supplies sometimes kept poorer children out of the college-preparatory high school called the *Gymnasium*.

From the first, schools were coeducational. A 1950 Law for the Promotion of Youth decreed that all children, regardless of gender, should receive the same education, vocational training, higher education, and access to sports. While equality could not be achieved immediately, of course, we must consider that the US did not formulate such goals until the passage of Title IX legislation in 1972. In contrast to the German Democratic Republic, some of West Germany's public high schools remained segregated by gender into the 1970s. As the American civil rights movement demonstrated, separate educational facilities are seldom equal.

Education in the German Democratic Republic began in kindergarten, which 95% of three- to six-year-olds attended. Viewed as the cornerstone of the country's educational system, and thus a state service rather than a private responsibility, kindergarten instruction went beyond the custodial care provided in the West. An official handbook of the German Democratic Republic (published in 1986) describes the crèche and kindergarten as teaching "respect for parents and for the achievements of the working people," developing such habits as "readiness to help, modesty, love of truth and order," and motivating children "to become useful members of their group" (*German Democratic Republic,* 178). These aims differ sharply from those taught in an American kindergarten, with its emphasis on self-reliance, development of the individual, and independence.

A 1965 law specified that the goals and content of education for girls were to be the same as those for boys beginning in pre-school (*Frauenreport '90,* 235). With respect to the content of education, a 1962 decision by the Council of Ministers decreed that works of art and literature should include the role of women, and that the artistic activities of girls and women should be promoted (*Frauenreport '90,* 234). Even allowing for the impossibility of realizing such lofty aims, their declaration alone is heady stuff. The presentation of women in exhibitions, magazines, literature, and film emphasized their role as workers as well as mothers.

In school, as in society, work in the collective was emphasized and valued above individual achievement. At an elementary school in Erfurt, I was told that the purpose of socialist schooling, and its most difficult task, was "*die Erziehung vom Ich zum Wir*" (educating from "I" to "we.") Young Pioneer groups and the Free German Youth reinforced this emphasis on group work, organizing study collectives to see that all pupils passed their tests. One drawback to this training was the lack of individual inventiveness or creativity; children simply did not learn to think differently. Individuality and entrepreneurship were not valued either; thinking outside the group brought censure and friction. This devaluing of personal initiative and innovative skills helps explain East Germany's woeful lack of progress in high technology fields such as computerization.

The foundation of the socialist system was the ten-year polytechnic school introduced in 1958, where all students followed the same educational path. Again we must stress contrasts to the West German system, where pupils completing elementary school (*Grundschule*) are sorted into separate institutions for those who will pursue a university education (the Gymnasium), those who will enter a middle school for management and technical programs (*Realschule*), and those whose education will end after ten years with an apprenticeship and vocational training lasting an additional two or three years (*Hauptschule*).

Polytechnic schools taught international solidarity and peace education, although compulsory preparation for military service for boys, and civil defense or first aid training for girls were introduced in 1978. Parents and other citizens opposed this move, and formed the first peace groups to protest, but to no avail. While Americans may criticize the military's intrusion into public education, we must consider the presence of ROTC on college campuses and of Junior ROTC in high schools in the United States.

Polytechnic schools taught Russian from grade five onward. A second foreign language, usually French or English, began in seventh grade. A few schools offered Spanish, Polish, or Czech. Language study was not limited to students destined for the university, and it began early enough to produce good results. Unfortunately, however, teachers who could travel only within the Soviet block seldom found an opportunity to converse in English or French with native speakers. Resentment against the Russians prompts many East Germans to claim that although they were herded through years of Russian language study, they never really learned to speak it.

Marxism-Leninism was an obligatory course from the middle school years upward, reinforced in extra-curricular activities as well as classes. Pupils in the first three grades were expected to participate in the Young Pioneers; those in grades four through seven were called Ernst Thälmann Pioneers. The familiar face of this communist hero, killed in Buchenwald, appeared on posters and camp signs everywhere. Between the ages of fourteen and twenty-five children belonged to the

Free German Youth. An after school program (Schulhort) offering sports, extra curricular activities, and homework study groups enrolled 81% of children in the first four grades. Depending on the viewpoint of the speaker, such institutions are described either as a way of providing childcare for working families, or as supplemental forms of indoctrination by the socialist state.

Article 38 of the German Democratic Republic's constitution required parents to raise their children with a socialist consciousness; those who failed to do so risked losing custody of them. Parents were encouraged to participate in elected parents' councils within the schools, and received time off from work to do so.

From their earliest years East German children were trained for production. Handicrafts in their elementary years developed manual dexterity and familiarity with common tools. The polytechnic school attempted to integrate theory with practice, and taught more specific industrial production skills. Children in the upper grades were required to work without pay one half-day a week to learn solidarity with the working class and to become familiar with the often monotonous routine of factory work. While instruction in the polytechnic school was largely the same for boys and girls, gender bias persisted in production training and textbooks. Girls at a collective farm might be assigned to weed vegetable beds while boys learned to repair farm machinery. Textbooks illustrated mothers at work, but not fathers doing housework (Hempel, 90-91).

In some respects (such as teacher preparation and gender balance on their faculties) these schools could be judged as falling short of western standards. Kindergarten teachers studied for only three years after completing the ten-year polytechnic school. Teachers in the first four grades studied German, mathematics, and a third subject of their choice at a teacher training college like Erfurt. Virtually all were young women. In classes averaging close to twenty-five pupils, discipline problems sometimes arose in the upper grades. Eventually more male teachers were brought into these grades to cope. Teachers qualified for upper grades by taking a five-year course at a teachers' college or university. The level of instructional technology available remained low. Pocket calculators were introduced into mathematics classes in 1985. American educators may react by bemoaning East Germany's technological backwardness, or by rejoicing that its waiters and waitresses can still add up restaurant checks in their heads.

One woman whom we will call Ingrid taught English in a polytechnic school for many years. She moved directly from study in

Leipzig into teaching, with no opportunity to reflect on other career choices. Beyond teaching her classes from eight in the morning until around two in the afternoon, she led Free German Youth and Young Pioneer groups after school. She felt pressured to discuss politics and current events with her ten- to sixteen-year-old pupils, and she admits now that she told them lies because she didn't know any better. Other teachers struggled with the gap between socialist ideals, which they were obliged to teach, and the political reality in which they lived. In one incident recalled in her interview, Russians had shot down a Korean plane. Following the official news reports, she assured her pupils that it was an accident; the Russians would never commit such a brutal act. Later she learned that wasn't true, and the memory of the incident troubles her now. She says she doesn't believe in any ideology any more. And students have become more assertive in questioning their teachers, a healthy development, she thinks. However, women teachers have to prove they are right; sometimes students will seek verification from a male colleague.

When asked about women's roles as teachers, Ingrid remembers that the staff in elementary schools was 80-90% women. She explains that the higher the grade level, the more males taught there, in the expanded secondary schools, for instance. Kindergarten and daycare workers were all women. In Erfurt in 1985 a school director explained that kindergarten teaching was purely a woman's profession ("ein reiner Frauenberuf"), and asserted that there were only nine male kindergarten teachers in the country! Only a miniscule percentage of department heads, deans, or college and university presidents were women, and the higher the level, the more exclusively male the personnel.

East Germany's special schools for athletes became famous in the West for their success in producing Olympic medallists, but not all of their pupils became competitors. A young man whom I met had been selected for training as a swimmer. He was placed in a special residential school at the age of seven; there the academic curriculum was structured around physical training. He was given steroids whose effects later caused minor health problems. When it was determined that he would never qualify as Olympic material, he was returned to the polytechnic school system and later apprenticed in a factory which manufactured bottles and bottled soft drinks. From there, favored perhaps by his father's position as a school principal, he moved on to study at the College of Education in Neubrandenburg, founded in the 1970s under the aegis of Margot Honecker, wife of the country's long-serving General Secretary.   He studied Russian and English and eventually moved West.

An integral part of the polytechnic school was vocational counseling during the last two years. While West German children were strongly influenced by their parents' choice of occupation, the socialist state's intention of overturning this class structure called for some revisions. Based on projected needs in certain trades laid down by the country's five-year economic plans, children were presented with certain vocational choices roughly corresponding to their talents and skills. A Council of Ministers decree in 1962 demanded increased recruitment of girls into technical trades and agriculture, and the establishment of quotas for their recruitment into regional industries. Government subsidies for all apprentices and the guarantee of free vocational training freed girls from the reluctance of some families to prepare them for any career but marriage and motherhood.

Girls who entered the vocational counseling process with one idea of a chosen career might be persuaded to change to meet the needs of the socialist state, or to better fit their own qualifications. A candidate with a weak voice or a hearing impairment, for example, might be directed away from a teaching career. This process, called simply steering (*lenken*), supposedly occurred in about 30% of the cases. Girls were more apt than boys to have to re-think career choices, for some aspired to occupations such as hairdresser or cosmetologist, which were already over-filled.

The lack of flexibility in the system of imposed career choices had some drawbacks. It left little room for late bloomers or for individual talents. Preference was given to protégés of the Free German Youth, or to males who served three years (rather than the minimum eighteen months) in the National People's Army. On the other hand, the system insured that no one was barred from higher education on financial grounds, since university education as well as technical training was fully supported. Of course my sojourn at Erfurt's College of Education showed me that facilities and lodging in higher education ranged between spartan and squalid.

In general East Germans seem to have accepted the career choices made for them. Many later pursued further vocational training, commonly paid for by state-owned enterprises, which also granted them paid time off from work. At the very least, polytechnic school graduates could take comfort in the fact that their career choice guaranteed lifetime full employment. After ten years of hindsight, some find that guarantee a fair trade-off to balance against their freedom in united Germany to choose an occupation.

Most students graduating from the ten-year polytechnic school entered a two-year apprenticeship, then received a skilled worker's certificate that qualified them to enter a technical school, and went to work. Others underwent a three-year apprenticeship that qualified them for eventual admission to a university. A third of apprentices lived in hostels near the workplace; the remainder usually continued living with their parents until marriage. From 10-15% of students left the polytechnic school without completing vocational training, and 20-30% did not find a suitable apprenticeship. Some were young women who married early. Some disliked the prospect of lifelong manual labor. Others aspired to careers in the arts or other areas for which they were judged unqualified.

Despite the noble aims of a single school for all intellectual and social classes, it became necessary to return to a partially stratified system: those destined for the university spent an additional two years after the polytechnic school in an *erweiterte Oberschule*, (an expanded secondary school) which prepared them for university work.

The German Democratic Republic's system of higher education offered fully financed study to anyone who qualified. Workers who had begun in a trade might be supported in evening courses or correspondence courses that later prepared them for entrance to a university. Most courses of study at the university lasted four or five years; medical programs lasted six. Coursework culminated in writing and defending a thesis. Exceptionally successful students might continue for a further three years or longer for the doctorate. Only about 8% of all employed people held university degrees in 1989 (*Frauenreport '90*, 38). Indeed a significant advantage of the country's system of directed career choices was that it left no opportunity for the rise of a highly educated, unemployed intelligentsia. Those are the people who foment revolutions, we were told in 1985. Ironically, the creation of a highly educated but under-employed intelligentsia is precisely what resulted from German unification. East Germany is now estimated to have the highest unemployment among intellectuals and the highest rate of intellectuals living below the poverty line in the world (Richter, 20).

Because socialism used the educational system as a way of overturning gender segregation, some women were urged to study chemistry and physics. One woman chemist interviewed in Berlin in the mid-nineties found her gender a greater hindrance in a non-traditional occupation than would have been the case in the old days. As a student she observed the candlelight peace vigils in Leipzig that preceded the political turnaround in 1989. In her class of sixty-three students, half women and half men, everyone received a monthly grant of two hundred marks that covered their expenses adequately. Now of course students are free to study anything they wish, but some cannot afford higher education. She found only advantages at first in unification, but now she recognizes disadvantages too. She knows many women who studied chemistry who are unable to find a job today. Applications from women in chemistry are considered second class, she says. That certainly wasn't the case in the German Democratic Republic; many already signed a contract with a factory while they were students.

How well did the German Democratic Republic meet its goal of implementing gender equality by re-designing the educational system? Answers can be found in a document from the last year of that country's existence, *Frauenreport '90*, commissioned by the Council of Ministers' office for gender equality. The inequality between women and men was attributed to remnants of the old capitalist division of labor, and statistics bear out this claim. For example, while three-fourths of those inhabitants without a high school diploma or certificate of vocational training were women in 1981 (the latest census available), their portion fell to 63% among employed people, who were younger. Older rural women comprised the greatest number of those without such qualifications; thus the country had also fallen somewhat short of its goal of overcoming differences between urban and rural residents.

The 1990 *Frauenreport* found that women were more likely than men to be employed beneath the level of their educational qualifications, particularly after the birth of a child. While women valued education and knowledge as highly as men did, they were more likely to place a career second to family concerns, making adjustments such as refusing shift work or managerial responsibilities to adapt to family priorities, their husband's job, or the availability of childcare near the workplace. For the same reasons they were less likely to accept re-training to qualify for a new position.

The polytechnic school and its vocational counseling achieved only modest success in re-arranging the gender balance in blue-collar trades. Over 60% of girls finishing the polytechnic school entered just twenty-eight professions. Those trades whose workforce was over 90% female included clerical work, shoe and clothing manufacture, textiles, sales, and postal work. Trades where the workforce was at least two-thirds female included chemical production, data processing, gardening, and animal production. Less than a third of the workforce was female in meat processing, machinist trades, woodworking, tool making, construction, and electronics. Twenty-five to thirty trades were closed to women, for "health reasons." Such trades, including high-rise and subterranean construction, excavation and mining, paid very well.

In occupations employing few women, few apprenticeships were opened for girls, in electronics, tool making, or office machine repair, for example. Seven times as many men as women held the master of trades certificate needed to train apprentices. Thus girls experienced a shortage of women role models in many skilled trades. However, girls' traditional views of female roles also limited their choices; often there were more apprenticeships open to them in male-dominated trades than there were girls ready to enter them. The microelectronics and computer chip production industries (the country's Robotron computer manufacturer was located in Dresden) offered new opportunities for women; because of their manual dexterity and attention to detail they are favored in such production facilities. However, the new jobs would require re-training workers who would work in shifts, both drawbacks to young mothers. Furthermore, highly paid trades were usually offered to men first. Factories viewed young women as a poor risk because of the maternity and childcare benefits they could demand. To some extent the effects of such occupational segregation were mitigated by the existence of affirmative action plans which had come into existence as early as 1962 in fields such as agriculture, where there was traditionally a shortage of women.

Twice as many women as men held the lower degree from a vocational-technical college, and by 1981 over 90% of students in such institutions were women, because this was the degree required for teachers in daycare through grade four, and for medical technicians and nurses. Here too socialist rejection of historical gender roles had relatively little effect: in 1971 about a fifth of women studied technical fields and the sciences; in 1989 the proportion of women students in these fields had only risen to 27%. Greater gains were reached at the university level where more women entered economics, mathematics, technology, and the agricultural and natural sciences. In general, the higher a woman's level of education, the more liberal her attitudes toward gender roles, and the more willing she became to pursue a traditionally male occupation.

Statistics on university students bear out the claim that socialism gradually overcame the inherited imbalance of women in higher education. German universities originally trained clergy, doctors, lawyers, and professors, all occupations that excluded women. Unlike America, where private colleges (such as Oberlin, in 1837) opened their doors to women, Germany had only public universities, and most began admitting women after 1918, with the beginning of the Weimar Republic. Women did not begin earning doctorates, however, until the early thirties, and their progress was cut off by the rise of fascism. While only one-fourth of East Germany's university students were women in the early sixties, that portion reached almost one-half by 1975. However, many continued in traditionally female areas such as the humanities and social sciences.

In 1992 I participated in a summer program for American teachers of German at the university of Leipzig. Germany's most famous author, Johann Wolfgang von Goethe, studied in Leipzig in the late 1760s and immortalized a cellar tavern, Auerbach's Keller, in his drama *Faust*. Remnants of the old university were razed around 1960 and replaced by new buildings housing the proudly named Karl Marx University. City residents dubbed its slant-roofed skyscraper "the wisdom tooth."

I arrived in the midst of academic upheaval. I lodged at the Haus der Wissenschaftler, a turn of the century villa on Georgi Dimitroff Straße which had been turned into rooms for visiting scholars during the German Democratic Republic. The Bulgarian Communist whom the Nazis charged with setting fire to the Reichstag in Berlin in 1932 had defended himself unsuccessfully in a trial held on this street. The courthouse now houses a city art museum. Before I left Leipzig, Dimitroff's name had been marked with a red slash, and a new street sign, "Wächterstraße" posted below it. Thus do heroes vanish.

I arrived in Leipzig's cavernous train station, one of the largest in Europe, and made my way by streetcar to my destination. An elderly housekeeper, appropriately named Frau Diener (Mrs. Servant) showed me to a double room that I was to occupy alone, a tribute to my status as Frau Doktor Professor. Professors outrank even medical doctors in prestige; their erudition is more highly valued than high earnings, and since only a minuscule percentage of tenured professors are women, I enjoy my exceptional status and the benefits it confers whenever I travel to Germany.

Nothing in the Haus der Wissenschaftler had changed in recent decades. Opposite my room across a large foyer were unisex showers, and toilets with an overhead water tank that flushed when the chain was pulled. My room was carpeted in a design of black-leaved orange flowers. It boasted four lamps, each with a thirty-watt bulb and a lampshade the size of a toilet bowl with pumpkin-colored fringe. By the radio stood an elephantine armchair that reminded me of Kruschev in a gray suit. In its crevices I found East German pennies and ten cent coins, the "aluminum chips" so lightweight they float. No one bothered to pick them up anymore, and they lay where they fell. My bed, ready to serve as a sofa by day, was covered with a feather puff buttoned into an embroidered cover, its satin brocade showing through the back of the featherbed cover like the backside of a plump dowager in a ball gown. Behind the massive desk stood double glass doors leading to the balcony. Its sculpted Corinthian columns had crumbled away below, revealing the metal bone inside the stucco. Other seminar participants found less comfortable lodgings, I learned. Next morning the seminar convened in the Jenny Marx dormitory where some participants were lodged on the seventh floor. The elevator was broken and the bathrooms stank of urine.

One evening I supped alone in the little tea kitchen at the Haus der Wissenschaftler. Another guest, a professor from Cologne who chanced to find me washing dishes, took me for the housekeeper. Once I explained that I was a visiting academic like himself, he apologized most heartily, and went on to describe what had brought him to Leipzig. He had been born in Silesia, formerly a part of Germany, but apportioned to Poland after the war. For his children, the GDR was a completely foreign country. He had come as part of a West German team charged with reviewing and consolidating the city's numerous faculties. The college for training physical education teachers had a faculty of forty-one; three could remain.

Later I met a professor whose life would undoubtedly change through this restructuring. She was on the faculty at the Karl Marx University and had given a lecture on teaching literature. She was applying for one of four positions slated to remain in the German methodology department, which presently employed twenty-four. She had never before applied for a job in her life, and the Leipzig university had never advertised any under the old regime. She had successfully completed her doctorate there after only three years, and was simply taken on. She had married at twenty and had two teen-aged sons, now studying for three weeks in England. By anyone's judgment, her prospects looked dismal.

The effects of unification in rolling back East German women's gains in education are twofold: first, massive unemployment among teachers caused by the drop in the birthrate and changes in political ideology. Of the country's 170,000 teachers, about 40,000 lost their jobs. Second, the imposition of the West German educational system means a shift in the subjects taught, and changing working conditions for those who do manage to stay employed.

The post-unification drop in births means that the new federal states will need significantly fewer teachers into the twenty-first century. While 82,000 pupils entered first grade in the East in 1990, only one-third as many began school in 1999. Women who worked in childcare or kindergarten face grim prospects. First, daycare centers have closed their doors. Many belonged to publicly owned enterprises which have ceased operation or been taken over by West German managers who don't expect to hire working mothers. Second, women who have lost their jobs care for their children at home and take advantage of united Germany's payments to stay-at-home mothers.

Mecklenburg-Vorpommern, which employed 19,500 teachers in 1995, estimated needing only 8,500 by 2010, because of its loss of population. The effects of this Wendeknick are working their way up the system; at the high school level for instance, Saxony anticipates an enrollment drop of 60% between 2000 and 2004 (Hofmann, 9).

In contrast, the number of first graders in the West increased by 23% in the nineties, and 19,000 new teachers were hired to teach them. The West, which already had an over-supply of teachers, recruited very few from the East, considering them under-qualified or politically suspect.

A quarter of all East German teachers above kindergarten level were fired, many because they were considered ideologically tainted, a condition called *persönliche Staatsnähe*. Teachers of civics (Staatsbürgerkunde), leaders of Young Pioneers, or socialist party unit secretaries were routinely sacked, even without evidence of their individual conduct. Older people who recall the firing of teachers at the end of the National Socialist regime feel an eerie sense of *déjà vu*. Women, who constituted about 80% of all teachers, specialized in traditional female fields such as the social sciences, now considered tainted by Marxist-Leninist overtones. In the humanities, a new culture chooses new standards and new interpretations of the classics in literature, drama, film, and art. In Saxony, 4,200 teachers (both female and male) were dismissed between 1990 and 1994 on personal grounds. Another five to six thousand women from the "para-educational community" (researchers, administrators, teacher's aides) in Saxony were also dismissed (Buddin, 9). Only around 10% of East Germany's social scientists have kept their jobs in academia, and only around 12% of academics in all fields held onto their positions.

Education, like abortion and pensions, is an area where the West German system has been superimposed on the East. Teachers and parents there welcomed greater flexibility and experimental elementary curricula such as Montessori and Waldorf schools. But a 1992 survey showed that most parents wanted to retain the unified curriculum of the polytechnic school, which provided the same education for all pupils in the first ten grades, and the availability of after-school programs. A significant difference became apparent in what parents see as the task of education: East German parents ranked discipline and courtesy high among the things children should learn in school, while West German parents instead emphasized factual general knowledge (Volkhard, 5). East German parents chafe at the loss of their cultural icons, heroes of the communist resistance to fascism, at the de-valuing of a Marxist-Leninist view of history as class struggle, and at the disappearance of their own literature and film industry.

The shift in subject areas taught means that the demand for teachers has shifted as well. Russian language teachers face empty classrooms and find themselves poorly equipped to teach English or French. The classical education of the Gymnasium requires knowledge of Latin, where teachers are now in short supply. Given Germany's location and its role in Europe's future, however, one wonders whether Latin or Russian will be more valuable to high school graduates in the coming decades. Teachers of mathematics, physics, and chemistry, all male-dominated areas less ideologically contaminated by *Systemnähe*, survived the Wende in a better position than women teaching humanities and social sciences. Yet today their future is jeopardized by the over-supply in these fields; Saxony has three times as many teachers of physics and chemistry and twice as many teachers of mathematics as it anticipates needing in the next five years (Hofmann, 9). These statistics mean slim chances for women teachers seeking to enter these traditionally male subject areas.

East German teachers who have held onto their jobs work in a different learning and teaching environment. They lack the job security assured under the old regime, and receive lower pay than their West German colleagues. While they welcomed video recorders, copiers, and computers, they have struggled to master and keep up with new technology. The hours of instruction have been lengthened and class sizes have increased from their pre-unification average of twenty-one pupils per class to over thirty. Discipline problems have become more common, exacerbated by stresses on parents and families, and the loss of extra-curricular or after school activities. Many teachers feel overworked and burnt out, particularly in the elementary school and Hauptschule, the institution for pupils destined for an apprenticeship and learning a trade. The concentration in one school of most pupils not planning to continue their education means that teaching here is more stressful and difficult than in the old polytechnic school, which mixed pupils of varying abilities.

In the ten years since unification, vocational training has undergone far-reaching changes. Today girls are far less likely to prepare for careers in animal or chemical production. Top career choices of girls remain concentrated in sales or services: retail sales, doctor's or dental assistant, hairdresser, banking, and food sales. Services have replaced manufacturing as the focus of the economy. Increasingly women find themselves in professions where helping, serving, or pleasing the customer is paramount.

Young people face heavy competition for a limited number of apprenticeships. At the start of the new school and work year in the fall of 1999, the number offered fell 140,000 short of the need. The only increase in the number of openings came from government-sponsored programs. The loss of industrial jobs and the closing of East German factories have further reduced the number of apprenticeships. High school students who know their prospects for finding an apprenticeship are dismal lose motivation to succeed in school. Young people unable to land a first job are not eligible for unemployment compensation and must continue to depend on their parents. At the same time many youth clubs or activity centers have been forced to close, leaving young people nowhere to go after school. A frequent lament in my interviews with older people was that today's youth are ill-mannered and unruly. People realize that the summer youth camps the GDR created for Young Pioneers and Free German Youth were a forum for political indoctrination, but they bemoan their disappearance, for at least children learned social values, a sense of responsibility, courtesy, and respectful behavior in these settings. Today juvenile delinquency is on the rise; a survey reported in a May 1997 newsletter of the Deutscher Frauenbund stated that 60% of East Germans are afraid of being out on the streets at night, compared to only 34% of West Germans reporting such fear.

In higher education, young women are less protected than in the old days of the GDR from financial, familial, and social pressures that limit their access to education. Having a baby before university graduation has become a rarity. The number of women students at East German universities is shrinking as daycare centers, once part of every campus, are closed. Many highly educated women will forego having children to maximize the earning potential that makes the investment of time and energy in education worthwhile.

Women constitute half of all university freshmen in united Germany, and make up 46% of those who graduate overall. But they represent only 12% of university graduates in engineering, 31% in math and natural sciences, and 39% in law, economics, and social sciences. Twice as many men as women study computer science. Women are less likely than men to pursue doctoral studies. The number of women earning a Ph.D. in West Germany doubled between 1982 and 1990, when they comprised 36% of new Ph.D.s in humanities and linguistics, 22% in social sciences, 17% in law, and 3.5% in engineering. Now women make up just 30% of all doctoral recipients, and constitute a majority only in art history and veterinary medicine (56%).

The under representation of women in academia is rooted in the long tradition of exclusion and discrimination which blocked their entrance to universities until the Weimar Republic. Today they constitute one-fifth of the *wissenschaftliches Personal* of West German universities, but only 9% of tenure-track professors and less than 6% of full professors. (Another source cites 3% of academic positions held by women (Hosken 1998, 72). In contrast, about 36% of American college and university faculties are female, although women constitute only a fifth of full professors (1999 statistics from the National Educational Association). Nine per cent of East German university professors were women, a rate three times higher than that for the West during the 1980s. Between 1989 and 1993 the ratio of women professors on the faculty at the University of Jena fell from 9% to 3%. The number of women professors at Berlin's Humboldt University fell by about half.

Many academics lost their jobs through the consolidation of institutions of higher learning, a necessary streamlining, in many cases. Dresden, for example, boasted not only a Technical University, but a separate medical school, a college of fine arts, and a technical college for transportation. Now the medical school and the college of transportation have become part of the University, with a resulting loss of jobs in administration and teaching. A June 1999 newsletter published by the German Academic Exchange Service contained the welcome news that the number of unemployed academics fell by 12.7% in 1998, to 198,300. Today one in ten young academics is unemployed, as compared to 17% in 1993. However, the greatest gains in employment have occurred in engineering, the natural sciences, economics, and public relations; in the first three fields, men continue to outnumber women. Germans have coined a new term for unemployment of the intelligentsia: *Intelligenzlerarbeitslosigkeit* .

As is true in other highly-skilled professions, women find it nearly impossible to combine a scholarly career with family life: 40% of women professors are single (versus 4% of their male colleagues) and 60% have no children.

To receive a tenured professorship, German, Austrian, and Swiss candidates must publish a scholarly work called a *Habilitationsschrift* in addition to the doctoral thesis. On average, successful candidates have spent four years in elementary school, nine in the secondary school, seven at the university, five years in the stage called *Promotion*, and an additional seven years in further academic service. Many are over thirty-two when they complete the doctorate, and over forty by the time they are promoted to a professorship. The candidate must seek grants or family funding to support these extended periods of research. Even after years of preparation, a *Habilitationsvater* (father-mentor) and the faculty of a single university judge the quality of the research and publication. Of the 1,915 scholars who successfully completed this process in 1998, only 293 or 15% were women. The complex stages and the need for personal sponsorship constitute further barriers to women, who are unlikely to find a *Habilitationsmutter. (Überholspur zur Professur*, 13). Education tends to reproduce the inequities within itself. The absence of women as role models reduces the likelihood that young women will enter research and university positions in the future.

To update my picture of changes in East Germany's education system, I returned in spring 2000 to visit Erfurt's College of Education. I instantly recognized the streetcar line I needed: Ulan Bator Street was its end station. The high-rise dormitory where I had lived in August 1985 looked much the same except for a fresh coat of paint and more parking spaces. The College still has about two thousand students, and continues to train teachers for elementary and vocational schools. Teachers for the college-preparatory secondary school now study in Jena or elsewhere. Dr. Theodor Neubauer's name has been dropped from the institution, though his statue remains near the administration building: a well-known educator and a communist member of the Reichstag, he was killed by the Nazis.

Less visible changes have had a deeper impact on the faculty and academic programs. Programs which were completely revamped include English and American studies, geography, history, education, philosophy and ethics, political science, psychology, romance studies, and sports. The faculties of science and mathematics were relocated to the University of Jena, but the Erfurt campus now offers prospective teachers the opportunity to minor in religion. After 1990 about 60% of the faculty was forced out and replaced by 110 newly hired professors, three-fourths of them from West Germany. Given the list of programs which were revised, we can assume that many of the faculty who lost their positions to westerners were women.

Later I traveled to Leipzig, where I found the university's "wisdom tooth" shrouded in scaffolding. The Haus der Wissenschaftler now houses the university's foreign studies office. The art museum which occupied the former courthouse in 1992 will be moved into a new building, and a federal court will occupy the renovated building, as it did when Georgi Dimitroff was tried there.

At Auerbach's Keller over Sauerbraten and red cabbage I spoke with Gerlinde F., a tall, energetic woman with a noticeable Saxon accent. She was born about fifty miles from the small town of Brandis east of Leipzig where she now lives. Frau F. has been principal of the elementary school in Brandis since 1992, and gave me a firsthand perspective on changes in schooling since unification. The story of her small town, as told in brochures and town histories she gave me, is worth recounting in some detail because it illustrates social as well as educational developments in the German Democratic Republic.

Brandis developed a significant industrial base during the twentieth century. A factory which manufactured packaging material was producing 90% of East Germany's cellophane by 1978. It employed around 125 women who worked in two shifts to utilize the factory's costly equipment more effectively. A natural pond was converted to a fish production facility, which caused some environmental damage and drove away the local waterfowl. Bituminous coal, used for huge heating plants in Leipzig, and sometimes mixed with clay to make porous firebrick, was mined until the deposits petered out in 1959. The manufacture of clay bricks, tiles, and masonry stove components from deposits of yellowish clay became the largest industry in Brandis. As the clay and firebrick plant expanded its state-owned production, it added social services in the pattern typical of such socialist industries. Apartments for its workers were constructed in the early fifties. The building which houses Frau F.'s elementary school today was completed in 1955 to accommodate eighty kindergarten places and an additional forty-five daycare spaces. Beginning in 1959, the plant offered up to 240 summer vacation places to its workers' children at a company-owned facility on the Baltic. The clay and firebrick plant had its own health clinic and dental practice too. Although residents of Brandis enjoyed such benefits, they suffered from the noise, dust, and air pollution which the plant generated.

A more ominous presence looming over the village was the nearby Soviet military base. Built by the Nazis in the early thirties, the airbase survived the war intact, sheltered by forests. The Russians moved in and expanded the facility, adding huge concrete block apartments to house around five thousand soldiers, airmen, and families. The self-contained base, with its own schools, commissary—even a bakery and a pig farm—was as large as Brandis itself. There was little contact between the Russians and the townspeople, except for a short-lived experiment begun by a teacher of Russian who invited the occupying forces to folk dances and festivals in his school. Higher authorities frowned on this informal arrangement, and it ended abruptly with the transfer of the Russian commandant, despite the fact that the Socialist Unity Party preached brotherhood and friendship with the GDR's "liberators." Sometimes residents of Brandis tried to sneak through the barbed wire and security system surrounding the base to buy champagne and caviar in the base commissary.

The expansion of a runway in 1985 to accommodate jet fighters and training flights aroused opposition in Brandis, though nothing could be done. In October 1987 a realistic simulated air attack terrified residents of Brandis, who feared a new world war had broken out. Frau F. and her husband watched a frightened young Russian land in a field, hastily bundle up his parachute, and run away. No explanation was ever offered, and the event could not be openly discussed until after the Wende.

The end of World War II marked a new era in education in Brandis. Schools reopened on October 1, 1945. Every teacher who had worked during the Nazi years was sacked. Qualified teachers were available at first only for Russian and sports; others had to be hastily trained. Beginning in 1958, pupils worked a few hours each week in agriculture or industries such as the clay and firebrick plant under a program called *Einführung in die sozialistische Produktion*. In 1979 military training was introduced for ninth and tenth grade boys; a uniformed soldier of the People's Army taught the course two hours each week. At the end of ninth grade, boys participated in a two-week civil defense training camp, and in tenth grade a course to prepare them for military defense took place during winter vacation. Given the presence of the Soviet base, some Brandis residents disliked this military training, but they dared not protest openly.

In the days of the German Democratic Republic, Frau F. and her family went their own way, somewhat apart from the mainstream. Frau F. taught in the first four grades and placed her children in daycare after spending the first year at home with them. While her daughter was an infant, this leave was unpaid, but shortly after her son was born in 1976, the Socialist Unity Party introduced the paid year of maternity leave. She would have liked to stay home longer with her children, but that was not possible. Mothers who were teachers taught twenty hours, at full pay, and when she finished teaching around noon, she could take her children home. Her son says he has no unpleasant memories of daycare; among the happy ones was building a large tower with a group of children. The children were confirmed in the Lutheran church, but also participated in the *Jugendweihe*, a socialist coming of age ceremony. Frau F. belonged to the Liberal Democratic Party, in part because participation in its political education circle exempted her from otherwise obligatory attendance at the Socialist Unity Party's monthly seminars.

She and her husband, a mason, bought an old house from a widow in 1972, but the widow retained the right to continue living there until her death. Because her husband's siblings included a number of skilled builders, they were able to renovate and maintain their house, and he worked many overtime hours at black-market building sites to earn extra income and obtain scarce building materials. The family kept a vegetable garden and slaughtered a pig every year to supplement the foodstuffs available in stores. They bought a used Trabant in 1977 and paid more for it than a new car would have cost, but at least there was no decade-long waiting period for the used one. Because their daughter had a heart murmur, they were finally able to obtain a telephone, which had belonged to a head gardener behind on his bills. Later Frau F. suspected he or someone else listened in and spied on the family for the Stasi: her Liberal Democratic Party membership might have made her suspect; the Party had only about 115,000 members. Moreover she opposed the Russian military base, and threatened to organize a petition drive against the runway expansion and simulation exercises. When candlelight vigils began in Leipzig, the family attended them. At first they feared reprisals, but the regime tolerated these peaceful demonstrations, swayed in part by the advocacy of Kurt Masur, director of Leipzig's world-renowned *Gewandhaus* Orchestra.

The years after the Wende brought massive unemployment. The masonry plant was taken over by the *Treuhand* (the government's trustee) agency in 1993, but the collapse of eastern markets and the advent of greater competition forced it to close. A West German manufacturer of paving stones, garden ornaments, and pre-fabricated garages uses a small part of the factory plant. The cellophane and packing materials factory closed in 1992. Overall, the town of six thousand residents lost 2,500 jobs. The five hundred ABM make-work jobs created were a mere drop in the bucket, or, as the Germans say, a drop of water on hot stone. Today the unemployment rate in Saxony remains about 20% (*Arbeitslosenreport 1999*, 165).

Russian troops moved out of Brandis-Waldpolenz on June 30, 1992. The 840-acre base they left behind was an ugly sight. Kerosene and jet fuel polluted the soil. Enormous barracks where families crowded together in small, poorly equipped apartments now loomed empty. Residents formed a private organization to promote transforming the site for use by private firms and civilian air carriers.

Schools underwent far-reaching reform with the passage of Saxony's new education law in 1991. Now that education and the curriculum are the province of the five East German states rather than a national government, Saxony has invested heavily in education. It retained the daycare and after school programs existing before unification, though now parents pay 20-25% of the costs for childcare. The old ten-year polytechnic school, housed in a typical concrete block building completed in 1976, was broken up. About three hundred children in the first four grades attend Frau F.'s elementary school in the renovated kindergarten and daycare building. Pupils sample their first taste of language instruction in third grade. Saxony's school system allows children to move freely among various types of schools, rather than sorting them early on into those destined for an apprenticeship and those headed for white-collar occupations. A new middle school accommodates children who end their education after either ninth or tenth grade. The Gymnasium, housed in a renovated school built in 1906, prepares children in grades five through twelve for college or university study. English instruction now begins in fifth grade, and Russian is no longer obligatory.

Frau F. considers most of the changes since unification positive, particularly the withdrawal of Soviet troops. Air quality has begun to improve, and swans, ducks, and loons driven away by the fish farm have returned. No one in her family became unemployed for long periods due to unification. She enrolled in a two-year program for further training as a school principal and found it useful in managing her faculty. This program in Meissen, sponsored by Saxony's Ministry of Education, trains the state's own school administrators, rather than bringing in West Germans. The old socialist political content of instruction has gone. In the old days a designated political theme had to be discussed before each parents' night; that is no longer the case. After unification, teachers with Socialist Unity Party functions were fired, and leaders of the Young Pioneers were demoted if they had no other training, or if they were hard-line ideologues.

The introduction of religious instruction has taken some getting used to. In Saxony parents can choose between ethics or religion, in the case of Brandis, Lutheranism. Catholic children receive religious instruction in a neighboring town. At first parents had difficulty understanding the difference between ethics and religion classes, and in accepting the fact that one or the other constituted a requirement. Because there were no trained religion teachers, nearby churches supplied temporary instructors. No one rebelled against religious instruction, and by now it has become widely accepted. It has not, however, produced any increase in church attendance, Frau F. asserts, and statistics bear her out. Her daughter's wedding a few years ago was the first church wedding to be held in Brandis since 1973.

Frau F. notes regrettable tendencies to greater class-consciousness among her pupils. The choice of religious or ethics instruction has made them aware of differences among them. Their parents' occupations or, in some cases, unemployment, determine whether they can afford popular new name-brand clothing. She thinks that school uniforms might be one way of counteracting the influence of such status markers.

Changes in the employment of teachers have occurred in Brandis, as they have everywhere. At first assignments were increased from the twenty-two hours standard in the GDR to twenty-eight hours. Fully employed teachers in the new federal states earn about 87% of the salaries paid to their colleagues in the West. As enrollments dwindled because of the post-unification drop in the birthrate, Saxony's school administrators decided to reduce teaching assignments to part-time, rather than lay off teachers. Now most of the elementary teachers in Brandis teach just sixteen hours a week, with a concomitant reduction in pay. Because of their part-time status, it is difficult to motivate teachers to take on extra duties such as organizing class trips. Given the low demand, there is little prospect of hiring newer, younger teachers: about half of the school's fifteen teachers are over fifty. Frau F. acknowledges that children might be better off with younger teachers, but sees little prospect for change. The year 2000 marks the nadir in the region's birthrate. As numbers of schoolchildren gradually increase, those teachers now working part-time will return to full-time status before any new hirings occur. The same money-saving policies prevail in her school as elsewhere: the maximum class size is thirty-two, and classes are not split unless a thirty-third pupil appears.

Overall, Frau F. welcomes the political and cultural opening of her country. A program sponsored by the European Union promotes partnerships with schools in Scotland and Austria organized around themes such as art or living with nature. She and her husband have traveled to Turkey and throughout Europe since unification. Her daughter married a Nigerian and moved to London. Her son worked as an au pair in New Hampshire for a year to improve his English. When his parents visited, he took them to see maple syrup production and housing constructed using post and beam timber framing techniques. The breadth and richness of such varied experiences are among the benefits of German unification which Frau F. values most.

What lies ahead for women in education? East German teachers have weathered the worst of the lay-offs caused by declining births and political changes, but new employment opportunities, especially in the natural sciences and mathematics, will not open up for another decade. Future initiatives affecting women in education come from the Social Democrats Frau und Beruf program introduced in 1999. Some of its provisions, such as the plan to promote vocational training for women in non-traditional occupations, resemble the policies of East Germany's old Socialist Unity Party. To broaden the spectrum of choices for girls graduating from high school, the program would increase funding for apprenticeships and for training women in fields such as engineering and information technology. In that field, women lag far behind. The proportion of girls studying computer science in high school ranks near the bottom of all academic subjects; only 2.5% of all girls choose to study it in the thirteenth grade (Bauermann, 17). Recognizing that information technology is key to future success, Frau und Beruf would increase funding for Internet instruction for women and girls.

In higher education the Frau und Beruf program aims to increase the number of women professors to one-fifth by 2005. Summer 2000 also features an experimental summer program in Hannover, the International Women's University for Technology and Culture. One third of the nine hundred women students will come from Germany. They will study broad themes such as migration, water, and cities, in addition to technology and culture. While such initiatives have value, the International Women's University may be largely symbolic because of the small number of women involved. Furthermore, the return to gender segregation in education can hardly be seen as a promising model for the future.

Instead what is needed is affirmative action to raise the numbers of girls and women studying mathematics, natural sciences, and information technology. As I interviewed older East German women, I was struck by the frequency with which they expressed a love of physics, statistics, or mathematics, sentiments women rarely express in America. Positive images and role models can create affective changes to encourage girls to enter these fields. There will be a time lag of at least a decade until their presence becomes more visible. Nurturing, mentoring students, and positive incentives will be needed to place women in the mainstream of German education.

Chapter Five
Religion: Is God Dead?

Frau Gisela Meise, who arranged a number of interviews for me in Berlin, explained that the club "Living Together" ran a housing complex for elderly people, some of them disabled, and organized coffee hours, calisthenics, and outings for its residents. At a high-rise apartment building in East Berlin the organization's director, a dark-haired woman in an open-necked, short-sleeved white blouse which showed off an excellent tan, ushered us into a large function room. Residents and guests greeted us warmly, as she shepherded people in from the breezy terrace and propelled them toward seats around a horseshoe layout of rectangular tables. I took my place at the head of the table, behind a vase of flowers and plate of cookies. A waitress in a white smock passed cups of steaming coffee. The director and Frau Meise knew most of the residents by name and inquired after their health, friends, and activities.

The roundtable gave me the chance to ask a question I had been considering for a long time: how had the German Democratic Republic become an atheist state? In America in the fifties and sixties, the assertion that the communists did not believe in God seemed one of the worst accusations one could make against them.

First a look backward is in order to understand the religious map of the lands which became the German Democratic Republic. In pre-World War II Germany, one's Christian denomination depended on geography. Martin Luther's Protestant Reformation gave rise to the Peasants' Revolt, which ended in 1555 with the Peace of Augsburg. The settlement stipulated that the ruler of a province would determine the religion of his people; if the duke, prince, or king became Protestant, his people were expected to convert as well. The bloody Thirty Years War (1618-1648) re-opened the question, as Germany became a battleground overrun by France, Sweden, and Poland. In the end the country's population had been reduced by two-thirds. The devastation of agriculture, infrastructure, and government set the country back by at least a hundred years. Once again the outcome, the

Peace of Westphalia, stipulated that the religion of a region's ruler would become the religion of its people. Fragmentation and religious persecution resulted, although the system was not unlike that of America's original colonies, where residents of Massachusetts needed to be Puritans (Congregationalists), Pennsylvania was settled by Quakers, and Rhode Island opened itself to many sects.

Frederick the Great, King of Prussia from 1740-1780, declared, "Es darf jeder nach seiner façon selig werden." (Let each one reach salvation in his own way). He offered freedom from persecution to French Huguenots, whose language he spoke. Voltaire, who played flute duets with Frederick, reported that everyone at his palace, Sans Souci in Potsdam, spoke French; German was necessary only to address servants and dogs. Today French names crop up among old Prussian families, one reminder of the legacy of religious freedom in East Germany's predominantly Lutheran territory.

The postwar division of Germany left the East largely in Protestant territory, a factor which contributed to the disappearance of religion. Had the wealth and structure of Catholicism been brought to bear against Marxist-Leninist atheism, the results might have been different. As it was, churches, Protestant and Catholic, lay in ruins. Scarce building materials went to rebuild factories and eventually dwellings, not cathedrals. On my first visit to East Berlin in 1967, I was aghast at the sight of pigeons flying in and out of the round domes of the huge cathedral on Marx-Engels Platz, a sight that confirmed my worst suspicions about communism putting religion to death.

"Religion is the opiate of the masses." Karl Marx's dictum expressed his belief that by concentrating on the afterlife as the place where rewards and punishments shall be meted out, Christianity quiets social unrest. The weary and downtrodden learn to offer up their privations, assured that in the next world "the meek shall inherit the earth." Furthermore, Christianity teaches submission to hierarchy, in the church, the state, and the family. Women, relegated to second-rank status ever since being created from Adam's rib and excluded from Catholic and Protestant clergy, had much to gain from the abolition of organized religion.

Looking around the circle of faces at the Living Together Club, I recognized that these war survivors, most of them women, constituted the first generation to grow up in the non-religious ethos of Marxism-Leninism. The club's director, born in the mid 1920s, answered my question about the demise of religion in the German Democratic Republic. She responded that children whose families had been torn apart by the war asked adults how a just God could allow their fathers to be killed. She voluntarily left the church at eighteen. Another woman described her family's situation at the end of the war: her father dead or in a Russian prison, her mother sewing at home and struggling to feed her hungry children in a dwelling reduced to rubble. "It was simply clear to me," she declared, "that there could be no God." Another elderly respondent commented that religion is a generational question: in old age, people naturally feel a reverence for the Creator.

One woman compared the principles of Marxism (world peace, international brotherhood, a society based on the greatest good for the largest number of its people) with the Old Testament's Ten Commandments. The oaths taken by Young Pioneers to honor father and mother, and not to steal, did resemble the Ten Commandments, and their moral purpose was similar. The director suggested that because of their similar ideals, belief in Marxism made a suitable replacement for Christianity; yet these ideas were never fully realized: "Nur Friede, Freude, Eierkuchen auf der Welt gäbe es, wenn man danach gelebt hätte." (There would have been nothing but peace, joy, and prosperity on earth if people had lived accordingly.)

For the first three decades of the German Democratic Republic's existence, the substitution of Marxism for Christianity was the rule of the day. Aside from religious objections to abortion, little attention was given to the question of how women were affected by the demise of Christianity. Life's rituals took on a secular character. A celebration of name-giving for a newborn infant took the place of church baptism. A new ritual, the Jugendweihe, was created to mark the transition to adulthood and the acceptance of citizen's responsibilities in the socialist state. Much like Catholic confirmation, it was celebrated as a coming of age ceremony complete with a family gathering, gifts, and a large dinner. Photographs were taken of Jugendweihe ceremonies in the People's Chamber in Berlin, or of Walter Ulbricht and Erich Honecker greeting these new members of the Free German Youth. At funerals the Arbeitskollektiv or work team of the deceased gathered with family to offer a eulogy and honor the dead.

People continued to celebrate Christmas, renamed *das Fest der Freude und des Schenkens*, a festival of joy and sharing gifts. Schoolchildren made sparkling stars and "winged year's end figures," i.e. Christmas angels. School choruses sang "O Tannenbaum" but not "Stille Nacht, heilige Nacht," though families might choose to do both. Easter did not signify an awareness of personal sin and redemption through human sacrifice, but a spring ritual of renewal and rebirth, in keeping with its pagan roots. Easter egg hunts, chocolate bunnies for children, and a large breakfast remained traditions.

Marxism-Leninism, East Germans learned, should be considered a rational, intellectually developed theory of social structure, in contrast to the hocus-pocus of spirituality. Its product, the socialist state, taught moral, ethical behavior to Young Pioneers and the Free German Youth. The government-supported People's Solidarity looked after the elderly and saw to it that the Golden Rule applied. Reverence for one's country and a belief in the superiority of socialism replaced reverence for a supreme being and belief in the afterlife, and the socialist alternatives enjoyed the advantage of being visible. Many Christians recognized the similarities between Marxism and Christianity: both repudiated materialism and wealth, advocated a classless society, peace, and international brotherhood. The stumbling blocks between them lay in how Marxism transformed these ideals into daily practice.

At the time of my 1985 visit, the churches themselves remained in a deplorable state of disrepair. I found both the Erfurt cathedral and the Saint Severi Church, a gloomy Gothic fortress, soot-blackened and locked in the center of the marketplace. Visiting Leipzig I saw bullet holes in the masonry walls of St. Peter's Church, and tufts of green grass sprouting between its steps. At the estate of the romantic poet Novalis, the chapel had been used as a granary. By the 1980s West German churches were permitted to send hard currency or building materials (many diverted to other uses) into the country to rebuild some churches.

Their position within the socialist state forced churches to find a delicate balance between activism and survival. In 1978 churches voiced opposition to the introduction of para-military training in schools and gradually became a gathering place for peace activists and opponents of the socialist regime. Albrecht Schönherr, Bishop of Berlin and Brandenburg, met with Premier Erich Honecker and achieved major concessions: churches could broaden their radio broadcasts beyond Sunday religious services, and newly built community houses in the satellite developments which had sprung up around cities would be opened for religious congregations. Collective farms would pay rent for the use of church-owned farmland.

The five hundredth anniversary of Martin Luther's birth, in 1983, brought about an odd rewriting of religious and political history. Socialists had no desire to glorify the Protestant Reformation as a re-kindling of religious faith, yet they realized that busloads of well-to-do Lutheran tourists from the American Midwest would flock to visit the castle church at Wittenberg where he posted his Ninety-Five Theses and the Wartburg fortress, where he sought safety, disguised as Junker Jörg, and translated the Bible. Therefore Luther came to be portrayed as a hero of the class struggle, who roused farmers and peasants to rebel against the landed aristocracy in the Peasants' Revolt of 1525. The fact that Luther was horrified by the violence he had unleashed and ultimately sided with the nobility against the peasants was not mentioned. Instead Luther's follower Thomas Müntzer, who remained true to the cause, was elevated to hero status and schools were named in his honor.

The churches came to fulfill some important social functions inside the socialist state. In the Erfurt seminar in 1985, I was told that they took primary responsibility for the care of the physically and mentally handicapped, a task requiring such devotion that only religion supplied sufficient motivation. Second, they accomplished the task of publishing the Bible and religious materials.

The German Democratic Republic's universities in Berlin, Halle, Leipzig, Rostock, and Jena offered theology studies, and the country's three religious colleges (in Leipzig, Berlin, and Naumburg) remained freer of state influence (Rogers, 133). In 1967 a ruling by the Lutheran church in Mecklenburg gave women the same rights and duties within the church as men. Thus women could be ordained as pastors and serve their own congregations, though for some years their ordination rights were suspended if they married (Rogers, 84).

True religious believers walked a fine line between kowtowing to the regime and keeping their faith. Pastors and their families were observed by the Stasi but seldom punished, unless they engaged in acts of open defiance or political protest. At the Living Together Club, one woman said she had belonged to the East German Farmers' Party; like most mass organizations, its purpose was not to oppose the regime, but to encourage the correct form of citizen participation. In that role, she had to urge the Lutheran minister to go vote, realizing that clergy who refused could be prosecuted.

Children of Christian families faced difficult decisions about joining the Young Pioneers and Free German Youth. Some became Pioneers, attracted by the group's activities for children and its sessions to help with homework. Some refused and belonged instead to the Lutheran Church's *Junge Gemeinde*. Entering the Free German Youth seemed a greater hurdle because its oath of allegiance expressed atheism and the willingness to fight for the Socialist Unity Party. At the end of the ten-year polytechnic school, Christian children were sometimes denied access to the final years of secondary school that led to the Abitur required for university admission, but others found ways around this hindrance. Another woman at the Living Together Club who had worked in the Labor Ministry in Brandenburg said that she remained in the church; reprisals consisted of her children being forced to take an alternative route to passing the Abitur. "It was possible to stay with the church as long as you behaved correctly," she said.

This need to behave correctly before strangers, at work, and among casual acquaintances led to a split in personality. Many East Germans suffered from the necessity of hiding their true sentiments and beliefs from possible informants. Children were cautioned to speak freely only at home, and not to reveal family discussions at school. Informants for the Stasi were planted in church groups, high school and university classes, in the Free German Youth, and in every factory, shop, and farm. A state-imposed schizophrenia led some to suicide. In Erfurt I was warned that two statistics were so damning that they could not be given out: the suicide rate and the divorce rate. The Samaritans had applied to publish their suicide hot-line number in public telephone booths, but permission was denied because its publication would have meant acknowledging that suicide was a huge problem. An East Berlin theater director who visited me in the mid-eighties claimed that every family he knew had been touched by suicide. Even today the suicide rate in the East (nineteen per hundred thousand inhabitants) remains higher than in the West (fifteen per hundred thousand inhabitants) (*Neues Deutschland* May 30, 1998).

By the mid-eighties, the churches assumed a role in the peace movement; opposing NATO's intention of stationing Pershing nuclear missiles in West Germany in the eighties aligned them with the Socialist Unity Party, even though the socialists were intent on suppressing the peace movement itself. Gradually churches became the chief refuge for political dissidents, many of them peace activists. Because anyone who applied for an exit visa was deprived of the right to work, churches supported dissidents with whatever wages they could scrape together, and sometimes a place to live. Clergy visited political prisoners. Because they were exempt from requirements that groups register their meetings with the authorities, Lutheran churches opened their doors to alternative political groups and protected them with the ancient right of sanctuary. Oddly enough churches also offered space and thus some protection or security to gays and lesbians who were sometimes the target of Stasi informers. However, the drawback, from the churches' standpoint, was that political dissidents and social outsiders were not necessarily Christians. Thus when unification swept over the land, those who had benefited from the church's protection were not always committed to strengthening organized religion.

An enormous collective sigh of relief greeted unification in 1990. It was no longer necessary to hide one's religious beliefs. If East Germany had been an avowedly atheistic state, West Germany was a largely secular society. West Germans seldom attend church and are not ardent believers in religion. They comfortably describe themselves as *Kulturchristen,* (cultural Christians) who observe Christmas and Easter and seek church validation for ceremonies such as birth and marriage and death. One of the reasons Germans failed to comprehend American President Jimmy Carter (besides his adult use of a childhood nickname) was his self-description as a born-again Christian. The notion of experiencing a spiritual re-birth was not as widely familiar to Germans as it is in the southern United States.

Two post-unification innovations were expected to strengthen the churches: the imposition of the church tax, and the introduction of mandatory religious education in schools. German churches are supported not by donations from the sparse congregation, but by a tax equal to ten percent of the payer's income tax liability. Germans grumble about it, but seeking an exemption from the tax can arouse suspicions that one is anti-Christian, and West German taxpayers seldom bother. The institution of this tax in the East after unification brought unexpected results: a sharp increase in parishioners leaving their churches. Because of the tax, both Lutheran and Catholic churches lost about 10% of their members in the early nineties. While the tax funded much needed repairs to the churches themselves, their pews remained nearly empty. Today there are about 3.5 million Protestants and a million Catholics in East Germany (*Sozialreport 1999,* 371-72).

Under the German constitution, church and state are not separate in education: public schools include obligatory religious instruction. In some of the new federal states, children or their parents can choose between ethics and either Catholic or Protestant religion. At the age of fourteen pupils can generally decide to cease religious education. While proponents assert that religion classes in schools teach about all of the world's religions and include non-sectarian ethical teachings, Turks, who are Moslems, and other minorities may feel uncomfortable in such classes. (There are still fewer immigrants from other cultures in the East than in the West). In Bavaria and the Rhineland, religion generally means Catholicism. In Hesse or Schleswig-Holstein, and in the new eastern states, it means Lutheranism. These divisions are one reason parents are allowed some flexibility in choosing their child's school.

Materials used in Saxony to teach the Protestant religion include chapters on Islam, Buddhism, and Germany and the Jews, a topic the German Democratic Republic largely ignored until the late eighties. Topics treated in ethics courses resemble those in an American health class: decision making skills, learning tolerance and respect for differences, friendship, love, and relationships, and career choices. In part such instruction replaces the values taught in East Germany's Young Pioneers and Free German Youth groups. The re-institution of religious instruction in schools has made little difference in the numbers of churchgoers, as evidenced by stagnating numbers of applicants for church ceremonies such as baptism and marriage.

In the wake of unification, churches have had to re-examine their role in a society which remains largely secular. Under the old socialist regime, persecuted and excluded from political power as in the era of the early Christian church, East Germany's faithful sometimes experienced tests of their religious beliefs and were forced to lead lives of poverty and humility. Liberated today from external political constraints, and having largely relinquished their role at the center of the anti-government peace movement, church leaders search for a new *raison d'être*.

Like the imposition of the church tax and the introduction of religious instruction in schools, church restoration is another result of unification, albeit a highly visible one. Yet ironically the East German churches resemble Germany's few remaining synagogues: the buildings are preserved for historic interest without any active congregations to sustain them. Most function as museums. The Berlin cathedral (whose site is now once again called Cathedral Square) houses organ concerts and a historical museum. Dresden's shabby Regiment Church (Garnisonkirche) once held both Protestant and Catholic services for the military. Today a Catholic congregation rents a third of the church, and the remainder houses a lending library and storage for costumes belonging to the Semper Opera House. The enormous red brick Gothic churches of Güstrow and Schwerin tower over their communities in undiminished dominance, but their pews are empty, save for tourists who visit Ernst Barlach's "Singing Angel" sculpture in Güstrow.

The consummate physical evidence of a religious reformation in East Germany is the rebuilding of Dresden's Frauenkirche, a Baroque Protestant structure built between 1726 and 1743. City ordinances stipulated that no building could rise higher than its dome; thus its existence preserved Dresden as a moderate sized city without towering skyscrapers to shadow its streets. The firebombing of 1945 reduced the church to a heap of rubble sixteen meters high. When I first visited Dresden in 1985, the nearly vacant church square had become a parking place for tour busses. Official guidebooks explained that reconstruction was impossible, and a plaque identified the site as a memorial to the horrors of war. Some Dresden residents say stones from the church were used in other construction. By 1992, efforts to rebuild had become a topic of debate. The hiring of a Japanese architect to oversee the work alienated some East Germans. And many insisted that not even West German money could erase the effects of war which the church's ruin had come to symbolize.

By 1998, opinions had shifted. The whole power of united German technology had been applied to the task of rebuilding, which should be finished by 2004 at a cost of 260 million marks (about 150 million dollars). Supporters equate that cost to building another ten kilometers of Autobahn, or buying five jet fighters. The reconstruction is being financed by private donations; one Dresden taxi company donates one Pfennig per kilometer driven to the effort. Computers have identified, numbered, and cataloged every salvageable brick and stone. Huge warehouses shelter the inventory, which will supply only about 45% of the building material needed. The remaining sandstone is being quarried along the Elbe river. Overall, the reconstruction and restoration project has created two hundred jobs. The crypt beneath the church has re-opened for religious services and won over more converts for the reconstruction effort. A glass-walled information booth opened at the worksite, selling videos, postcards, and posters. Most Dresden residents have become convinced that the Frauenkirche belongs in the Canaletto image of their city beside the Elbe River. Cynical residents say that at least the church's rebuilding might increase tourism and revenues.

Ironically, the church has no real congregation to take possession of the building once it is completed. Its complete destruction and forty years of Marxism erased any religious community surrounding it. When its silhouette returns to the city's skyline, the church's facilities will be used for concerts and exhibitions. The Lutheran Church will lease space from the private foundation which will own the church for the next ninety-nine years, paying rent on the same terms as other groups.

The continuance of the Jugendweihe illustrates another difference between the secular East German mentality, and West German culture, which, while not deeply rooted in personal faith, remains grounded in religion as a social framework. As late as 1993 the Jugendweihe attracted 70,000 participants, more than in 1992, and more than the number who participated in any religious confirmation ceremony.

In a land without a central belief system, some East Germans, disillusioned with the collapse of Marxism-Leninism and with the failed promises of capitalism alike, search for a new system that can provide meaning. One young woman I met was exploring wicca. An older woman said she was studying world religions now and reading the Bible. She quoted a bishop who said that socialism failed because people are too selfish to work for the common good. Her parents taught her that Christians believed someone else, such as Jesus Christ, would improve their lot, while socialists believed they would have to do it themselves. While some observers assert that post-communist Poland has been saved by its traditional Catholicism from the social disarray that has swept across Russia, older East Germans, those no longer interested in reviving religion, deplore the moral effects of socialism's demise. They trace the increase in juvenile delinquency not only to youth unemployment, but to the disintegration of the Young Pioneers and the Free German Youth with their mission of teaching youth social responsibility. Furthermore, East Germans look around them and see that neither capitalism nor socialism lives up to its promises of social justice. The question of how to reconcile West German Christianity with West German capitalism remains a riddle to many in the East.

What difference does it make to East German women whether they live in an atheistic or a Christian state? In the Christian myth of creation Adam appears first; Eve is created from his body afterwards. Thus man becomes the norm, that which defines humanness, and woman is the other, secondary, an afterthought. (The prevalence of this attitude has shaped centuries of human biology and medical research.) The depiction of woman as man's helpmeet relegates her to a secondary position in marriage, where she becomes the secondary earner, the homemaker. Man, in contrast, becomes the head of the family, the lawgiver, the leader of the social group. While men certainly held this function in the German Democratic Republic's Politbüro, their role was limited to political power; they were not simultaneously revered as moral authorities. In a Christian state, on the other hand, political and religious leaders often become one and the same, e.g. the Pope in the Vatican, the head of the Anglican Church in England; even America's presidents are expected to fulfill this role of moral and spiritual leader to some degree.

Since unification, the debate over abortion has drawn new attention to the role of priests and bishops as secular authorities who wield political as well as religious power. Because church hierarchy excludes women from these powerful positions, they particularly resent the churches' role in opposing abortion. Both Protestants and Catholics opened counseling centers to provide the mandatory counseling for women who want to avoid legal prosecution for ending an unwanted pregnancy. The debate between Germany's liberal bishops and more conservative Catholics (and the Vatican) ultimately resulted in the decision that these Catholic centers would not distribute certificates proving that women had undergone counseling, a protracted dispute that drew considerable media attention to questions of women's right to control their sexuality.

The Bible presents two supremely powerful images of women's sexuality: Eve the seductress and Mary the Virgin Mother. Christianity confines women's sexuality within the single permissible framework of heterosexual marriage, while allowing freer play to male sexuality. Within traditional Christianity, the goal and purpose of female sexuality is not personal pleasure or gratification, but fertility and motherhood. Bearing children may be portrayed either as a reward for the virtuous confinement of sexuality inside of marriage, or as a punishment for sin (as Eve's expulsion from Eden is accompanied by the threat that she will bring forth her young in pain and suffering). Uncoupling women's sexuality from the risk of childbearing alleviates both the threat of punishment and the likelihood of pregnancy and motherhood, which make women more vulnerable and more needy of man's protection. Therefore Christianity condemns abortion because it makes women sexually autonomous, as men are, and the Catholic Church forbids even the regulation of female sexuality through birth control. (Depiction of the fetus as a sentient being with a human soul is a fairly late development in the abortion debate). Since motherhood is the fruit of female sexuality, Christianity honors it, *provided* it occurs within the patriarchal framework of male-dominated marriage. Christianity glorifies images of women in their secondary role, as stay-at-home mothers, economically dependent, submissive, obedient to wage-earning husbands who provide for them and their children. No wonder the East German women described West German Christian strictures on abortion as backward and primitive (*hinterwäldlerisch*).

As we have seen, the reconstruction of churches and the introduction of religious instruction in schools, as well as legislation against abortion, signal a re-imposition of Christianity in East

Germany. If it has not increased the numbers of believers, what purpose is served by the re-introduction of Christianity, with the limitations it places on women, into this formerly atheistic state? The most obvious gain for western capitalism is that the idealization of stay-at-home housewives and mothers, favored in social policy and the tax code, relegates women to secondary status as wage earners. They can be brought forth to work in temporary, unskilled, low-paying jobs and sent home again when no longer needed. If home life becomes their central focus, giving birth and rearing children become an easier fit for that female role. The ensuing growth in population feeds capitalism by increasing the labor force and consumer demand. As daycare is reduced, mothers' responsibilities to young children increase their economic and personal dependency: in the days of the GDR, a dependency on Vater Staat, today, dependency on their husbands or partners. Women who become economically dependent, and eventually passive and obedient to their husbands, also lose their decision making power and more easily accept political authority. Such women no longer define themselves by what they know and what they do for work. Instead status becomes visible through possessions, creating a greater need for consumer goods and luxury items, and increased demand further strengthens the capitalist economy.

Our excursus into the matter of religion in East Germany opens more questions than it answers. To what extent did the Socialist Unity Party intend the demise of religion in the East as a means of transforming women's position in society? Did women recognize a direct connection between the weakening of Christianity and their own greater sexual and social emancipation? Asking this question in my interviews elicited no meaningful answers. Women seemed puzzled about describing the effects of something that simply wasn't there. A more significant question looms ahead for the future: will women's independence and self-sufficiency prove to be a bulwark against the re-imposition of Christianity from the West? Or will economic uncertainty drive the flock back into the fold, and reconcile women to their position of helpmeet and self-sacrificing mother?

Chapter Six
After the Fall

What led ultimately to the collapse of the German Democratic Republic? Nowhere in the American intelligence apparatus did the alarm sound that the world's most prosperous and most highly developed communist state was on the verge of collapse: thus the causes can not have been military or technological. The events seemed almost serendipitous: the opening of Hungary's border with Austria in August 1989 enabled East Germans on vacation to drive into freedom, displaying bracelets of barbed wire from the Iron Curtain on their wrists. The political events, Honecker's abdication, the brief reigns of Egon Krenz and Hans Modrow have been documented in the history books.

Better remembered are the images of candlelight vigils in Leipzig, held on Monday evenings. Almost everyone in East Germany watched the West German news on television and formed their own conclusions about the true state of affairs. The Federal Republic beamed its televised messages, which some might call propaganda, along the border dividing the two Germanies, and from West Berlin. The Dresden area alone remained unreachable, and other Germans called it "das Tal der Ahnungslosen," the valley of the clueless. On Monday evenings the German Democratic Republic aired its own corrective program, exposing the falsehoods and distortions of West German television. Perhaps for this reason, candlelight vigils opposing the moribund socialist regime occurred on Monday evenings.

It was in Leipzig that Kurt Masur, revered conductor of the city's Gewandhaus Orchestra, pleaded with the government not to fire on its people. What other culture could elevate a musician to such political prominence that his voice would be heard at such a moment? And to the Socialist Unity Party's chiefs, with their palaver about the "people's" army, the people's factories, and the people's state, the protesters called: "We are the people!" (Wir sind das Volk).

Seeking causes behind the sweeping changes, I asked everyone who would hear me in East Germany what had caused the political turnaround called simply "die Wende." Two answers predominated: the isolation of the country's leaders, and its devastating economic state.

Calcified (verkalkt) was the word used to describe the old men of the Politbüro whose black limousines drove from the residential district of Pankow into Berlin and back each day. Observers said the streets were cleared to remove any likelihood that the gentlemen would confront reality during their daily commute. Few women held any office in the impenetrable, overlapping layers of Socialist Unity Party bureaucracy (Central Committee, Politbüro, Secretariat) which ruled the country. While some observers might consider the demonstrations in Leipzig, where women comprised 40% of the participants, a call to remedy their exclusion from power, most women simply considered themselves as part of the disenfranchised populace at large. After a decade of reflection, many of them cite the existence of two completely separate worlds: the optimistic forecasts of SED propaganda and the reality of shortages, dilapidated infrastructure, and things that just didn't work. The German Democratic Republic's real existent socialism collapsed into the void between ideal and reality.

Economic collapse, not visible in the American press, appeared to the East Germans as the inevitable result of their country's high subsidies for basic necessities. Housing costs remained stable while communal landlords failed to collect their rents. Government funds which should have paid for renovation and repair shored up housing prices instead. The high subsidies for maternity and childcare benefits have already been described. For every mark consumers spent on common foodstuffs, the government paid an additional seventy-five Pfennig in subsidies to lower the costs of bread, cheese, potatoes, and the ubiquitous cabbage. Fares for public transportation remained low so that everyone could get to work, while high prices for cars and gasoline discouraged joy riding or spontaneous travel. Meanwhile a second market for luxury items which the privileged few bought with hard western currencies undermined the socialist economy. The cost of supporting the country's military does not appear to have contributed significantly to economic downfall. According to the *Statistisches Taschenbuch* for 1990, the GDR spent about as much throughout the 1980s for defense as for housing and education, and only one-third as much as the cost of subsidies for food and consumer goods.

New economic costs, for environmental cleanup, appeared after unification. The Elbe River, called Germany's sewer, carried municipal and industrial wastes. The Gera River in Erfurt flowed beneath a scum of chemical suds. Waste from collective farms raising cows and pigs pooled in malodorous lagoons, beside fields polluted by heavy applications of fertilizers and pesticides. West Germany regularly paid the East to store its toxic and nuclear waste, and the East Germans stored it along the border, as close as possible to the West. Today these sites too are being cleaned up, while East Germany's nuclear plants and open-pit coal mines have closed.

In the euphoria surrounding the opening of the Berlin Wall, East Germans believed for a few brief months that they could gain a real voice in shaping their country's future. What they wanted, many of them assert today, was the third way: not the continued existence of their moribund state, not a hasty buyout by the West, but an indefinite period of democratic, independent existence as a separate state. The Social Democrats, and notably Nobel Prize winning author Günter Grass, also espoused this hope. What they got under the leadership of Helmut Kohl's Christian Democrats, East Germans now lament, was a sudden economic takeover, a merger some view as colonization.

The seduction of a sudden currency union in 1990, with the opportunity to exchange East for West German marks at the one to one rate, seemed too good to resist. (The actual provisions of currency union were complex, governing how much of individual savings could be exchanged at this equal rate, and how much at progressively less advantageous rates.) East Germans threatened that if the *Deutschmark* did not come to them, they would go to it, and West Germans feared a sudden influx of new settlers they could not easily accommodate. But currency union did not equal comparable costs and prices. Increases in rent and food prices quickly outstripped raises in pensions and wages. Consumers bought cars and video recorders and then found themselves hard pressed to make ends meet each month.

The Treuhand agency was established to sell off state-owned industries to private developers, a task largely accomplished by 1994. Today East Germans bemoan the low prices paid in this huge sellout of their property. Often the buyers were foreign firms, such as Sony and the Hyatt hotel chain, or West German giants such as Daimler-Chrysler which built on East Berlin's Potsdamer Platz. Sometimes the buyers created a new merger of East and West branches of an original parent company split since the Second World War, such as the Reclam publishing house in Leipzig and Frankfurt, or the Zeiss optical works in Jena. All too often the new owners of factories disregarded their pledges to retain jobs. Sometimes the subsidies they received to keep newly acquired East German factories afloat were channeled instead into the West German parent companies. In the aftermath some researchers conclude that the Treuhand's efforts amounted to a wholesale destruction and exploitation of East German industry and agriculture. The country's clothing, leather, and housewares industries employed about 460,000 women, but 90% of them went bankrupt or ceased operation in the early nineties. The disappearance of GDR products, and consumers' preference for those from the West fueled a buying boom that postponed until around 1992 the recession that had appeared imminent in the Federal Republic (Behrend 1996, 26-29).

Various sources estimate East Germany's labor force at around 9.7 million. Without counting the million who moved West and the half million who commute there to work, only five million were still working in 1993. Thirty-eight per cent of the employable East German population was unemployed in July 1993. Women's share in the labor force fell from one-half before unification to one-third afterwards. By 1995, 69% of women with children under four were not working (Pfitzner, 45). Between 1991 and 1995 about half as many as the total number of unemployed were temporarily at work in ABM jobs, but two years later this proportion had fallen to one-fifth (Pfitzner, 44). In the summer of 1998 Helmut Kohl's re-election campaign boosted funds for re-training and make-work schemes, but the numbers fell again after his defeat. One-half of all jobs in the East, 80% of all jobs in agriculture and in industry have been eliminated. For the past five years, Germany has counted an average of four million people out of work. In February 1999 the rate was 9.7% unemployment in the West, and 19.1% in the East. In December 1999, it was slightly lower, 8.6% in the West and 17.7% in the East. Unemployment figures fluctuate but they do not go down. A downturn in the unemployment rate does not signal an increase in the number of people working; rather it suggests a decrease in the numbers of people looking for work, as older workers accept early retirement or young women resign themselves to stay-at-home motherhood.

A vigorous campaign against the elimination of jobs in the East is being waged by the Society for the Protection of Civil Rights and Human Dignity, whose Lichtenberg offices I visited in 1998. Today the Gesellschaft zum Schutz von Bürgerrecht und Menschenwürde, or GBM, counts 4,500 members (nearly all of them in the East) and defines itself as a leftist human rights organization which also concerns itself with international human rights issues. It demands self-determination, job security, affordable housing, equitable pensions, social justice, and defense of the constitution of the Federal Republic of Germany. Specifically, the East German Society for the Protection of

Civil Rights and Human Dignity accuses the West of human rights abuses resulting from unification: unemployment, the political ban on certain occupations, and the destruction of East German culture.

From a western capitalist perspective, defining unemployment as a human rights issue seems a novel idea indeed. Examining what is meant by human rights forces us to recognize that what constitutes such rights depends on our political perspective. To the Germans, the United States violates human rights when it imposes the death penalty, and to the East Germans, both the US and the Federal Republic of Germany violate human rights when capitalism promotes an enormous income gap between rich and poor, forcing a working underclass to subsist in poverty and squalor, and making it impossible for others to find any meaningful work.

Results of a survey published in 1996 by the Society for the Protection of Civil Rights and Human Dignity illustrate the central importance of work in one's self-esteem and identity. Over 97% of respondents agreed with the statements that work was essential for their personal fulfillment, as well as a means of earning money. Such people find it difficult to grasp the capitalistic depiction of work as the means of obtaining greater consumer goods. Indeed a fundamental opposition becomes visible between those who work merely to earn a living and those who live to work. Ironically, it is the latter group who has been left unemployed by the political turnaround.

Battling the *Berufsverbot*, or ban on certain occupations, is a particular initiative of the GBM. Professional bans affect 1.5 million East Germans who lost their jobs and are banned from further employment because of their Staatsnähe, or proximity to the regime. This ban affects diplomats, scientists, engineers, civil servants, researchers, telecommunications and railway personnel, teachers, police, military personnel, workers in political parties, and artists (most of whom received state support from the German Democratic Republic).

The Society for the Protection of Civil Rights and Human Dignity points out that the Berufsverbot has a long tradition in Germany; while communists and Social Democrats, as well as Jews, were banned from the civil service during the Nazi years, the Adenauer era in West Germany saw renewed bans on communists and Social Democrats, as well as ex-Nazis. Of course the German Democratic Republic banned and persecuted not only former Nazis but committed Christians, political dissidents, and those who had applied for emigration. Overall, the Germans have considerable experience observing how political allegiance can cost workers their jobs when the old regime gives way to the new.

Because political culpability was a charge commonly applied to teachers, especially those who taught history, sociology, civics, economics, or literature, women have been hard hit. East Germany is estimated to have the highest unemployment among intellectuals and the highest rate of intellectuals living below the poverty line in the world (Richter, 20). When I participated in a seminar on the German Democratic Republic in Erfurt in 1985, I was told that the country's system of guaranteeing jobs for everyone who finished school or vocational training was intended to prevent the build-up of a large number of unemployed but educated citizens who might foment a revolution. United Germany seems to ignore this lesson. Everywhere I met highly educated East Germans who had left specialized careers to deliver newspapers, sell wares in shops, or offer services to tourists and the nouveaux riches. Some could barely conceal their bitterness at the devaluation of their years of study and experience, yet the level of material comfort provided by the social welfare state seems adequate to forestall any semblance of revolution.

Loss of public and private property, another accusation leveled by the Society for the Protection of Civil Rights and Human Dignity, may seem an odd complaint in a formerly communist state. But the Treuhand agency sold to West German developers about nineteen million acres of forest in the East, much of it in nature preserves (Behrend 1996, 33). Unification agreements established the principle of restoring publicly and privately held land to its former owners rather than compensating them from public coffers for its loss, a step which has complicated property ownership enormously. Fifty-three per cent of all East German households had a small plot of land for gardening and recreation. Typically families cultivated these tidy, flower-bordered plots on weekends and used the fruit and vegetables they raised to supplement the produce offered in state-run groceries. Or their produce could be sold through collective farms, or from a roadside stand. Traveling in rural East Germany in the 1980s, one often saw lines of Trabbis stopped beside a farmer's cart at the roadside, selling cherries or apricots. These privately-owned plots were so successful, in fact, that they accounted for up to one quarter of the total agricultural production of the country.

An additional 600,000 families owned their own homes. In many cases they rented land cheaply in long-term agreements with the town or district which owned the land, and then built modest homes. Under the provisions of the unification treaty, people who fled East Germany during the Hitler regime, or after 1949 when the GDR was founded, as well as those who left after the building of the Berlin Wall in 1961 could all reclaim real estate that had been left behind. This group of former property owners (who had already been compensated by the Federal Republic during the forties and fifties) wielded considerable political clout during unification negotiations. By 1994, 2.5 million property claims against property in the German Democratic Republic had been filed, most of them by West Germans. In several cases, two or even three former owners are claiming the same piece of property. Unraveling the legal morass will take decades. Homeowners may be able to purchase or rent the land beneath their homes at prices which gradually increase to market value over nine years, but even so the cost is beyond the reach of many ordinary people.

In 1985 in Erfurt I visited a reception hosted by Volkssolidarität, the quasi-volunteer organization which provided services to the disabled, the elderly, and shut-ins. The organization was housed in a handsome, partially restored villa that had belonged to a wealthy shoe manufacturer. In 1992 in Leipzig I stayed in a similar edifice, Haus der Wissenschaftler, on Georgi Dimitroff Straße. Bullet holes were still visible in the stucco surrounding the balcony. Clearly both villas had once belonged to rich owners who fled West. Now both may be reclaimed by descendants of their former owners. In Berlin in 1998 I lodged in Weißensee in a building which looked so decrepit I hesitated to get out of the taxi. My hostess, who welcomed me into her comfortably renovated apartment, later explained that the building's ownership was contested and no repairs could be undertaken unless there was a serious emergency. A week later I traveled to Dresden, where I attended a Goethe Institute seminar, I lodged with a family in a turn of the century villa on Reger Straße. My hostess sold Meissen porcelain in the city's new Hilton hotel, while her husband delivered newspapers and advertising circulars in the predawn hours. She explained that they had bought the house as soon as unification occurred, only to learn that its former owners had filed a claim against the property. Paralyzed by the fear of losing their home, they made few repairs, and the building became increasingly dilapidated. Now at last they had begun renovations, yet fear of losing their hold on the house increased.

Intolerance and loss of cultural freedom also figure among the charges which the Society for the Protection of Civil Rights and Human Dignity levels against united Germany, further demanding "respect for the dignity and identity" of the populace of the former German Democratic Republic, and "an end to the victor vs. vanquished mentality." A few examples will illustrate what these charges mean.

The language with which East Germans describe unification and their reactions to it reveals their true depth of feelings. The appearance of West German managers and entrepreneurs in the early nineties gave rise to *Besserwessi*, a pun on *Besserwisser*, meaning a know-it-all, and *Wessi*, or westerner. The wave of longing for the old days as seen in hindsight through rose-colored glasses is dubbed *Ostalgie*, nostalgia for the East. Writing in English, East German scholars describe the fusion of East with West Germany as *colonization*, a term loaded with capitalist imperialist nuances. Writing in German, they say the West German way of doing things was superimposed on them. Their usual term for this process, *übergestülpt*, would describe an act like putting a brown paper bag over someone's head; it's an act in which the victim plays no part.

The gradual elimination of East German culture has taken many forms. By 1992, street signs with a red diagonal slash through the name had become common. Names like Karl Marx, Clara Zetkin, Rosa Luxemburg, Karl Liebknecht were replaced by innocuous names like Berliner Straße or Leipziger Straße. Other street name heroes, like Georgi Dimitroff, would be less familiar to western capitalist tourists. Ernst Thälmann, whose name was often invoked on schools or playgrounds, was the head of the German Communist Party who perished at Buchenwald. Wilhelm Pieck led that party into union with Otto Grotewohl's Social Democrats in 1949; Pieck then became head of the Socialist Unity Party and first president of the German Democratic Republic. Schools were sometimes named after Thomas Müntzer, Luther's follower who sided with the peasants against the feudal nobility in 1525. East Germans as well as West Germans recall that streets were re-named in 1945 too, as Hermann Goering and Heinrich Goebbels were consigned to disgrace. Nevertheless, East Germans feel that obliterating their heroes means obliterating their history and destroys part of their identity. In the interests of tolerance and fairness, they ask, couldn't some names such as those of Clara Zetkin and Rosa Luxemburg stand alongside women like Bertha von Süttner?

East German television stations were liquidated, (as was the radio station for young people, DT 64) although 80% of the populace wished them to continue broadcasting. Of the German Democratic Republic's major daily newspapers, only *Neues Deutschland* has managed to stay afloat; the others have been bought out by western publishers, or have ceased publication. Theaters and houses of culture (some maintained by large state-owned factories) have been forced to close, causing massive unemployment among actors, musicians, and theater technicians, who were usually supported by the state.

East Germany had its own film studio, DEFA, whose films are now available through the film archives of the University of Massachusetts. While films of the fifties and sixties offered entertainment in line with socialist realism (presenting heroes of the workers' and farmers' state, for example) by the nineteen-seventies greater latitude was allowed, even encouraged. Films began to depict women's issues such as the double burden of housework and childcare shouldered by many working women, violence within marriage, and the quest for personal fulfillment. Most of these films were unknown in the West, and they reach only a limited audience today.

During the seventies and eighties East German authors, many of them women like Christa Wolf, Irmtraud Morgner, Monika Maron, and Helga Schütz, to name only a few, produced the most prominent works of new German literature. Today Christa Wolf is the only one still widely discussed, and chiefly because she was exposed as an informal collaborator with the Stasi, an experience she describes in her book *What Remains (Was Bleibt)*.

Americans may feel smugly that they enjoy complete cultural freedom; our schoolchildren learn about heroes and heroines who represent a variety of cultures. Or do they? Did American schoolgirls in the nineteen-fifties and sixties learn about Elizabeth Cady Stanton, Susan B. Anthony, Harriet Tubman and Sojourner Truth? Did their history books devote a chapter to the Seneca Falls convention of 1848? If these historical figures were invisible in mainstream American culture before the women's movement of the nineteen-seventies and eighties, can we trust completely that we see an unbiased, impartial picture of our own history? East Germans' experience reminds us poignantly that it is the victors who write history, and they omit much that may be of importance to future generations.

Andrée Fischer-Marum, whom I met in August 1998, exemplified what the East Germans mean by of the loss of their cultural heritage. As member of the intelligentsia, she had averted the professional ban black-listing others who had worked in state-owned media and publishing, and she had skillfully navigated her way through oceans of red tape, clinging to a series of temporary make-work jobs. Frau Fischer-Marum's background as the editor for a government run East

German publishing house made me want to know more about her. She was someone with not only her own story to tell, but a woman who had influenced the reading habits of thousands of others in that "Leseland DDR" (country of readers). I telephoned her before coming to Berlin and learned that she had also conducted interviews with women making the transition to life in united Germany.

Frau Fischer offered to meet me at a streetcar stop on the way to her home in Friedrichshain, and I set out punctually, navigating my way through the spaghetti of East Berlin's streetcar lines. It was possible to reach every destination in the former socialist republic cheaply by public transportation, provided one had plenty of time, patience, a sense of direction, or in my case, the ability to ask directions. Frau Fischer was easy to spot; a short, plump woman, she wore a black and white polka dot tunic as she came bowling along to meet me. Her dark eyes expressed lively curiosity, but her brow was furrowed beneath her short salt and pepper hair.

We walked over a trestle and along sandy roadbanks dotted with red poppies and blue chicory weeds toward a new housing development. Frau Fischer had recently moved into a smaller apartment in a brand new building, in part to save money. Her old apartment, measuring about seventy-five square meters, cost 930DM (about $550 at the time) including utilities. East Germans seldom moved; newspapers contained no house or apartment classifieds, for the only way to find new lodgings was to be assigned them by employers or government entities. Newlyweds might be able to move out of their parents' homes, and workers might be rewarded for exceptional achievements by the award of a newly constructed flat in a high-rise building. Otherwise people simply stayed put. What Frau Fischer had dreaded the most in the upheaval of moving was parting from some of her books. Now she ushered me into her tiny, book-filled home with a jangle of keys and chains. Her husband, she explained in a hushed voice, was sick at home and unemployed just now. Later she quoted what he had told her when he lost his job: "Bilde dir bloß nicht ein, daß ich jetzt den Hausmann spiele." (Just don't imagine that I'm going to play the house husband now.) That changed later, she assured me.

Herr Fischer is a historian and had also worked for the army. After unification he spent a year and a half creating a memorial at the former women's concentration camp, Ravensbrück, to the wives of the conspirators who attempted to assassinate Hitler on July 20, 1944. This task ended in 1991 and he became unemployed at the age of fifty. For two years he had an ABM job in an institute for conflict resolution, where he investigated dissolving East Germany's armed forces, including the police, army, border control officers, and the state security officials, the much-dreaded Stasi. At the same time, he edited a journal called *Europa Dialoge* dealing with political developments in Eastern Europe. Later he found another eighteen-month ABM position researching the Germans who had settled in Russia, where Stalin dispersed them to avoid their uniting to join Hitler. Unification had affected Herr Fischer so poignantly, his wife told me, that he could no longer vacation anywhere in East Germany, because he could not bear to see the changes. Instead the Fischers have traveled together through West Germany, France, and Spain, and he has been to Italy and England. But the feeling of a homeland lost lingers between them.

Frau Fischer showed me into her study while she tended to her husband's needs and made us a simple lunch of pasta, salad, and orangeade. I looked around her cluttered desk and bookshelves: the usual classics of Russian literature, obligatory in East German homes, as if above socialist suspicion, then numerous more recent works including several statistical works about women. Clearly she was a *Leseratte*, a bookworm. Later she kindly set aside a large stack of pamphlets and books that would be useful to me, things I couldn't have gotten anywhere else. We ate on her tiny balcony seated among the plants and housekeeping utensils that would fit nowhere else in her crowded rabbit warren. Overlooking the rooftops, the scaffolding, and the cranes she told me her story.

She began working at the age of twenty-seven for the Dietz publishing house which brought out 150 to 160 titles a year. She had full responsibility for one small segment of the business, and feels proud of what she achieved. And yet some things just didn't work any more: she compares the frustrations to running up against a rubber wall and bouncing off, undamaged, but unable to make any headway. On the other hand, the final months of the GDR's existence were a heady time, the most productive and wonderful time of her working life. Peter Marcuse (son of the philosopher Herbert Marcuse) was her first western guest, and she suggested that he keep a journal of his experiences as unification unfolded during his year-long stay in Berlin beginning in August 1989. Her publisher brought out the book, an accomplishment she reflects on with pride.

In the days of the socialist regime, she admits, some hair-raising things occurred in cultural politics. But she says nothing specific about repression or expulsion of dissidents. Nonetheless, she would have continued working in publishing until retirement at sixty. Then she would have kept busy as a proofreader, a museum guard, or a theater usher. She had her dreams. She dreamt of editing a journal of cultural politics, or she and her husband would have taken over and built up a small museum of regional history somewhere in Saxony or Thuringia. At the publishing house she voluntarily contributed 3% of her salary to a political party pension. The scheme was advantageous: she would have received 90% of her salary as pension, and after the age of sixty, one no longer had to pay into social security. When she first entered the business, she smiled at the oldsters who kept working there, but as she aged, she saw their advantages.

Instead, the break-up of the GDR left her bewildered. She was fifty years old then. She found it incomprehensible that the society she had devoted herself to in order to create a better Germany should collapse. In 1991 she was laid off. Money in special pension funds like the one she had contributed to was swallowed up into the state coffers and disappeared, her hopes for a comfortable retirement vanishing with it. She decided it would not be worthwhile at her age to learn a new profession such as real estate agent, which hadn't existed under socialism. She and her husband decided not to work in any capitalist profession: it was no coincidence that they lived in a socialist state.

Since 1991 she has had five government-subsidized make-work jobs, so many that she calls herself the world champion of ABM positions, make work schemes called *Arbeitsbeschaffungsmaßnahmen*. My hostess in Weißensee told me the East Germans interpret the abbreviation cynically as "arbeite bis Mittag," work until noon. With varying degrees of success, these ABM jobs were designed to match the skills of the unemployed to the work to be done. But in the year or two which most of these positions lasted, it was impossible to learn one's way into a new job; again and again the process was interrupted by change, usually termination and a new round of applications, making contacts, and anxiously awaiting the outcome. Most recently Frau Fischer had found work moving and re-organizing a sociology reference library.

When the GDR collapsed, it swept through her children's lives as well. Her son had completed the usual ten-year polytechnic school, and then an apprenticeship in data processing. While it would have been less common for the son of West German intelligentsia to learn a trade, East Germany encouraged the process as a way of breaking down class barriers; indeed during the nineteen-fifties, such children were forcibly excluded from universities to make space for progeny of the farmers' and workers' state. Quite shaken by the breakup of the National

People's Army, young Fischer reversed the process, returning to finish
his Abitur before entering a university.

His younger sister just finished her tenth grade schooling when
unification swept over the country. She had planned to become a travel
agent and sought an apprenticeship in that field, but three contracts
offering her an apprenticeship were canceled. She too returned to
school for another two years, finished her Abitur, and then went to
Paris as an au pair. While she suffered the uncertainty and rapid
changes in fortune brought on by the collapse of communism, the
opening of the GDR brought her new opportunities and the freedom to
make her own decisions. She wanted to work in data processing at the
Academy of Sciences, which she and her parents assumed would
survive the changes intact. But it too was dissolved, its scholars and
researchers thrown out of work. With her Abitur and knowledge of
French, she was considered over-qualified for a library apprenticeship.
At last she found work in the administrative office of Marzahn, an East
Berlin city district. She hopes to become a permanently employed civil
servant, and wishes to continue her education. Frau Fischer commented
that both of her children were very critical of united Germany, but
unlike their parents, critical of the GDR as well. She conceded that the
GDR had driven away many of its young citizens, bored by an
uneventful life in which most decisions were made for them.

Frau Fischer's own situation was complicated by the fact that she
had worked for a state publisher, an activity which left a stigma on her
resumé. She remained loyal to the ideals of socialism. Her Jewish
parents had emigrated to France, and the family later moved to Mexico
and to Mecklenburg-Vorpommern. She grew up in the section of East
Berlin known as Prenzlauer Berg, now given over to artists' studios,
galleries, and chic boutiques among the aging factories and turn-of the-
century apartment houses. Her childhood was overshadowed by an
awareness of the Cold War, and she remembered the building of the
Berlin Wall. But she learned that her own country worked for peace
and would keep its people safe from war, secure in brotherhood with
the Soviet Union. In kindergarten she sang peace songs, and when
soldiers from the National People's Army appeared, they were hailed as
peacekeepers. War as she had experienced the Second World War
became unthinkable.

In the GDR women had gigantic opportunities, she said. Their
education and work went deeper than those open to West German
women, and more of them got involved in politics. Parent advisory
groups were at least 80% women (how could it be otherwise?) and

women were well represented in trade unions, in Volkssolidarität caring for the elderly and shut-ins, and in residential block organizations. The latter, she conceded, formed part of the state's plan for integrating its citizens smoothly into local politics, and watching over their activities. Yet at the same time such organizations promoted the interests of individuals to improve conditions for their children, neighbors, and residences. Women accomplished most of this grassroots political activity, on top of their paid labor and endless hours of shopping and housework. It served as a social outlet for some, as a way of bettering their chances for the perks (new apartments, access to vacation lodgings) distributed by local party officials, and as a way of strengthening the network that provided scarce commodities such as building materials or tires through an informal black market. Nowadays, she lamented, these parents' groups and residential political cells have been denounced as propagandistic, and have been replaced by a heavy-handed bureaucracy, laws that no one knows, and money must be connected to everything. Citizens' lobbies have no new ways of attracting participants.

Unification struck women harder than men, she asserted. First, there was the matter of children. She knew that many women had given up their wish to have children, or had had themselves sterilized; a gynecologist had told her so in an interview. While she herself did not actually know anyone who had given up having a baby in order to work, when she looked around among her children's friends, she saw that there were simply no babies at all. People want stable employment first and foremost, and they are pessimistic about the environment. Furthermore, the war in former Yugoslavia frightened Germans. The precipitous drop in births, she says, is simply due to complete uncertainty about what is going to happen, "die totale Unsicherheit, wie das weitergeht."

The infamous paragraph 218, the law outlawing abortion revised by Germany's Bundestag in 1995, makes her bitter. Her mother and her daughter, bracketing either side of the generation that fought for abortion, simply can't grasp that it has once again become a political issue. She went to a demonstration at Berlin's Rotes Rathaus, the red city hall famous in old newsreels as the site of Hitler's speeches. She thought, now surely women will turn out. Two or three hundred appeared. That was even worse than the parliamentary decision. That was the point where people should have declared, "We've had enough." But nothing much happened. She condemns outlawing abortion as reactionary, nineteenth century. "We can't just accept it," she says. But she looks tired.

For years she had helped organize an annual Berlin gathering opposing fascism, where she arranged publishers' booths and authors' appearances. After being laid off she held true to her habit of attending this demonstration on the August Bebel Platz, and there she made the contact which led to her next ABM job. Thus she circumvented the employment office; East German women often learned to use their networking skills in place of the cumbersome state bureaucracy. This time twenty women worked on the project together; some had been unemployed for four years. As a kind of hobby, or perhaps as an effort to understand what had happened to her generation, she undertook a project similar to my own. She recorded interviews with about twenty women who moved West after unification. What struck her was their universal lament that they found no one in the West with whom they could discuss the art, music, or films they had grown up with. The correspondingly alien experience of West German women who moved East, she told me, was that they could not understand the animosity of East German colleagues, when they took the job of an Ossi woman. She had also interviewed women trained in technical fields: construction engineers, and horticulturalists, for example. They found it especially difficult to get work now, she said.

Women were hit harder by unemployment, she found. They often worked in the humanities, jobs that were dissolved after unification because of suspicions that fields such as publishing, literature, art, and history were tainted by socialist precepts. Women's jobs in farming or in textile manufacture have simply disappeared. Now at least a quarter of all bank tellers are men, and more men work in the bank's offices; in the GDR only women worked in banking. Born in 1941, she remembered that many women drove streetcars in East Berlin during the post war years. But when they reached the West Berlin border, they were required to relinquish the driver's seat to a West German man. Today once again men have replaced women as streetcar drivers.

A year and a half later Frau Fischer-Marum met me for tea in a café at the Alexanderplatz, and gave me more recent news of her situation. Her demeanor seemed brighter, cheerful despite the torrent of rain pouring down outside. Because Germany is raising in stages the retirement age for women from sixty to sixty-five, she needs to work nineteen months longer than she had originally planned. Fortunately she was still employed and would continue working until her ABM assignment expired in August 2000. Her current project was a sociological survey of the overall level of satisfaction among people aged eighteen to forty-five. A journal was publishing her article based on interviews with East German women who had moved West, and her husband had just written an article about the structure of Nazi leadership in Berlin. Her daughter had become the European Commissioner for the Berlin district of Marzahn. After spending four months in a special European Union training program in Brussels, she believed she had a good chance of holding onto her office when Berlin's twenty-three administrative districts were combined into twelve. But she had just parted company with a West Berlin boyfriend, and Frau Fischer lamented that her hope of having grandchildren had receded further into the distance. Her son worked assisting companies making the transition to better computer technology, and had recently returned from a trip to San Diego. In his line of work, she said, only those who have worked in America rise to success.

Before we parted, Frau Fischer announced she was about to depart for France, a journey in the footsteps of the author Anna Seghers, who had emigrated to Mexico, as her own family had done. She described her pleasure in observing the arrival of spring over Berlin. Walking home across a bridge she pauses each day to look out over the Spree River and the trees bringing forth their new leaves. "Beautiful," she says, "simply beautiful."

Her story is not an uncommon one; she has survived the overturning of two regimes governing her homeland and is coping with the third, which she views as not necessarily more permanent than fascism or socialism. While unification has presented her with some personal losses and some broader gains, elderly women and rural women, whose conditions we will consider next, must be ranked among the losers of German unification. A more optimistic light appears to shine on new women entrepreneurs who have launched their own ventures into the uncharted waters of capitalism. Finally we will consider the feminist movement in East Germany and its prospects for fruitful cooperation with West German feminists.

Chapter Seven
Pensions: A Women's Issue

Pensions are a bone of contention in unified Germany, and East Germans believe the injustices are numerous. Until 1992 German women on both sides of the Wall retired at sixty and men at sixty-five. In that year a pension reform raised the women's retirement age in stages to sixty-five. Since women outlive men by about six years, they spend longer than men living in retirement. Thus there are more women pensioners–283 retired women for every hundred retired men–for these reasons, in addition to the after-effects of World War II. In united Berlin in 1994, for example, over 70% of retirees aged seventy or older were women (Haupt, 15). The preponderance of women at this age, and among those over fifty-five forced into early retirement by economic dislocation after unification, explains why pensions are such a hot political issue in the East. And they can be expected to remain so: 12% of united Germany's population is over sixty-four, the third highest proportion of elderly in Europe, behind Sweden and Belgium.

Pensioners occupied a paradoxical position in the German Democratic Republic. Unlike any of its other citizens, the country allowed them to travel freely to the West. Since they no longer performed productive labor, the country could easily afford to get rid of them, and if they chose to stay away, the Federal Republic paid their retirement pensions. Thus they were truly free to leave the country. Yet because most elderly people cling to their homes and families, few chose to remain permanently in the West. Most preferred to travel to visit their relatives and then return, carefully keeping track of any surviving family members on the other side of the Wall who might host a visit. In my travels into East Germany, I encountered these solidly built, carefully dressed Omas in trains, where I helped them hoist valises filled with oranges, bananas, and chocolate onto overhead luggage racks. Ironically the elderly were among the few people in the German Democratic Republic who really knew how living conditions looked in the West.

Retiring women at sixty had certain benefits for the German Democratic Republic's centrally planned economy. Their departure made way for a younger generation who needed to begin working, and was more highly trained. The Socialist Unity Party attributed lack of vocational skills in women to the traditional gender division of labor inherited from capitalism. Statistics confirm that three-fourths of those without skilled worker certificates were women, many of them elderly and living in rural areas. (*Frauenreport 90*, 177). Besides getting rid of less skilled workers, and preventing unemployment by limiting the labor supply, it was cheaper to pay retirees a pension than wages.

Women earned less than men in the German Democratic Republic, but the country's pension schemes made provisions for mothers' unpaid contributions. Women with five or more children who worked only at home received a basic pension. Those with several children who continued in paid labor were credited with extra working years when their pensions were calculated to compensate them for their dual contribution to society as mothers and as workers. Those who cared for elderly parents or relatives, or participated in special training courses for women, or who worked alongside their families in agriculture, forestry, crafts, or self-employment were also protected by supplemental provisions. Anyone who had worked a minimum of fifteen years, regardless of interruptions for family care, or working only part-time, received a pension. These basic pensions paid only 500 marks per month; those based on wages averaged just 45% of workers' net pay.

People who earned over six hundred marks per month in wages could contribute voluntarily to a supplemental fund (*zusätzliche Altersversorgung*), which provided a total pension equal to 55% of average net pay. A third of all workers contributed to such funds, which existed for twenty-seven occupational categories, from SED party functionaries to teachers to chemical workers. These supplemental pension funds were supposed to be protected by complex special provisions in the unification agreement, ensuring that retirees received half the amount owed them, with the remaining half going into the general coffer to increase basic pensions for everyone. Instead, monthly payments from these supplemental plans were capped at lower amounts, depriving East German workers of their hard-earned benefits. Those who worked in the Socialist Unity Party and its organizations, or members of the intelligentsia have lost the most, through measures which East German sources describe as blatantly punitive.

For women, retirement in the German Democratic Republic meant living on a shoestring. In 1989 three-fourths of all pensioners were women, and 90% of all pensioners received five hundred marks per month or less. Pensions were not indexed to cost-of-living increases; instead minimum amounts were raised every three to five years. In the meantime, retirees fell further beneath a reasonable standard of living. Fortunately the German Democratic Republic's health insurance system provided full coverage to all retirees, including prescription drugs, eyeglasses, hearing aids, dental work, and dental replacements.

The discrepancy between men's and women's pensions was greater than the wage gap: as of July 1990, men received on average 800 DM per month, and women only 550 DM. While women's earnings more closely approached men's in the final years of the GDR, pensioners represented the generations of less-skilled women who had received their vocational training before socialism. The average retired woman in East Germany in 1990 lived alone and spent a third of her income on food, a fifth on rent and utilities, 10% on clothing and shoes, 17% on other consumer goods, and 9% on taxes and insurance. West German retirees spent a larger share on rent, utilities, and transportation, and less on food, clothing, and shoes.

The right to work guaranteed to all citizens extended to retirees also. Ten to fifteen per cent of retired women continued to work until they turned sixty-five. More men than women continued working after reaching retirement age; but the discrepancy between the sexes evened out in the 1980s, and smaller percentages of retirees overall continued working, probably because their standard of living improved. Postal and communications workers and farm women were the retirees most likely to continue working. Those who worked for private companies or were self-employed were more likely to go on working than those employed in state-owned enterprises. Employees who continued working after retirement enjoyed the highest earnings of their lives. Free of deductions for health coverage or pensions, they received their wages plus their full pension payment each month. As of 1988, these older workers were protected from firing and received an extra week of vacation each year. A fourth of the women who continued to work agreed in a survey that they had always enjoyed working, a fourth wanted to supplement their pension with wages, a fifth believed that their companies still needed them, and about 15% continued working because of good relations with their co-workers (*Frauenreport '90,* 187). Because so many elderly women were widowed or divorced, social contacts developed in work collectives played an important role in their lives. From the employer's standpoint, hiring older women made good sense because they no longer demanded maternity or child-rearing leave. As part of the first generation to create the socialist state, older women felt pride in its achievements, and theirs, although the media paid little attention to their contributions.

Unification struck a sharp blow to women who wanted to continue working until sixty. Already in February 1990 *Vorruhestandsgeld* (pre-retirement pay) was introduced for workers five years away from the retirement age whose companies were downsizing, closing, or could offer them no suitable re-training. This pre-retirement pay amounted to 70% of average net pay for the previous twelve months–thus it was advantageous for employers to push workers out before their wages rose in the aftermath of unification. Transitional payments called *Altersübergangsgeld* equaling 65% of wages were paid to women fifty-five or older until they became eligible for their old-age pensions. This arrangement means that the years between fifty-five and sixty are not counted toward a woman's eligibility for a pension, nor is she counted among the unemployed (Haupt, 170). People between the ages of fifty-five and fifty-nine who are still actively seeking work comprise one-fifth of the unemployed in the new federal states (*Arbeitslosenreport 1999*, 167).

Pension inequities stem not only from gender-related causes, but from the fact that lifetime earnings determine the amount of pensions for all retirees; thus in 1992 the average pension in East Berlin amounted to only 57% of the average West Berlin pension, despite guarantees made during unification that pensions would be equalized in both Germanies. In 1992 new pension reform legislation was passed to narrow the discrepancy, and West German pension regulations became the law of the land, following a period of transition. The effects of the reform have placed women at a considerable disadvantage, both because the western economic system is geared to stay-at-home married women–who earn less than men–and because special provisions favoring working women in the East were eliminated.

West German retirees derive 72% of their income from pensions and the remainder from savings, real estate ownership, or other investments, so that their actual retirement income is greater (49% higher for men and 61% higher for women) than that of East German retirees. Four million West German retirees received additional pension funds from civil service or government careers, or from private pensions payable after a minimum of ten years with a single company (*Betriebsrente*). East Germans, in contrast, drew 98% of their retirement income from pensions. They lost or saw greatly reduced contributions from special supplemental funds, and from the few private funds administered by a handful of East German companies. (Winkler, "Volkssolidarität," 16).

The pension reform of 1992 altered the East German system in ways relating to family circumstances. Under pre-1986 West German law, if a spouse died, the survivor, usually a widow, could claim the deceased's pension, or receive her own, whichever was higher, but was not entitled to both. Thus widows received their husbands' pensions, but widowers received nothing from the pensions of their deceased wives. To benefit men, the system was altered in 1986 so that either surviving marriage partner receives the higher pension, plus a portion of their spouse's pension. Because of this provision, some East German widows now live from their husband's pensions, plus a small supplement from their own, an arrangement which they feel devalues their own earnings and forces them into a kind of post-mortem dependence, although they supported themselves for years.

Another provision of the 1992 reform law affects divorced mothers. In the West, a stay-at-home mother who divorced after 1977 can claim a share of her husband's pension (called *Versorgungsausgleich*) as compensation for running the household and caring for the family during the duration of the marriage. However, the 1992 legislation specifically denied this provision to the 800,000 women who divorced before 1992 in East Germany, whose old law remains in effect. Although these women were considered self-supporting (and thus not entitled to alimony unless they had small children) most earned lower wages or worked fewer hours because of family obligations, thereby reducing the pensions they now receive. Divorced women who had children face the highest risk of poverty in old age; nationwide 10% of them depend on welfare to live (Ottow, 1999). Divorced mothers became angry enough to organize their own new political lobbying group in 2000. Of course neither the system of survivors' pensions nor these supplements based on child-rearing work within marriage will benefit East Germany's large numbers of single mothers.

East German women were entitled to count years of part-time work toward their eligibility for pensions, which was not the case in the West. Credits for special women's vocational training courses, child-raising, care of the elderly, and similar duties, which raised the value of their pensions, were eliminated in the 1992 reform. As partial compensation for these reductions, supplemental pension payments (*Auffüllbeträge*) were made to two-thirds of East German retirees (84%

of them women) between 1993 and 1996, but these payments were reduced at the rate of 20% per year beginning in 1996 (Winkler, "Volkssolidarität," 14). Another provision which worked to the disadvantage of East German women was the ruling that distance learning courses, such as that taken by Susanne W., were treated as regular periods of study rather than as working years. While few West Germans worked full-time as students, many East Germans did so, and were furious that these years of carrying a double burden should be discredited in the pension system. The matter was rectified in 1999, so that years of distance learning were counted as periods of employment.

Despite these setbacks imposed by the West German pension system, East German women actually receive pensions (not total monthly retirement income!) about a third higher than those of West German women, chiefly because they worked longer. Two-thirds of them worked for more than thirty years, while only 37% of West German women worked that long (Winkler, "Volkssolidarität," 16). Pensions paid in Berlin in 1993, for example, were based on an average of twenty-six years at work for women in the West, compared to thirty-four years in the East. And of course, far more women worked in the East; when the Berlin Wall opened, 81% of women of working age were employed on its eastern side, in contrast to just 49% of women of working age in the West. Even in retirement East German women come closer to parity with their male counterparts. With a monthly pension of 1,169 DM in 1998 East German women lagged behind men, who received 1,906 DM a month, but the gap was not as wide as in the West, where pensions averaged 1,970 DM for men, compared to only 868 for women (Ottow, 1999).

The results of the imposition of the West German pension system caused consternation and resentment among women, particularly acute in the early nineties. A survey of 956 Berlin women ages thirty-six through seventy-one conducted in 1993 found that 55% of those in the West and 70% of those in the East did not believe their present income corresponds to the value of their life's work (Haupt, 150-51). While the value of East German pensions has now risen to 75% of West German ones, women must cope with a tighter budget: 94% of the East Berlin women surveyed received 2,000 DM or less per month in total income, while only 56% of West Berlin women received so little. Furthermore, East German women resent the way that the present system undercuts their hard-won economic achievements, because it is based on capitalistic assumptions about stay-at-home mothers and economically dependent wives.

In recent years the campaign for fair pensions has been waged by both old and new organizations. First is the Volkssolidarität; founded in 1946 to care for widows, war orphans, and the elderly; it continues today to provide social services for senior citizens. Second is the Demokratischer Frauenbund Deutschlands, the old Socialist Unity Party's women's association, which in 1995 made common cause with West Germany's housewives' union in the latter's campaign, "Rente statt Rosen" (Rohmann, 36). Its chief initiative is to recover better pension compensation for women who raised children and worked as well. The third advocate for fairer pensions is the Society for the Protection of Civil Rights and Human Dignity, which includes inequities in the pension system among the human rights abuses resulting from unification of which it accuses the West.

To learn more about the pension debate, and the lives of older women in East Berlin, I accepted Gisela Meise's invitation to meet with a local chapter of the Society for the Protection of Civil Rights and Human Dignity in August 1998. The Lichtenberg offices which the group occupied in 1998 lay in the ground floor of an office building whose renovations hadn't been completed. Industrial extension cords lay across the hallways, and the walls showed cracked plaster, and chipped paint. But the place sparkled with energy, in the swinging gold earrings of its director, Professor Grandke, who greeted us, and welcomed me warmly to her organization. I was ushered into a warm, street level room prepared for ritual German hospitality: flowers, and plates of cookies at every place. Mineral water followed, and excellent dark coffee.

A look around the table confirmed that the participants were all women. Undoubtedly Frau Meise's advertisement of my research in the organization's newsletter had drawn women rather than men, yet their presence reminded me that millions of men of this age cohort were killed in the Second World War, disappeared into Soviet prison camps, or died early as a result of war injuries. These women were the survivors, and their brief introductions impressed me. First was a lawyer for foreign trade who had raised three sons. Next came a lawyer and chemical engineer who had worked in health care for twenty-five years, raised her children as a single mother, and managed to hold on to part-time work now at the age of sixty-five. The organization's director, Professor Anita Grandke, held a chair for family law at the Academy of Sciences in women's research and taught until 1994, while raising three children. She also wrote a study of single mothers for her task force, Woman in Socialist Society, at the Academy. She passed her post-unification evaluation, and continued to work in the reform of family law. Here I also met Dr. Christa Anders. Next to her sat a state's attorney and judge who was forced into early retirement in 1990 and prosecuted for three years because she ruled on violations of state law. She had three children. Another woman had fled her native Poland at war's end and studied economics at an Arbeiter- und Bauernfakultät, a special course intended to overturn Germany's conservative class structure by educating peasants and workers. She negotiated foreign trade agreements and worked abroad until she was fired in 1990, a year before earning her full pension. A former teacher of belonged to the Union for Education and Science, one of the organizations whose supplemental pension funds were poured into the common fund after unification. She explained that although teachers earned only a modest salary, they expected a more generous retirement pension would reward their years of service. Now that hope was gone.

These were remarkable women indeed: lawyers, judges, doctors, scholars, economists, teachers from a generation which, in the US, included too few women in such prominent, powerful roles. They identified themselves both by profession and by family status, as proud of their children as of their other achievements. Patiently they answered my questions about the pension system they expected to provide for their retirement, and its erosion during unification. They made it clear that they refuse to accept the capitalist rationale that equalizing retirement income East and West would cost too much; they will persist in demanding what is fair and right.

Another woman dissatisfied with her present retirement income is a vigorous widow in her nineties living just outside East Berlin, Frau Geiger. As she greets visitors at the door, her voice can scarcely be heard above the twittering of parakeets who now provide her most cherished companionship. Born in 1906, she survived the last years of the Wilhelmine monarchy, the Weimar Republic, the Nazi Socialist dictatorship, the German Democratic Republic, and now lives in united Germany's social market economy. Like other women of her generation, she received only a limited education. Her husband died a year after the Berlin Wall closed access to West Berlin; Frau Geiger has outlived him by thirty-six years.

She worked as a saleswoman for twenty years and retired at the age of sixty, with a pension of 550 marks. She experienced unification on television, expecting that everything would improve, more money, more things to buy. Her pension increased to 868 marks, but she expresses bitterness over the fact that it represents only her widow's pension based on her husband's earnings, "nothing from my own work, twenty long years," she says. The new capitalist system has forced her into a symbolic dependency that did not exist during her husband's lifetime. He worked until he died and never received a pension, but he earned what was an uncommonly high salary for the German Democratic Republic: two thousand marks a month.

Her daughter Beate looks after her, and she has a younger sister, eighty-two. Frau Geiger's sister has broken her arm twice and can no longer cook; a community program brings her meals. Frau Geiger is proud of maintaining her own independence, but complains that prices have risen so that even with her higher pension it has become difficult to make ends meet. She's cynical about her new political freedom; politicians do as they please, she grumbles: the people's initiative against expanding East Berlin's Schönefeld airport did no good.

She says women have lost ground with unification. In the German Democratic Republic husbands of working women helped with the cooking; her husband's specialty was Fleischrouladen (stuffed rolls of meat). She knows all about her country's declining birthrate and its causes: the dilemma of unemployed mothers.

One volunteer who assists elderly residents like Frau Geiger is Jutta Freiberg, and she says unification altered many aspects of their lives. Before unification she worked with People's Solidarity helping elderly people with housecleaning, shopping, and meals, or carrying coal up from the cellar. Many elderly live in older housing, some of it heated by coal-burning tile stoves. People's Solidarity still exists and lobbies actively for fair pensions, but its monthly dues have risen from fifty Pfennig to four marks a month. Today, Frau Freiberg says, the whole process has been crippled by bureaucracy; old people needing help must present their savings passbook before receiving services, and many would prefer to just stay in an unheated apartment rather than seek help from strangers. Because of new privacy laws, it's hard for Frau Freiberg to know who might need help. People's Solidarity has an office and open hours, but few people seek it out. She too carries an official identity card. In the old days, Frau Freiberg says, people performed services for the elderly voluntarily; singers from the Volksoper entertained gratis at the Christmas party; today everyone must be paid. Then people got a birthday bouquet and gift basket when they turned eighty or eighty-five. Now the days are long gone when people do anything for free, and she bemoans the fact that all relationships turn on money. In the old days she offered a payment to someone who found windows for her garden shed, when there were none to be had anywhere, but today she's embarrassed when the elderly people she helps try to pay her for her efforts.

Most pensioners in the former German Democratic Republic share the sentiments expressed by Frau Geiger and Jutta Freiberg. In 1996 the Society for the Protection of Civil Rights and Human Dignity reported in its journal *Icarus* the results of a survey of 2,277 retirees. Most identify themselves as citizens of the former German Democratic Republic, not as citizens of the Federal Republic, a society they view as spiritually bankrupt. Two-thirds of them believe socialism was a good idea, but imperfectly realized. In conversations, East Germans sometimes point out that while socialism rests on the theories of Karl Marx, capitalism has no such theoretical underpinnings.

Three-quarters of those responding to the survey were married and living with their spouses in an apartment in a city of 100,000 or larger. About 95% had received higher education or vocational training. Seventy percent received less than 2,000 DM per month in pension payments; another 20% received less than 2,500. About 65% had household incomes of 4,000 DM per month or less (around $28,200 per year). Three-fourths had filed a protest against their pension allotment, and only 15% had additional resources such as savings, life insurance, or income from rental property. A 1995 survey found that only one-fifth of East German retirees felt that their pensions compensated them fairly for their life's work, a declining percentage from the 1993 survey quoted earlier (Winkler, "Volkssolidarität," 17).

Over 80% of the retirees in the 1996 survey agreed with statements such as "The world has become alien to me," or "Society has become hardened and less just, cold and unloving." Between 70-80% of them felt threatened by violence and criminality, social uncertainty, injustice at the hands of the legal system, the unaccountability of government, and the destruction of socialism. The Volkssolidarität survey points out that the social security which pensioners enjoyed under the old system meant not the amount of their pension, but mental security about their stable position in society and trust in policies for the elderly that were comprehensible and reliable (Winkler, 17).

The prognosis for resolution of this issue looks poor indeed. In the new century, the numbers of retirees will continue to grow, while the surplus of women in this cohort shrinks, particularly if the German government follows through on its intention (debated in January 2000) of lowering the retirement age to sixty. While raising the retirement age for women to sixty-five was intended to reduce the high cost of pensions, lowering the retirement age now looks like a way to reduce unemployment. In the year 2000 there are about 2,912,000 pensioners in the East, 70% of them women, and pensioners outnumber children under the age of fourteen. That means that there are fewer young workers paying into the pension system, and of course fewer workers of any age, given the continuing high rate of unemployment. In Saxony retirees constitute about 17% of the total population, as compared to 12% in Berlin. Younger people move from rural areas into cities, while the elderly tend to stay put.

The chief factor which will continue to shape pension inequalities in the future is the fact that pensions are based on earnings, and progress made in closing the wage gap is eroding as the present economic crisis pushes women out of the labor force, or into poorly paid service industries, or relegates them to part time work. In West Germany's first half-century women made little progress in closing the wage gap. In 1957, for instance, white-collar women employees in the Federal Republic earned 42% less their male counterparts earned, and in 1988 they earned about 36% less. In other words, every five years they came one percentage point closer to closing the wage gap, a feeble gain by any measure. During the same year, West German women working in industry narrowed the gap slightly more, from earning 42% less than men in 1957 to 30% less in 1988. Women in the German Democratic Republic (where the socialist regime repudiated the class distinction between white- and blue-collar workers) gained more ground. While they earned one-third less than men in 1957, they earned only 18% less in 1988 (Haupt, 109). However, unification has broadened the wage gap and erased these gains. In 1994, for example, women white-collar and blue-collar workers in East Germany earned about 24% less than men. In West Germany white-collar women employees continue to earn about 30% less than men, while industrial workers earn about 27% less (a gain from 30% less in 1991) (Haupt, 109-112).

Lower earnings mean lower pension contributions, and thus lower retirement income. For example in East Germany at the time of unification, women paid an average of 29% per month less into their pension funds than men; by 1994 they were paying 35% less as their earnings fell further behind. In West Germany the gap is both considerably higher–57%–and more stable (Haupt, 60). In the aftermath of unification, more women than men were pushed into early retirement, or into jobs paying 600 DM per month or less, which did not require pension or insurance contributions. The limit for these jobs has now increased to 630 DM, and pension and unemployment contributions are required. More mothers accept the three-year child-rearing payments which likewise do not include pension contributions. East German retired women will derive smaller gain from their working lives because of post-unification provisions basing widows' pensions on their husbands' earnings, adding supplements for West German mothers who divorced after 1977, and phasing out pension eligibility based on part-time work and extra years credited for child-rearing by the old socialist system. All of these factors decrease women's average lifetime earnings, and doom them to an old age of poverty and dependency.

Today united Germany is forced to consider revising its pension system. Between 2020 and 2030 it will undergo serious strain because the baby boom of the sixties and early seventies (the years before contraceptives and abortion became accessible) will reach retirement age, while the cohort of twenty- to thirty-year-old workers will remain small (particularly in the East) because of the Wendeknick. Basing retirement payments on the standard male biography of a forty-five year work life has become unrealistic because of high unemployment affecting both sexes, and child-rearing leaves which interrupt women's paid labor. The East German Party of Democratic Socialism advocates reducing pensions for those in the highest brackets to increase monthly payments to those at the bottom, a proposal which would benefit 80% of German women. This proposal illustrates the socialist belief that wealth should not be considered private gain won through individual competition, but rather a social benefit to be distributed for the greatest good of the greatest number.

Pensioners for the most part represent the generation that built the German Democratic Republic and felt greater loyalty to its achievements than younger people. They regard the western capitalist system with distrust and skepticism. Workers who were forced into retirement at age fifty following the political turnaround will remain active and discontented for another quarter century. And unlike young working parents, older people have the time and energy to organize, network, and protest. It is unlikely that the German government can placate such people with the excuse that offering fair pensions would simply cost too much.

Chapter Eight
Founding a New Existence: the Women Entrepreneurs of Hasenwinkel

Plainly Frau Meise was a master of networking, I reflected, rocketing northward on the Autobahn through the flat grainfields of Mecklenburg-Vorpommern. East Germans considered personal contacts an essential ingredient in the success of any undertaking; "Beziehungen," contacts, were jokingly referred to as Vitamin B. By chance Frau Meise had encountered her former boss, Professor Dr. Helmut Voigt, whose wife I had met in the Gesellschaft zum Schutz von Bürgerrecht und Menschenwürde. Professor Voigt had been Frau Meise's last employer, charged with the sorry task of letting her go, a proceeding which caused him as much pain as it did her. After a few reminiscences, she told him about my project, and he agreed to bring me along to Güstrow and Schwerin, where he supervised women entrepreneurs in a special project designed to lift them out of unemployment and into the capitalist market economy. With a willingness and cordiality that I had rarely experienced in the West, he called to explain that we would leave Berlin in the evening after rush hour and drive north. We would spend two nights at Schloß Hasenwinkel. The name meant Rabbit Corner Castle–who could fail to be intrigued? I packed my knapsack and agreed, filled with curiosity at the prospect of another unique experience.

Professor Dr. Voigt materialized on the doorstep precisely on time, and stowed my knapsack in the trunk of his navy BMW. He threaded his way out of Berlin and picked up the Autobahn which now spans the former East-West border. Some East Germans find it cheaper to live in Schwerin, he explained, and drive to work in Hamburg, Germany's largest port and its media and press center which lies about fifty miles to the west. Hamburg residents, on the other hand, visit Schwerin on weekends because of its inexpensive theater and concert tickets. The city of 130,000 boasts a fine state-supported theater, two orchestras, a number of museums, and a Baroque palace surrounded by a lake.

Professor Voigt had an easy, unassuming manner, and I told him about my project, trying to mask my terror as we rocketed along at 180 kilometers (108 miles) an hour unimpeded by rush-hour traffic. We swept past flat fields of wheat and rye and then a wind farm, a series of tall, slender turbines used to generate electricity. After unification, all of East Germany's nuclear power plants, built on the same model as Chernobyl, were closed. The country's per capita energy consumption rivaled that of the US because so much voltage was lost in poorly maintained transmission lines. Now renewable sources, in this instance wind, provided some energy. The windswept coastal plains of Mecklenburg-Vorpommern seemed ideally suited, since the former agricultural areas were only thinly settled. But people complained of the low frequency hum emitted from the turbines, or of the shadow of gigantic propeller arms sweeping darkly over the landscape.

We stopped at an antique windmill looking like something out of a Dutch picture book. Once used to grind grain, its arms stood still. Sitting outdoors in the soft twilight, we ordered a beer. Herr Voigt ordered a Warsteiner, a non-alcoholic beer, I noticed, feeling a little guilty as I sipped a tall Pilsener. Germany's stringent drunk driving laws mean that a driver who has had even one beer risks losing his license. In any case, driving over a hundred miles an hour on the Autobahn requires one's full concentration.

Darkness had settled by the time we reached Schloß Hasenwinkel. It turned out to be an early twentieth century hunting lodge built of yellow sandstone, its pseudo classical facade facing a simple gravel walkway and an expanse of lawn. Like most property of Prussia's wealthy Junker class, it had been confiscated by the communists, who let its flower gardens go and converted it for use as a school and a camp for children of the workers' and farmers' state. Inside it had been modestly restored, and re-opened in 1996 as the seat of an institute for education and economics of the state of Mecklenburg-Vorpommern. This Bildungswerk der Wirtschaft, founded after the Wende, offers training courses in several cities in Mecklenburg-Vorpommern. Herr Voigt pointed out the breakfast room where we should meet next morning, and led me up the graceful, oak-railed staircase. On the landing between floors he paused for a moment. There was another stairway, he explained, intended for lodgers such as ourselves. But just once every visit he liked to walk up this stairway and imagine he was one of the landed gentry who had originally owned the place. Now he revealed that we were the only guests and had the entire place to ourselves. I fell asleep to the music of crickets beneath the linden trees.

Next morning I entered the breakfast room where a generous meal of bread, cold meats, cheese, and a boiled egg had been prepared. Soon Frau Doktor Quilitz, Herr Voigt's co-worker, joined us to accompany us to Schwerin. She told me that she had been born in the early fifties into a working class family and studied Russian and German at the ten-year polytechnic school in Güstrow. At the age of twenty-four she had earned her doctorate. She worked for ten years educating teachers in the Baltic seaport of Rostock. Married at the age of twenty-four, she had a seventeen-year-old daughter who was interested in languages, and a fourteen-year-old son. She and her husband, a military officer, both lost their jobs after unification. Unemployment reached 20% in Mecklenburg-Vorpommern, and on the island of Rügen in the Baltic it ran as high as 26%. While politicians planned ways to increase tourism, inhabitants of the area emigrated westward. Eventually Dr. Quilitz found work in the women's project in Schwerin we were going to visit.

In the late nineties the state of Mecklenburg-Vorpommern, the German government, and the European Union joined forces to support an initial group of thirty unemployed women who wanted to open their own businesses. Women who could prove they had fulfilled an apprenticeship and had some business skills would be able to borrow start-up money for up to ten years at 3% interest. While banks found the sums women wanted to borrow too small to bother with, or their qualifications inadequate, the government-sponsored program offered them help. First they enrolled in a management training course (initiated and organized by the Bildungswerk der Wirtschaft) taught by free-lance instructors such as Professor Voigt, trained as both an economist and a foundry engineer. Then they developed a business plan, secured a loan, and opened shop. Professor Voigt and Dr. Quilitz and other consultants working with the program visited them and stayed in touch by letter or telephone, offering help with hiring employees, filing taxes, advertising, or customer relations. While this assistance was scheduled to last only for the first year, the two found that the second, third, and fourth years presented the greatest risks to start-up ventures.

Our first stop took us into the countryside outside a small village called Käselow to visit Frau Schwaß, a former bookkeeper who had purchased a roofing company and now employed seven people. The BMW bounced over a rutted driveway past a pond and a goat pasture. Children, dogs, and chickens greeted our arrival with a cacophony of confusion. Setting a table outdoors with coffee and cookies, Frau Schwaß explained that she had bought the former children's camp to house herself, her four children, and her sister and brother-in-law with their brood of three. During the heyday of the GDR, city parents could send their children to such a camp in a healthful rural location to spend their summers in supervised sport, play, and educational activities. On the one hand, camps for the Young Pioneers or the Free German Youth, offered parents a way to care for their children while they continued to work. On the other hand, it was no secret that summer camps furthered the political indoctrination begun in schools. And not all children enjoyed such activities as harvesting cucumbers on a collective farm and "voluntarily" contributing their proceeds to the Nicaraguan Contras.

Frau Schwaß, a tall, energetic redhead, watched the events of 1990 from home. As the mother of new twins, she had been granted a two-year maternity leave from her bookkeeping job in a kindergarten. For a year she remained unemployed. Then she found work as a bookkeeper in the roofing company. At the hiring interview she hid the fact that she was the mother of four children. While it is forbidden to ask prospective employees if they are pregnant, questions about the number of children are included in written applications. Mothers, employers assume, may be called away from the workplace to care for sick children, so any children constitute a liability. In 1994 the roofing company closed its doors, throwing its sixty or seventy employees out of work. Ten of them, including Frau Schwaß, decided to buy the roofing equipment, rent space, keep the company's telephone number, and fill its remaining orders. At first things went well enough. But there were difficulties in working together, and problems securing a loan. Supported by a small inheritance, Frau Schwaß bought out her colleagues. Only the master roofer continues to work for her. But other problems followed. Some customers couldn't or wouldn't pay. She had to write off 70,000 DM in bad debts, and is pursuing another 30,000 in litigation. She opened an office in Schwerin, closed it about a year later, and moved the office into the former summer camp, renting warehouse space for roofing materials in Tressow.

Now the company's seven employees roof houses and commercial buildings in slate, tin, and cement fiber shingles, and install gutters and downspouts. Frau Schwaß feels the handicap of knowing too little about the roofing business; in contrast to most roofing company owners, she did not learn in an apprenticeship and rise through the ranks. But her eighteen-year-old daughter has apprenticed herself to a roofer and is learning the trade. Meanwhile, the master roofer whom she employs calls on clients with Frau Schwaß to lend the necessary voice of experience. Undoubtedly his male presence also carries weight with prospective customers.

In Dresden I was told that the GDR's last long-term head of state, Erich Honecker, a roofer by trade, had at least seen to it that the roofs of historic buildings were repaired, although funds for other necessary renovations were lacking. Now Frau Schwaß tells Herr Voigt that after a few lean years, things have begun to pick up. People are eager to move to the country. While little new construction is being started, many old buildings need re-roofing. He is happy to learn that she has devised a new twist in marketing: she is offering to extend credit to those who do business with her company. The advertising flyers are ready to be put into people's mailboxes: she doesn't feel able to approach people directly. She gets some work from a company in Hamburg, and now orders from local people have begun to trickle in.

She has another small victory to report. She wanted to join the association of independent roofers, but they hesitated for two years to accept her, and then made her feel out of place among them. Such trade associations are important; Germany has over 360 recognized trades, and these organizations determine apprenticeship procedures, set professional standards, and license competent tradespeople.) Two months ago at a trade seminar on advertising and marketing Frau Schwaß found the opportunity to describe what she had accomplished in marketing her services, and finally she was allowed to join the roofers' association.

Later we go inside to visit the company office upstairs. The household appears in a constant state of either construction or destruction, it's hard to tell which. Frau Schwaß's brother-in-law uses office space here too, selling computer and communication systems. He says that there was a slight advantage to the GDR's technological backwardness. Its citizens waited a dozen years for a telephone. Now that new telephone cables are being installed everywhere, they're putting in a fiber optic system which can carry both telephone and computer modem signals at the same time.

His wife learned the tool-maker's trade, joined the Free German Youth and lived in an apprentices' dormitory. She wanted to study in the Soviet Union, and entered the Arbeiter- und Bauernfakultät in Halle, but rejected the experience because of the political indoctrination she was subjected to. After meeting her husband, she gave up the idea of studying abroad and they settled into life as married students in Magdeburg. The Wende came when she was home for the baby year. While she received the usual government scholarship, her husband received no financial assistance and had to break off his studies. It had become difficult to care for their three children while continuing to study. She found work as a technical writer, then in advertising. She hoped to found her own business and entered Professor Voigt's management program. She wanted to help unemployed women using feminist techniques, such as creativity, networking, and intuition. But she aimed too high, she confesses, in starting with women who already had difficulties finding work, and now she must re-think her concept. Overall she judges unification as a positive development, because it has offered her the chance to try different careers.

After we leave the summer camp–cum–farm–cum–roofing company, Professor Voigt, Dr. Quilitz and I express our wonder at what Ria Schwaß has achieved. She is struggling to make her own way as a woman in a classic male profession; both the roofing trade and ownership of a business which employs mostly male laborers are atypical. Will she be able to hold her own in the weakened economy, and in a united Germany which is not kind to women who break such barriers? What about the challenges of supporting and running a household of three adults and seven children? She is not yet forty, I calculate, and there is no husband in evidence. She said she was married at eighteen and gave birth to her daughter at nineteen. But she had no time to play around. "We had it easier in those days," Dr. Quilitz says. "Life was orderly, and we knew what was expected of us."

We drive into Schwerin, to the headquarters of the women's project, located in a vocational center. En route Frau Quilitz points out the city's extensive leather industry, developed during the GDR. Now the huge factories, warehouses, and railyards stand empty. We eat lunch in the building's cafeteria and Dr. Quilitz meets her secretary, who asks her a few questions and addresses her informally as "Du." The easy interchange between them contrasts with the formal style of West German businesses I have observed. In the afternoon we drive into the shopping district in Schwerin to visit two more new entrepreneurs.

First we visit Susanne Fähnrich, a slight, delicate woman who opened a candy store under the Arko franchise eighteen months before. She pays 3.5% of her sales revenues to Arko and must purchase 80% of her wares from the company. In return she receives advertising materials and window-decorating tips aligned with the holiday calendar. A nursery school teacher and former art teacher, she has re-directed her talents to arranging store windows and holiday displays of chocolate, hard candies, gumdrops, and specially wrapped packets of coffee and champagne. This is no penny candy counter; most of her wares are too expensive to attract children. Much creative thought goes into the artful presentation of her wares. She explains that customers frequently shop for *Presente*, small presents to give a hostess when one is invited into someone's home. (Such English words, their meaning slightly askew, lend a certain cachet in East German conversation.) The elderly, with their leisure to stroll by and look into shop windows, constitute another important part of her clientele, and she stocks special candies for diabetics. We sit in a back workroom piled high with cases of candies and from somewhere she produces strong demitasse and little biscuits. At first her husband worked with her, helping unload shipments of candy and champagne, but now she has two full-time employees. During her busiest season, Easter and Mother's Day, she works fourteen-hour days, with no time to catch up on bookkeeping. But she has been able to afford a two-week vacation, and in the summertime she can sometimes work as little as five hours a day. She asks Professor Voigt's advice about expanding her business: she's thinking of opening a second shop in the new mall being built in the city center. Arko plans to open a shop there, and if she doesn't open the franchise, she'll have a competitor nearby.

At our next stop in Schwerin, Birgit Graumann presents a different picture. A large-boned young woman, she opened her "Chance Nr. 2" boutique in another part of the pedestrian zone. She explains that the name of her secondhand clothing store is meant to sound elegant, and its sign's typeface to evoke Chanel Number Five. Generously spaced racks and rounders of clothing stand about. Displays of handbags, shoes, and scarves suggest how shoppers can create ensembles. We talk upstairs in a gallery overlooking the boutique where Frau Graumann can keep an eye on shoppers. When women come into the store, she waits to judge whether they need help, leaving them free to browse, a contrast to the usual German custom, where salespeople promptly approach every customer. She says she's especially pleased that the same people who bring her their used clothing to sell buy from her too. She keeps her accounts on a computer sitting on her desk; customers who bring her used clothing to re-sell receive 50% of the price when an item is sold. Merchandise that hasn't moved in two months is returned to the owner. She shares business space with a woman who offers consulting on colors and styles based on the four seasons, a system popular among American women ten years earlier. At 200 DM per session, this consulting service isn't cheap. But women who have managed to stay employed in these difficult times are eager to look their best.

Frau Graumann's twelve-year-old son comes to the shop after school so she can keep an eye on him. She has lost one convenience offered mothers in the GDR: the after-school program of homework, sports, and activities that cared for children until the close of the workday.

Frau Graumann's enterprise presents a curious mixture, an atmosphere both intimate and businesslike. Professor Voigt asks her to reflect on what works for her. She replies that her shop's location is a definite asset: near city hall and lawyers' offices, where women can browse during their lunch hour. Women relish the thought that they are getting a bargain. In fact Frau Graumann knows that some of her customers are compulsive shoppers, a psychosis which certainly never existed in the GDR! She is flattered to notice that some women don't notice it's a secondhand shop. And she can afford to be choosy; she doesn't accept all consignments, but she can tell sellers who approach her which other stores might buy their used clothing. She makes it clear she's not serving the needy. She has to find ways to distinguish herself from other secondhand shops.

I ask Frau Graumann how her education in the GDR prepared her for becoming an entrepreneur. She replies that she was trained as a painter and developed an eye for color. Although she got good marks in school, she had no desire to continue studying; she always knew that she wanted to be self-employed.

We drive more slowly back to Schloß Hasenwinkel, where I have just a few minutes to rest before a shared supper of sandwiches and wine on the terrace in front of the hunting lodge. A dozen women settle into the metal chairs. Many know each other from Professor Voigt's seminars and exchange shop talk. Then we go around the circle as I ask each of them to summarize the education and career choices that led her to found her own business.

Frau Bosse completed the polytechnic school without an Abitur and entered an apprenticeship in a chemical laboratory. She received further training in education and instructed apprentices in a factory training center. She became an inspector for training centers, went West after unification, but ultimately came to help develop the program in Schwerin for women entrepreneurs.

Frau Dr. Gudrun Fechner came from a Mecklenburg village. Because her parents were poor and she had four siblings, she was sent to a state-run boarding school on scholarship. She studied economics in Berlin for four years and got married. Married for the second time, she brought up three children, despite furthering her education. Work times were flexible so that she was able to care for her children, and they all turned out well. She succeeded so well as a teacher that she was offered a tenured professorship when the Wende came and she was laid off. She became a free-lance management consultant in 1993 specializing in advice on investments and taxes and teaches besides. Today women have it harder than she did, she thinks, and she feels sad to contemplate her daughter's future. Today it would be unthinkable to have three children and a successful professional career at the same time.

Christiane Wilhelm, the next speaker, is a shy, quiet woman. Her entrepreneurial leanings have not taken her far from woman's traditional role: she opened a beauty salon. She learned the cartographer's trade, but her husband, a physical education teacher, traveled frequently, and she needed to care for their daughter. For a while she delivered newspapers, then took advantage of the management seminar to open her own beauty shop.

Christina Schwarz came to a similar field, fashion and image consulting, via a different route. She wanted to breed horses on her family's fifty-acre farm near Güstrow, but she was considered too small-boned for such heavy work. Through the career counseling typical of East Germany's educational system, she was re-directed, and and learned drafting instead. She studied mechanical engineering and met her husband; the couple had two children. She worked in communications design in Glewe, but her job was eliminated after unification. She celebrated with champagne, she announced, to the giggles of the other women. She continued her education, studying image building, fashion, and makeup in Munich. Now she works as a free-lance consultant in these areas and has been able to afford to build her own house in the countryside, where she hopes at last to raise horses.

Rosemarie Krummsee learned drafting and mechanical engineering, then patent law, then heating technology. Forty-three when unification came, she has managed to hold onto her job thus far. But because her company wants her to take early retirement, she's looking to open her own business. Her twenty-six-year-old daughter has re-located to Switzerland, and she is one of the few women I meet to express guilt over having sent her child into the state-run daycare and after school programs.

As the child of capitalist parents (her father's business was taken over by the state in 1972), Ulrike Leben had difficulties furthering her education in the socialist system aimed at breaking down barriers between proprietors and laborers. She worked in a collective fish farm, met her husband, and moved to Wismar on the Baltic Sea. The laboratory for fish diseases where she worked closed in 1991, and she became unemployed at the age of thirty. Judged over-qualified for a retail apprenticeship, she worked at various ABM jobs which pushed her into traditional women's work in a theater and in an adult education program. Now she has work in the city management office in Wismar, at least for the time being. But her boss is a "Besserwessi." Ulrike Leben, who fought for respect at the fish farm, argues with his attempts to make her conform to a subservient female role: he expects her to make the coffee. She has achieved only a modest compromise: she submits only if he says "please."

The next speaker, Laima Möller, is a slim young woman with a noticeable accent. She comes from Lithuania where she worked as a kindergarten teacher. Because the late hours made it difficult to raise her two children, she became director of a kindergarten instead. A widow, she married a German with whom she spoke Esperanto until she learned his language. She has been living in Germany since 1991, and first found work in a cleaning company to supplement her husband's meager wages. In Hannover she learned the professional cleaning trade, but encountered difficulty as a woman when she tried to continue her training to become a master tradesman, a step which would have given her the right to train apprentices. The company where she worked employed three women and thirty men. When she was laid off, she began studying at her own expense to qualify herself as a master cleaner. Her training course took place on Fridays and Saturdays, which meant that the employment office judged she was not available for hiring in a new position and therefore not entitled to unemployment benefits. After a year in her training course, officials at the employment office suggested she give it up so that she would qualify as available and have a right to benefits. She did not apply for welfare, because she had no wish to subject herself to the oppressive atmosphere of the social welfare office. Eventually she successfully completed the training course and became qualified as a master cleaner. After two years of hard work, she founded her own cleaning business, which now employs two people.

As I listen to these women describe their experiences, I marvel at their resilience, their determination, and their pluck. They have shelved their dreams, re-figured their options, gone back to school, taken enormous risks, and re-shaped their lives to survive in a new market economy so very different from the cradle to grave care-taking of the old German Democratic Republic. We sit talking on the terrace of Rabbit Corner Castle until nearly ten o'clock, as the late evening sun sets over the flat plains that stretch northward to the Baltic.

The next morning our two site visits send us rocketing over narrow paved roads in Professor Voigt's BMW once again. We are en route to a poultry farm and a donkey farm, and both of these women entrepreneurs live "JWD" Herr Voigt explains. Berliners are famous for pronouncing the consonant G as a J, so what he means is "GWD: ganz weit draußen," (way out there). Mecklenburg-Vorpommern is the most sparsely settled region in Germany. While the West boasts about 254 inhabitants per square kilometer, about the population density of Connecticut, the East outside of Berlin is closer to the population density of Pennsylvania.

Frau Hübner lives in a low stucco house surrounded by pens of ducks, geese, peacocks, rabbits, and chickens. "Broiler," as she calls them, meant young birds weighing less than three pounds. In the heyday of the GDR, rabbit was frequently served in cantines and cafeterias as an inexpensive source of protein. Rabbits could be cheaply raised in backyard hutches and fed kitchen scraps until they were ready for the kitchen themselves. Frau Hübner was an exception in the GDR, a housewife, an occupation she sustained for fourteen years while her husband worked and she cared for their four children. Housewives were a rarity, not only for economic reasons, but because women who stayed at home were sometimes portrayed as parasites in the socialist media. Nevertheless, she did not consider herself marginalized. Evenings she took part in social events such as the German-Soviet Friendship Club or Volkssolidarität. Now Frau Hübner delivers eggs from her free-range chickens to customers. At a price of two dollars for ten eggs they are expensive, but Professor Voigt explains he never visits without bringing home a box of eggs. After some good-natured teasing (she wants to give him the eggs, but he insists on paying) we go into the house.

Frau Hübner brings us coffee in living room, while houseflies buzz above the sticky table. She tells me that she was trained in animal husbandry in the GDR, and fought her way to the top as one woman working with thirty men. Her husband earned good money in the army so that she could eventually afford to stay home with their four children. Now her husband works in Hamburg where he earns around ten dollars an hour as an automotive mechanic. But he has to live there during the week. Thinking back on how they lived on his army pay, she comments that today they have a lot of freedom, but she wonders if they need all of it. Today, for example, people must work harder to buy the name brand clothing their children demand. Are they better off than in the old days when everyone wore the same things from the local state-owned clothing store?

Professor Voigt asks Frau Hübner about plans for the future. She rents her house and land, and she shows us through the attached barn and the poultry yards, admonishing us to watch where we step. Her fourteen-year-old son brings in armfuls of grass for the birds. She would like to raise ostriches, she says. She would like to expand operations by building a sanitary, tiled slaughterhouse with a smoke room above it so that she could sell smoked meats. Already people are ordering their ducks and geese for Christmas dinner. She sells dressed poultry and eggs from her free-range chickens in a nearby town on market days.

Frau Hübner's farm is small, but runs in the black. Free-range poultry and wholesome eggs would have been impossible to obtain from the huge collective farms that supplied food in the GDR. In the Erfurt seminar in 1985 I was told that most people ate preserved cold cuts once a day and were happy to get any fresh meat; even a rabbit stew for Sunday dinner was a small luxury. Berliners, in contrast, said only certain cuts of fresh meat were difficult to obtain. In the aftermath of unification, western media highlighted the shortcomings of collectivized agriculture. Nevertheless, Frau Hübner, who grew up in East Germany's agricultural regions, believes people in the GDR ate more healthfully than is generally the case today.

Even further out than Frau Hübner's poultry farm we locate the donkey farm belonging to Frau Regina Werner and her husband; Eselhof Fincken, its bright yellow signs pointing us the way, has been open for three years, another product of Professor Voigt's management seminar. Regina Werner chain-smokes as we talk in the little shop or visitors' center at her donkey farm. She lived for years in Neubrandenburg in a tenth-story apartment without so much as a balcony. She married late, a man eighteen years older than she, and because she was thirty when her son was born, she was unable to take advantage of the baby year; the age limit for new mothers was twenty-five. She worked in several executive positions within the Free German Trade Union (FDGB; the West German institution and its initials were similar, but omitted the "Free"). She worked in the division of youth and sports, then as functionary in the trade union for textiles, clothing, and leather. In both East and West Germany, trade unions are unitary, that is, organizing all the workers within a single company into one union. In the trade union for textiles, clothing, and leather, for example, secretaries, truck drivers, and janitors, as well as stitchers in a clothing factory would all be represented by the same union. Of course East German trade unions played no role in opposing management. Instead, they beat the drums for support of the central economy's five-year plans, set goals for competing to fill or surpass production quotas, channeled workers into political participation and, in return, rewarded loyal employees with educational opportunities for their children, better housing, or vacation lodgings.

After unification, Frau Werner successfully retained her executive position in a different style of trade union, but the factory closed down and her office was eliminated in 1995. She became a student in Professor Voigt's management seminar, interrupted by a one-week vacation which she and her husband spent in Tunisia. Her husband had taken early retirement. The two thought of opening a camel farm in Mecklenburg-Vorpommern, but when she returned to the management seminar, people laughed themselves silly at the idea. Nonetheless, they returned to Tunisia where her husband received training as a camel driver. The Tunisians, she says, made her husband an offer: they would exchange several camels for her. He declined. She learned French to communicate with the Tunisians. But their dream was shattered by import restrictions on camels: there were none in Mecklenburg-Vorpommern, and thus any imported camels would be subject to quarantine.

When the Werners took their son to the Hansapark (Germany's Disneyworld) in Schleswig-Holstein, they discovered the nearby donkey farm Nessendorf, and the idea of raising donkeys quickly supplanted the camels. The Nessendorf farm had 150 donkeys, and the Werners were able to buy ten of them, along with advice and assistance in learning to care for the animals. They rented a farm in Fincken, a hamlet near Röbel, and opened their donkey farm, the only one in East Germany, they tell me proudly.

Today the Werners offer buggy rides in the spring, summer, and fall, and sleigh rides in the winter. They take in summer campers who can tent nearby, or children who live with them on the donkey farm for a week or two. The donkeys are so gentle that children can drive them around a mile-long track outside a pasture. The summer camp children love to unharness them and brush their shaggy coats. Families celebrate birthday parties at the donkey farm, and several couples have even gotten married there. In the US, birthday parties at bowling alleys or pizza parlors are common, but in Germany the notion of celebrating a child's birthday at a donkey farm is a novel idea. Frau Werner is onto something.

But the work is hard: the Werners are up at 6:30 to feed their donkeys, and the farm is open from ten a.m. to six p.m. Frau Werner greets guests, urges them to sign the guestbook, sells popsicles and cold drinks, or little stuffed donkeys and souvenirs. Herr Werner does many of the barn chores and harnesses or saddles the donkeys. Summer campers learn to feed and brush the animals; some are dwarf donkeys less than three feet high at the shoulder. The original ten donkeys the Werners purchased have multiplied so that they now sell some foals. At the moment they own nineteen donkeys, worth from $900 to $2000 apiece. Their fourteen-acre farm provides pasture for the stock, but they must buy hay and straw. They entertain two to four summer campers per week with campfires, boat rides, and swimming, besides riding and driving the donkeys. Today, a Thursday in mid August, two hundred guests have visited the donkey farm, saddled and ridden donkeys, and have driven on twenty-two buggy rides.

Frau Werner has profited from Professor Voigt's management seminar; she has thought of some clever gimmicks to increase business, such as advertising in the local newspaper that a new donkey foal will be born and inviting readers to write in and name the baby. The small town radio station Ostseewelle (Baltic wave) reports news of the donkey farm, and the business has grown enough to hire a part-time bookkeeper. Regina Werner helps create advertising flyers and then distributes them to local mailboxes.

I ask what she has lost through the Wende, and she replies that her family has lost its security; in the old days there was no juvenile crime, and life has become more expensive. "My homeland has been taken from me," she says. But the people in her village are as friendly and ready to help as ever; that hasn't changed. She was happy living in the GDR; if only the political system hadn't destroyed people's initiative, she believes it could have worked. From the political turnaround she gained the freedom to travel by car and camper. She has visited France, Italy, and Greece as well as Tunisia.

We drive back toward Berlin as daylight fades golden over the flat wheatfields. We agree that the Werners' success is assured, in large measure due to their hard work. But what has made the concept of the donkey farm such a certain winner? First, families could rarely afford to keep pets in the GDR. The country fed its populace; food was abundant and nourishing, though not always delicious or well prepared, and seldom attractively presented. But there was little excess for pet food. Speaking at a poetry reading in Leipzig in 1992, poet Barbara Köhler commented on her impression of American capitalist decadence after seeing supermarket shelves stocked with countless varieties of dog and cat food. Cramped apartments in the GDR afforded no room for pets. By contrast, in the uncertainties brought on by unification, some families have opted for a dog rather than a child, a choice many landlords prefer. In fact East Berliners complain of their united city that now they must step around dog droppings everywhere. So pets, or at least the chance to fondle and pet gentle animals, are a real treat for children. Frau Werner understands what animal companionship can give a child; she's even considering a riding program for emotionally disturbed or retarded children.

Second, riding and driving animals, even little donkeys, satisfies a human urge for control. Ordinary East Germans were seldom were seldom able to drive anything. Cars were not only expensive, but difficult to obtain; a ten- or twelve-year waiting period was the norm.

Used cars, even those in poor condition, were more expensive than new ones, just because buyers didn't have to wait for them. Gasoline was costly and sometimes hard to get. Most workers rode the inexpensive public transportation network, jolting along on ancient, rattling streetcars. Bicycles were the ultimate subversive vehicle, as I learned from a Dutch participant in the Erfurt seminar I had attended in 1985. Border guards obstructed his entry into the GDR because he brought his bicycle. Bicycle tourists were not bound by a train timetable. Their whereabouts could not be controlled like those of automotive tourists by controlling where they could buy gas. Bicyclists might stop anywhere and talk to anyone. While bicycles provide cheap transportation everywhere in Western Europe, they were frowned upon by East Germany's socialist regime and therefore rare. Imagine the delight of a child learning to balance on a two-wheeler, and then convert that image to a child driving a little donkey cart: the rapture becomes visible.

Riding offers a similar feeling of control, control over one's speed and direction. To combat the tendency of East German youth to flee the toil and confinement of life on collective farms, the socialist regime made riding lessons available. Horseback riding has always been the sport of the wealthy landed gentry in Germany. Thus the donkey farm's opportunities to pet, drive, and ride its animals appeal to young and old.

Another aspect of its attraction is the fact that Germans associate donkeys (rather than horses) with vacation travel. Because Germany's climate tends to be cool and rainy, they love to visit warmer climes. Immediately after the fall of the Berlin Wall, East Germans headed south, to Greece, Italy, Spain, or Tunisia. On southern mountainsides some of them saw donkeys grazing or carrying baggage or baskets of olives and grapes. And like the Balkan grill restaurants and Turkish Döner kebab stands that have sprung up throughout Germany, donkeys remind people of holidays in the sun.

As Herr Voigt drives back into Berlin, we speculate together about the future success of the women entrepreneurs whose ventures into capitalism he is guiding. I've heard that half of all start-up ventures in the US fail within the first few years, and I pray that these women, who had to overcome so many more obstacles to begin, will prove more successful in united Germany's market economy.

Eighteen months later I meet Herr Voigt again and have a chance to ask him about the present fate of these women entrepreneurs. I am pleased to hear that all are still in business, though they've weathered a few setbacks since I met them. Frau Schwaß's roofing company is still in business. Frau Fähnrich did open a second candy store in the new shopping center in Schwerin, and as she expected sales in her original store fell off somewhat. But at least she owns her own competition. The Chance Nummer Zwei boutique still sells used clothing in Schwerin, although Frau Graumann's sales were a little lower than she would have liked. Frau Hübner expanded her poultry business to sell smoked meat, as she had intended. She made the mistake of hiring two neighbors to work for her, but found it hard to preserve the structured supervisory relationship at work and the neighborly friendliness in her village; the problem of addressing one another as "Sie" at work and "du" at home is how Herr Voigt explains it. Finally she had to let them go. She terminated her business dealings with one bank before establishing herself with another. But those are beginner's mistakes, he says, and can be ironed out. The donkey farm continues too.

Later I reflect on these women and their prospects in united Germany's market economy. The Social Democrats' governing coalition has pledged to support women's start-up ventures in its "Frau und Beruf" program, which supports management-training seminars and offers low interest loans. Laudable as such intentions seem, they circumvent the larger issue of transforming the male-dominated workplace to give women a fairer chance to succeed. They do nothing to combat sexual harassment or gender discrimination there. The program offers no guarantee that women-owned firms, like Frau Schwaß's roofing company, will get a fair percentage of contracts. The high risks which such entrepreneurs take become clearer in my next round of visits to women in the beauty business and rural women.

Chapter Nine
The Beauty Business

One of the most significant changes confronting East German women as they experience the transition from communism to capitalism has been the new emphasis on physical appearance and dress. In the new marketplace, a woman's looks become a commodity, part of her human capital, and can determine whether she finds work in the new service businesses that may offer her only chance of employment. Women's appearance is one more area where western tastes and standards have gained ascendancy over East Germany.

To gain a clearer understanding of the prevalent images of women in the German Democratic Republic, I examined copies of the women's magazine *Für Dich* published through the Wende. In the late eighties it cost just sixty *Pfennig* for around forty pages of feature stories about women and families, black and white photographs, health tips, and housekeeping advice. With a print run of 926,000 copies, the magazine appears to have been widely read. While its lack of advertising was typical of all East German publications, it reminded me of America's *MS. Magazine* and its struggle to exist without paid advertising in order to remain free of profit-oriented attempts to influence women.

Für Dich contained a wealth of information that I tried to absorb before turning my attention to the beauty question. Its articles on foreign countries featured women in Cuba, Chile under Salvador Allende, Armenians coping with a terrible earthquake, and racism in South Africa. Nearly every issue in 1989 featured negative coverage about West Germany: the lack of housing for large families, container housing for the homeless, high unemployment, the difficulty of obtaining an abortion, child poverty and child labor, religious cults, and Neonazis. Undoubtedly these features, like all effective propaganda, contained grains of truth, yet at the same time they contributed to the misunderstandings and suspicions East Germans harbored against the West when the two countries were united only a few months later. The magazine frequently pointed out to its readers what they had gained under socialism: one article reminded them that what the German Communist Party had demanded had become reality in the GDR (January 1989); another in July described how women entered the workforce during World War I only to be pushed out when it was over, something that could no longer happen under socialism.

Articles about the German Democratic Republic featured women in a few glamorous professions such as graphic designer and software engineer, but also showed women cleaning fish, milking cows, laying railroad track, supervising cranes in Rostock's harbor, and checking hygiene conditions in food production. Human-interest stories described large families, education and child raising issues, and single parenthood.

Für Dich's portrayal of women was refreshingly honest: there were women in wheelchairs, large women, older women, and real bodies instead of fashion models. Women appeared nude in articles about pregnancy and the sauna, but the photographs appeared factual rather than titillating. Health tips described nutrition, pregnancy, and the evils of smoking. Most fascinating was what the magazine did *not* contain: it had no articles on weight loss, increasing bust size, sculpting muscles, or reducing hips and tummy. There were no tips on tweezing eyebrows, coloring hair, manicuring toenails, or applying make-up.

Für Dich changed suddenly as the political turnaround began. Its January 1990 issue provided television listings for West German stations, which many East Germans had of course watched for years. Letters to the magazine insisted that women's equality had *not* been perfected in the GDR and openly criticized discrimination against mothers of young children and the lack of male teachers in kindergarten. Older women complained about younger co-workers taking advantage of the baby year. By spring and summer of 1990 the magazine was reporting on drug and alcohol consumption, women in prison, and sex in the GDR. It also reported on newly emerging feminist groups and identified itself as an advocate for women.

The West German publishing house of Gruner and Jahr bought the magazine, expanded it to sixty pages, filled it with color photographs, and raised the price. Some articles continued to address working women: features on unemployment, job-hunting, kindergarten closings, and tenants' rights reflect the changing conditions for East

German readers. The women who appeared in color photographs became younger and more glamorous as coverage of hair, grooming, and makeup expanded. Instead of writing about the dangers of smoking, the magazine published cigarette advertising. Features about working women and the burgeoning feminist movement disappeared and the space devoted to recipes and home-making advice increased. Travel coverage now included exotic vacation destinations around the world. Clothing appeared more elegant and leisure wear edged out some work clothing; readers were informed about where cosmetics and clothes could be bought. Too cheap and flimsy to gain a foothold in the West German market, *Für Dich* simultaneously became irrelevant to its East German readership and soon ceased publication.

To probe further into the question of how changing beauty and fashion styles affect East German women, I sought out two women who opened a beauty salon and image consulting business in Berlin Mitte. To reach them I threaded my way through a construction site: workers in blue overalls, trucks, plaster debris in the street, buildings blocked off by plywood sheets, and industrial extension cords snaking across the sidewalk. I located the house number and entered a small, ultra-modern beauty salon. The shop's proprietor, whom we will call Frau Bachmann, greeted me and introduced her partner, Frau Lindner. I sat in a stainless steel chair, its cushions a lovely shade of midnight blue that matched Frau Bachmann's silk blouse.

These women have made the transition from the GDR's production-based economy into the more service-oriented economy of united Germany. At the end of the country's existence, about the same proportion of its workforce, 45%, was employed in production as in the services. In 1998 63% of workers were employed in the services, and only 33% in production, a transformation which has affected more women than men, as they tend to lose production jobs (*Sozialreport 1999*, 137). Since I was curious to learn how these women had been affected by the transition, I asked them to describe their education, the division of household labor, and their prior careers.

Both Frau Bachmann and Frau Lindner came from households of five children. Because Heidrun Bachmann's mother suffered from rheumatism and her father was a student, she spent a few years in a children's home, an experience with no negative associations, she says. She attended the Karl Marx University in Leipzig from 1982 to 1987. When she married as a student, her husband took over most of the household chores. In Leipzig, she says, people could discuss politics freely. She had contact with Russians and also with the Central Committee of the Socialist Unity Party. She studied cultural politics; she knew what got published and what did not. But she too would be subjected to what Nietzsche called "die Umwertung aller Werte," the re-evaluation of all values. After completing a degree in education, she worked in Berlin at the Institute for the History of the Workers' Movement. That institution closed in the wake of reform. At first she reacted with enthusiasm to the Wende. She continued to work as a historian and created an exhibit on Rosa Luxemburg, who, together with Karl Liebknecht, founded the German Communist Party, and was murdered in 1919, her body thrown into Berlin's Landwehr Canal. But she came to understand that history is only written within the framework of a ruling philosophy, and she became disillusioned when she realized how the GDR had functioned. She went to work for the Party of Democratic Socialism, heir to the former Socialist Unity Party.

Then her life changed in other ways. She got divorced and became a single mother. She found an ABM job as a historian and worked on an exhibition about women after the Second World War. She observes the similarities between that era in and her own, as women were first obliged to labor clearing away the war rubble, and then pushed out of the workforce to make way for men. She had been a physical education teacher at one time and now she became interested in health and fitness. She decided to open a beauty salon and to use her experience in education to help other women become independent. She began working from her home, reluctant to borrow money to start her business. She began offering beauty consulting, and training other women to follow in her footsteps. Her present husband buys groceries and does the housework to support her business. The move from education into business cost her some friends, who considered her entrepreneurial venture a comedown for a highly educated university graduate. But like the women entrepreneurs I met at Hasenwinkel, her willingness to abandon old ways of thinking and to leave the educational and career path chosen for her may prove the keys to her success.

Frau Bachmann's colleague, Ursula Lindner (not her real name) came from Kremitz, a town of eleven thousand with a large chemical industry. Her mother stayed home to raise her five children. While the German Democratic Republic discouraged stay-at-home motherhood, women with four or five children were esteemed as full contributors to society, and the country provided them with their own old-age pensions even if they had not earned wages. Because Frau Lindner's father worked the night shift, he had no time for housework, but took his family on skiing trips and outings. After the erweiterte Oberschule Ursula Lindner wanted to continue her studies, and since she was the eldest of five children in a working class family, the Party supported her. In Lausitz, the area closest to the Czech Republic, she studied automation, then returned to chemical fiber technology, a male-dominated industry where she worked for seventeen years.

The demands of her occupation overturned the traditional gender roles in her marriage: she never learned to cook. Her husband can sew, knit, darn socks, and does the cooking. Until her son was three they lived with their parents because they had no apartment of their own. When the boy became ill with bronchitis, her husband took leave from work to care for him because he earned less than she did.

The company which employed Frau Lindner closed after unification; Frau Lindner was supposed to work part-time, but there was so little to do that she was really paid for not working. Anyway, she was able to continue supporting her two children. Next she studied data processing, but became disillusioned with her fellow students; paid by the employment office to take the course, they showed little interest. A West German boss told her she must learn to market herself, to name her own salary. She found work in Brandenburg (the federal state surrounding Berlin) but technology changed so swiftly she was unable to use much of her experience. She used some vacation time to improve her qualifications, and worked successfully for the next year and a half. But she wanted to become independent, and settled on the business of beauty consultant.

She began working from home in 1993, after gaining the approval of the husband and two children who share her small apartment. She continued to work forty-five to fifty hours a week for her West German employer, then saw her own clients in the evening. Weekends she attended beauty seminars while her husband booked appointments, shopped for groceries, and did the housework. The Monday through Friday work gave her no satisfaction at all; she was simply told what to do by her West German boss. She preferred the East German approach: teamwork in which brigades or groups of workers carried out projects together. When she quit, her boss, knowing nothing of her new business venture, paid her for the half-year she would have continued to work after giving notice.

Today she supervises fifteen women from various professions who are learning to become beauty consultants like Heidrun Bachmann and herself. She also directs their education center. This change of occupation, she admits, has created some family conflicts. Her mother is dissatisfied to have a highly educated daughter working in the cosmetics field. Nonetheless she helps with ironing and supports her daughter. Her husband works as a mason and carpenter and is away from home from 6:00 A. M. to 7:00 P. M. Under the capitalist economy their roles have reverted to the typical gender-based division of household labor. She does the laundry and mows the lawn. Their son, who is twenty-six, has become a carpenter and their daughter, twenty-one, a florist, traditional male-female roles in their–now free– choice of occupations. At the age of forty-six, Frau Lindner is a grandmother.

The most important aspect of her work, she says, is human relations. She works with women who are unemployed, early retirees, or struggling to hold onto their jobs in a highly competitive, fast-paced environment. She plans to develop a network in Brandenburg for women who work as independent beauty consultants. The consulting sessions these women offer are free, but the sale of cosmetics they recommend generates a profit.

Frau Lindner too, is on to something. She says that women have been made insecure by job losses and profound economic and social changes. They seek new places to put their trust. When she touches a woman's skin, she can feel the trust being placed in her hands. Now that the collectives that formed these women's base in the workplace have vanished, they lack the opportunity to communicate with others like themselves. There is no one to turn to to discuss divorce, troubles with unruly children, a husband's lost job. Nor is there anyone with whom to share the good times. East Germany's factories and stores held annual company parties, *Betriebsfeste*, where everyone celebrated and danced and ate and drank together. They organized theater visits, concert tickets, or picnic outings with families. The collapse of the workplace has left an enormous void, and Frau Bachmann and Frau Lindner are prepared to spread a net over some part of it.

I ask how these women judge the overall impact of unification. Frau Bachmann feared for her livelihood during the unification process, which she criticizes as undemocratic. The present economy, she says, wastes the potential of its citizens because of massive unemployment among well-trained workers. Of course her present independent venture would have been impossible in the old system. She sympathizes with the insecurity of kindergarten and elementary teachers, and agrees that women over forty when the Wall opened have lost a great deal. She herself had to undergo a painful process of determining her own identity. She was forced to acknowledge that her learning no longer stood for much. She does not identify herself as a citizen of united Germany; Mecklenburg-Vorpommern is her homeland. Her daughter has experienced unemployment, and Frau Bachmann wants to will her business to her. While she was sensitive and gentle as a child, her daughter has grown up stronger and sharper.

Frau Lindner asserts that she was more critical of the GDR before its collapse. She knew things couldn't go on as they were, and she finds it senseless to pretend things were all right. She agrees that women are the losers in unification, if you judge by the unemployment rate. But people must learn to think differently, not keep looking to the past.

Frau Bachmann and Frau Lindner are typical of many East German women in being obliged to abandon their technical education to meet the demands of a new economy. While I know from my research that women are far more apt than men to be employed beneath their qualifications, or to be required to learn other skills to get a new job, I marvel at their acceptance of change and their lack of bitterness. I can well understand the perspective of Frau Bachmann's friends and Frau Lindner's mother, who regret that the education these women worked for has become devalued in today's new labor market. Compared to Frau Lindner's technical know-how and Frau Bachmann's scholarly qualifications, their cosmetic enterprise seems superficial and even trivial.

However, they are realists, and ready to adapt. Like Frau Graumann in her Chance Nr. 2 boutique in Schwerin, they sell to women who are suddenly obliged to market themselves in a newly sexist culture that places new demands on women's appearance. In the GDR beauty salons remained open from early morning into the evening to accommodate working women, but their shops were often shabby and poorly equipped. Women often looked as if they needed a haircut, or just a shampoo, but traveling by streetcar to a beauty shop at the end of a long day in the factory sometimes became just another burden. Cosmetics and imported perfumes could be bought in luxury *Exquisit* shops where buyers paid in hard western currencies at prices beyond the reach of most working mothers. East German skin creams smelled like the petroleum from which they were derived. Some women smiled cautiously, trying to hide a missing tooth. Most were reasonably thin, not because of any fashion standards, but simply because treats like ice cream, chocolate, coffee and pastries were not cheap, nor sold on every street corner as they are now. In Germany today as in the United States, women are targeted by food advertising at every turn, while being simultaneously persuaded that they are too fat. A survey conducted by the German federal agency for health education (*Bundeszentrale für gesundheitliche Aufklärung*) recently determined that 40% of twelve- to sixteen-year-old girls believe they are too fat and have tried dieting. Two-thirds are dissatisfied with their bodies.

Huge changes have unraveled the German Democratic Republic's fashion industry. The country manufactured women's clothing for practicality and durability. Working women needed clothing suitable for going from work to parent-teacher conferences in the afternoon and theater in the evening. A little research in the German Democratic Republic's *Statistisches Taschenbuch* for 1988 reveals that in 1987 the country produced about 170 marks worth of clothing (excluding underwear, hosiery, and shoes) for each of its approximately seven million women over age eighteen. Clothing was expensive: women's panty hose cost fourteen marks a pair, and a cotton jogging suit 146 marks (*Statistisches Taschenbuch 1988,* 114)!

Photographs of clothing in *Für Dich* showed items that working women could wear on the job or on a date. However, instead of information on prices and where clothing could be bought, the magazine supplied information about sewing patterns. Many women were obliged to sew clothing for themselves and their families, yet another chore that added weight to their double burden. Synthetic fabrics were common, natural fibers a rarity. In Leipzig in 1985 I paused in front of a window in the Mädler Passage, wondering why the swaths of fabric displayed there were marked "second quality." Then another participant in the Erfurt seminar explained that first-quality fabrics were often sold directly to the Soviet Union. Many women dressed in light colors: beige, gray, light blue, so that garments could be combined easily without their colors clashing. "It was hard to put together a sensible outfit," one younger woman told me. State-owned clothing stores offered little variety, and items such as lingerie and stockings were sometimes in short supply. Women simply bought what was available nearby, and that varied considerably between large cities and the hinterland.

Men's clothing and fashion fared no better. It was rare for men to wear suits. In 1985 I found the absence of white shirts and neckties among college faculty both odd, judged from a West German perspective, and refreshing, from an American one. I soon learned that formal attire was expensive and not always easy to obtain. Once visiting Weimar I was surprised to see a half-dozen men, all wearing dark suits and white shirts. Then I realized that they were a funeral party.

Some East German women complain that clothing has become wildly expensive, flimsy, and not always available in tall sizes. Those who work are expected to appear in fresh attractive outfits, and looking elegant or tastefully dressed has gained in importance as older women are eased into early retirement and West German male bosses dominate the workplace.

Unification opened the country to competition from cheap imported clothing. Advertising and store displays make everything suddenly accessible, at least to those who can pay. Today American retailers such as Lands End and Eddie Bauer mail their catalogs into Berlin and Leipzig and Dresden, and through the wonders of electronic shopping, everything is for sale everywhere.

The inroads made by foreign competition have dealt a death blow to the country's textile industry. About 460,000 women worked in East Germany's clothing and leather industries, but 90% of the manufacturers which employed them went out of business in the early nineties (Behrend, 28). During the same period, the amount East German families spent on clothing and shoes declined by one-half to one-third (*Sozialreport 1999*, 217). The gain in lower expenses for clothing a family has come at the cost of thousands of women's jobs. East Germany's clothing factories employed large numbers of workers using outmoded production methods. Computer driven pattern and cutting machinery easily replaced women textile workers, who are among the occupations hardest hit by unemployment. Textile manufacture, less automated or computerized than in the West, required a fairly low level of skills, meaning that workers needed extensive retraining to find new jobs. Some, of course, were considered too old.

One attempt to salvage a small part of the country's clothing industry occurred in the town of Zehdenick about an hour north of

Berlin. There a clothing manufacturer closed in 1992, throwing three hundred people out of work. Several factors contributed to the failure of the company, which made jeans. Its climate prevented East Germany from growing cotton, and the lack of convertible currency curbed imports, as was the case in most Soviet block countries. Synthetic fabrics, which were often used instead of cotton, bore little resemblance to real denim. In fact when I visited Erfurt in 1985, I packed a new pair of jeans, certain that if I needed money, they would fetch a handsome price on the black market. Real Levis cost as much as a hundred dollars in the Exquisit shops.

To provide some jobs in the Zehdenick area, a make work project was started to produce stylish, high quality children's clothing made from natural fibers. The concept appealed because West Germans spare no expense when it comes to outfitting their few, precious offspring, and because consciousness of environmental damage was taking hold in the East. Two hundred women applied for fifty openings. Those hired included single mothers and women over forty-five, both considered hardship cases. They participated in training that included computer-assisted design, mastery of all phases of the production process, and a philosophy of ecology seminar, meant to create identification with natural fiber projects. Many women considered the natural fiber concept a peculiar tic of their West German bosses, but if the scheme produced jobs, they were ready to try it.

When the project moved into its next phase, founding an independent company, the ranks of women thinned. They learned that such a company offered no guarantee of job security. Furthermore, the concept of investing their personal savings, and assuming debts as well, frightened most potential investors. The prices for their products, such as three hundred marks for a child's snowsuit, seemed prohibitively high to mothers who were accustomed to their country subsidizing the cost of children's clothing and shoes.

In the end four women, all highly educated and experienced, three with children in the age group targeted by their natural fiber clothing, assumed the role of owner-managers. The new company, YoYo Kid, was incorporated in 1994 and took over machinery and orders from the job-creation project. They hired women from that project, again including three under twenty-seven and one over fifty, women whose wages of 15,000 DM (about $900) per month would be subsidized by state programs because they were considered difficult to place.

Production workers earned between five and six dollars an hour, and were given bonuses for extra productivity, but not paid for overtime.

Financing the new company proved all but impossible. Seventy banks turned down YoYo Kid's application for credit. Shares of 5,000 DM were sold to individuals, some of them feminists, and to a catalog company in the West which then advertised its support for the women's project. Finally state and national guarantees enabled the women to secure financing, but at a rate of 11% for short-term credit, 8% for a long-term loan. In addition, lenders demanded the women's husbands assume liability for their wives' financial obligations. The company's owners promised to create five more jobs within the next two years.

Four years later YoYo Kid closed its doors. The project's failure suggests several lessons. First the women who worked there couldn't afford to buy their own product, nor could their neighbors. In an area where three hundred workers had been laid off shortly before, buyers could not afford to concern themselves the environmental benefits of vegetable dyes and organically produced cotton and silk. A second major factor was certainly the country's falling birthrate. Immediately following unification, births fell by 60%, shrinking the market for children's clothing. Almost half of the births which did occur were to single mothers, who could ill afford the luxury of natural fiber clothing. And the workers themselves had difficulty identifying with the natural fiber concept at the heart of their enterprise.

Above all, competition from the country's new market economy sounded the project's death knell. While YoYo Kid could sell its wares tariff-free in other European Union countries, Spain, Italy, and France could sell theirs in Germany too. East Germany's largest trading partners had been the Soviet Union, Poland, Czechoslovakia, and Bulgaria. They could no longer afford trade with Germany after the valuable West German mark became the valid currency. Thus currency union, combined with the disintegration of the economies of the former Soviet block countries, destroyed the market for East German exports. High financing costs demanded by the Dresdner Bank added to YoYo Kid's overhead. Taken together, these factors brought about the failure of a concept that had conformed to feminist consciousness: concern for families, the environment, and ensuring a fair living for workers.

To assess whether Heidrun Bachmann's beauty consulting business had fared better than YoYo Kid, I decided to seek out her shop when I returned to Berlin in early 2000. My search in the telephone book failed to turn up either Frau Bachmann or Frau Lindner, and a perusal of a directory of women-owned businesses in Berlin brought no results. I sought out the beauty shop itself. Plywood sheathing and dumpsters full of plaster blocked the sidewalk as other buildings were being renovated. I found that the beauty salon had changed its name, and acquired new owners. Its display window now advertises Master Cut and Top Stylist, leading me to wonder just what the creators of such trendy English phrases intend to convey. Other little services have sprung up in the street, but the tattoo parlor nearby is not busy, nor is the little secondhand bookstore next door. Frau Lindner and Frau Bachmann are gone.

Chapter Ten
The Plight of Rural Women

Elke Goltz, whom I met in Berlin in 1998, was a doctoral candidate in cultural geography at the University of Potsdam whose research focused on unemployment, emigration, and social relations among inhabitants of the East German countryside. When she learned of my interviews with the entrepreneurs of Hasenwinkel and the beauty consultants in East Berlin, she wanted to be sure I got a glimpse of the women's dislocation in the market economy from the perspective of rural women, and offered to share her research with me. Many rural women, she said, were poorly educated, inarticulate, uncomfortable in group interviews, and lacking in self-confidence. From 1996-1998 she worked with a pilot project funded by the Federal Employment Office in Nürnberg, designed to lift rural women out of poverty. Most of the women in this re-training project had been employed in agriculture and lost their jobs in the post-unification break-up of East Germany's large collective farms.

In the seminar on the German Democratic Republic which I attended in 1985 in Erfurt, I had learned something about communist agriculture. Land reform began under Soviet occupation in the fall of 1945. Members of the Prussian Junker class, or anyone who owned more than a hundred hectares (about 247 acres), lost ownership of their land. Some land was redistributed to Germans forcibly resettled from Hungary, Czechoslovakia, and the newly delineated Poland. Between 1952 and 1960, agricultural holdings were re-organized into 3,844 state-run cooperative farms called *landeswirtschaftliche Produktionsgenossenschaften* or LPGs. Other land was converted to public ownership and formed into 464 additional agricultural entities. Farmers who placed their land, livestock, and machinery in these cooperatives were assured a market for their products, supplies of necessary seed and fertilizer, and access to heavy farm equipment. They retained a half hectare (about 1.2 acres) for private use. This allotment of private land was later reduced by half. Yet these tiny plots produced 29% of all the fruit grown in the GDR, 11% of its vegetables, 40% of all the eggs, and nearly all the honey and rabbits (a cheap and common source of meat protein). Private profit turned out to be a greater incentive than anything the state could offer to increase agricultural production.

According to East Germany's official handbook for 1985, 57.5% of its territory was farmland, and 87% of that area was cultivated by these collectives. The handbook describes the improvements which the collectivization of agriculture had brought into the lives of farmers: liberation from the boom and bust cycles of a capitalistic supply and demand economy, easier working conditions, and better educational opportunities. Through the sixties and seventies the state added other amenities to attract and retain workers in farming regions. Many collective farms had their own apartment buildings, daycare centers, health clinics, vocational schools with housing and dining facilities for apprentices, and huge kitchens which fed workers in these facilities as well as pensioners and school children. They owned vacation lodgings and children's camps and sponsored leisure activities like riding clubs, sports teams, restaurants, and houses of culture.

Newspaper accounts regularly featured stories about the fulfillment of production quotas outlined in the five-year plans that formed the framework of the centrally planned economy. Many collective farms developed their own research laboratories to study animal diseases, effective land use, and better strains of seed. East Germany achieved the best agricultural production yield of any Soviet block country, but its per hectare yields were lower than those of West Germany or Britain because the acreage included infertile land tilled to export foodstuffs to earn hard currency (Panzig, 163). Another drawback was that the country shortchanged its own farmers in order to sell tractors and heavy equipment to the Soviet Union in exchange for petroleum. By 1980, it became difficult to obtain chemical fertilizer and spare parts for machinery; many collective farms maintained their own repair facilities and stock-piled spare parts, even resorting to dismantling one new thresher-combine to keep three old ones running (Panzig, 164).

I visited a collective farm not far from Erfurt in 1985. Workers lived in gray stucco barracks constructed in the fifties. I learned that socialism made a point of employing women in agriculture either as technicians (for example as chemists developing herbicides and pesticides), or as heavy equipment operators, so that they played a key role in providing the nation's food supply. Farm women also continued laboring in the fields as they had always done. Thirty-seven per cent of agricultural workers were women. At the LPG I visited, women sat indoors at a conveyor belt inspecting potatoes which had been peeled by a machine. They bagged the potatoes in clear plastic sacks for transport to the farm's cafeteria and the local school. Mechanized or not, potato peeling was still women's work.

Through large-scale food production such as this collective farm and its potato peeling operation, the state ensured that workers and schoolchildren received a hot noonday meal at the workplace or in school or daycare. If there was little incentive for workers to show up at a job site where the lack of materials had brought production to a standstill, the expectation of a warm dinner motivated them to report for work. All cooks could depend on a supply of necessities such as bread, potatoes, carrots, onions, and the omnipresent cabbage. Hard sausage and cheese could usually be found. But fresh meat and perishable fruit and vegetables were in chronically short supply. (Nevertheless, East Germans ate better food more regularly than American welfare recipients at the end of the month.) One day everyone on the streetcar in Erfurt seemed to be carrying small round watermelons, which had just appeared at the market. Another day it was cauliflower. Some people made a practice of simply getting into line to wait for their share of whatever was to be had. Grandmothers who had time on their hands stood in line for hours to bring home fresh cherries or peaches in harvest season. People carried a bag with them at all times so that they could bring home whatever had suddenly become available. A decade later East Berliners told me that such folded cloth shopping bags were one characteristic distinguishing East from West Germans.

Because imported food would have cost the country precious hard currency, produce was limited to what would grow in East Germany's central European climate. That excluded such delicacies as oranges, bananas, tobacco, and coffee. Sugar was produced from sugar beets, as it is in much of western Europe. While tobacco and coffee could be had for a price, perishables such as citrus fruits and bananas were rare indeed. Furthermore, when bad weather affected the food supply (for example, heavy rains in 1987 which reduced the production of fresh fruits and vegetables), imported foodstuffs were not brought in to supplement the meager harvest; people simply ate more potatoes.

With sardonic humor, East Germans poked fun at the lack of fresh foodstuffs. The Socialist Unity Party's German initials, SED, were transliterated as "selten etwas da" (seldom anything there) a reference to the empty shelves in the state-owned grocery stores, or Handels-Organisationen, abbreviated HO. One joke told of a man who returned unexpectedly from work to find his wife in bed with her lover. "This is awful, this is terrible," he exclaimed. "Didn't you know–in the HO grocery store they have oranges for sale!"

Participants in the Erfurt seminar, viewed as guests from the capitalist west, enjoyed such luxuries as fresh tomatoes and new apples, about the size of a child's fist. Grandmothers, (retirees over sixty were permitted to travel to the West) brought home treats like chocolate and bananas. East Germans who streamed through the newly opened border in 1989 were greeted with bananas. In the summer of 1992, New Zealand kiwis appeared in Leipzig's markets. They cost around a dollar apiece. Restaurants served them halved, cut side up, and people dipped into them with a spoon as if they were eating a boiled egg. A young East German father who visited me in 1998 observed wistfully that for his four-year-old daughter it meant nothing at all to eat a banana.

Under socialism, the scarcity of a commodity was not allowed to drive up the price; prices of staples such as bread, milk, butter, cheese, eggs, and vegetables were held stable from the 1960s on. As desirable as this arrangement might appear to the consumer, the women I interviewed commented that they realized that the system could not continue. By 1985, every hundred marks worth of foodstuffs really cost an additional seventy-eight marks in subsidies that the government added to hold prices down. In 1987 a kilogram of carrots, red or white cabbage, bread, or a liter of milk cost less than one mark. At seven to ten marks a kilogram, meat was reasonably priced, though better cuts were not always available. A half-pound of butter, however, cost nearly ten marks, a dozen eggs four marks, and a kilogram of coffee was seventy marks (*Statistisches Taschenbuch 1988*, 113). While it is impossible to specify dollar values for these prices, the same source gives average monthly wages for 1987 as 1,250 marks.

Centrally managed agriculture caused some environmental degradation. Farmers who joined collective farms saw the hedgerows that had bordered their plots disappear as huge agricultural combines took over planting, fertilizing, and harvesting. The bird population dwelling in thickets disappeared too, or was decimated by heavy applications of pesticides. Huge swine warehouses kept animals in inhumane conditions, and were forced to rely on large doses of antibiotics to prevent the spread of disease. Lagoons of animal waste caused ecological damage. The overuse of fertilizers and herbicides in the farming regions of Mecklenburg-Vorpommern contributed to the highest rates of cancer in the country.

Under unification agreements on farming passed in July of 1991, East German collective farms had six months to reorganize or break up, distributing land, machinery, and livestock to their members based on their length of service, salary, and land originally entered into the collective (Panzig, 167-68). The majority succeeded in continuing to produce as some type of cooperative, albeit with very different economic and working conditions. Some East Germans rail against the idiocy of obliging their agricultural system to conform to the already out-dated West German model of the family farm, with its heavy reliance on federal and European Union subsidies. Many East Germans suspect that the intent of the unification agreement on agriculture was to dismantle their food production, opening the East as a market for West German and European Union imports (Panzig, 169). Opening the country's markets to imported foodstuffs has lowered prices for some commodities to a range where its own farms can sometimes no longer compete. To shore up prices, some farmers receive payments for taking their land out of production. The result is that as much as 70% of all fallow land in the European Union lies in East Germany, which comprises only 3% of the European Union's land area. While a far richer variety of produce and meats are now available than before the political turnaround, small grocery shops previously subsidized by the state have been unable to make a profit and have had to close. Rural residents must often travel several kilometers to buy bread, milk, and potatoes, an inconvenience in areas where public transportation has also been reduced, and some elderly inhabitants cannot afford a car.

The most significant effects of the break-up of the collective farms are emigration and massive unemployment. Most of the 1,144,000 people who left the new federal states in the decade after unification were young, and most came from the countryside. Mecklenburg-Vorpommern has only seventy-nine inhabitants per square kilometer, and Brandenburg counts eighty-six, although it has recently experienced an influx of Berliners moving out into the countryside. In

West Germany, by contrast, as many as 268 inhabitants per kilometer crowd together.

One of the emigrants who moved away from a collective farm was a young woman whom I met in 1998. Karin (as we will call her) was a tall, thin woman in her early thirties who had grown up on a collective farm in Wusterhausen, a town of 4,500 in rural Brandenburg. The oldest of three children, her father headed the LPG and her mother worked in its chemical laboratory. Karin was sent to daycare, and one of the few things she remembers about it is walking around with a broomstick held between her arms and behind her back to correct her poor posture. She remembers a happy childhood in the country, where she enjoyed sailing with her family on the region's many lakes. She would have liked to study textiles and clothing, but when she and her father attended career counseling, only certain occupations were presented. And so she served an apprenticeship in Klotze, near the West German border, where she studied fertilizers and pesticides. Later she spent four and a half years at Berlin's Humboldt University studying plant production. When the Wall opened in 1989, she was twenty-three years old. She finished in February of 1990, one month before the unification vote, and worked about six weeks on an LPG before returning to Berlin, ending this phase of her career.

Determining the next phase was not so easy. After five months of unemployment, she embarked on a new field of study which had not existed in the GDR: environmental protection. Next came an ABM job in a nature protection office, then three years' study of law and public administration. By then the students' atmosphere had changed. At the Humboldt University students worked and studied together in close-knit groups. But as a student after unification she found a competitive atmosphere where everyone worked for herself. She says she observed the same thing when she toured Harvard: no groups, just individuals sitting alone in the café.

Now she works in the Berlin district of Weißensee in property management for the office of excavation and construction. She considers this kind of administrative (probably also clerical) work a comedown from the science and technology area in which she trained. She was not the least bit interested in new occupations in retail sales, insurance, and banking, which have become new areas of employment for women, albeit often poorly paid.

Karin says that she doesn't know any West German women, although she has lived in Berlin for about ten years. For seven years she lived with a West German man, but felt uncomfortable in his better West Berlin neighborhood. Unlike the West German women she met there, she rejects religion altogether; even her mother did not receive any Christian education.

Her sister and mother, rooted in the same environment of rural Brandenburg, were not so fortunate in their desires to continue working. Her sister trained as a technician for the layout of production facilities and designed assembly lines. Now she works as a finish carpenter, but steady work is hard to find. Her mother lost her job in the chemistry lab and was unemployed for a while. She receives a modest pension now that she is sixty, and used it to buy a car for her small podiatry practice. She drives to homes, often homes for the elderly, and offers podiatry care. But she earns little, and she misses the contact with women she used to work with.

I ask Karin how she judges the overall impact of unification. She replies that it brought her enormous freedom, above all the freedom to travel. At the age of thirty-two she's ambitious and hopes to rise in her profession. At the same time, she's eager to have a child, and considers her job secure enough to risk it, even if she stayed home for a year and a half. She has participated in the employment office's training sessions on interviewing skills, and she knows that while employers may ask if she has children, they are not entitled to ask about her future plans to start a family, and she is not obligated to tell the truth.

Several factors enabled Karin to succeed better than most rural women, who often fall into the ranks of the long-term unemployed. First, the opening of the Berlin Wall caught her at the end of her education and the beginning of her work life. She was flexible enough to adapt and young enough to retrain, and had acquired the technical skills and study skills she would need. She no longer lived in Wusterhausen, but in Berlin, where opportunities were most numerous. She was unattached and childless, conditions a West German employer viewed as positive, since she was unlikely to claim maternity leave or be absent from work to care for a sick child.

In Karin's hometown, Wusterhausen, the situation of working women continued to deteriorate after she left. In 1989, 930,000 people worked in East German agriculture. Ten years later, 80% of those jobs have been lost. The 402 people unemployed in Wusterhausen in 1996 grew to 614 unemployed the following year (60% of them women), and even today the number is not going down (Goltz, 13). The loss of agricultural jobs in East Germany in the five years after unification was proportional to the loss of agricultural jobs in West Germany over the preceding forty years. Forestry and fishery industries were equally hard hit. Because the socialist regime of the GDR wanted to create equal living conditions for rural and urban communities, industries with little connection to agriculture were sometimes located in rural areas. These too have now proven unprofitable and have been forced to close. Unlike West Germany, where the unemployment rate is higher in the cities, in the East it is higher in the country hovering around 20%, due in large part to the collapse of collectivized agriculture.

Here as elsewhere women comprise about two-thirds of the unemployed. Their chances of finding work worsen with age. Only 8.5% of those under twenty-five are out of work; these people are young enough to have finished their education or vocational training after unification, that is, in keeping with West German standards. Over one-fifth of women between forty-five and fifty-five are out of work; these are the women considered too old to retrain. A fifth of women over fifty-five are out of work too, but the real number is far higher; about 45% of those who lost jobs in agriculture accepted early retirement. A third of the unemployed have been out of work longer than one year, and their chances of finding new work sink rapidly the longer they are out of the workforce. Throughout the East, three-fourths of the long-term unemployed are women.

Germany's national employment office in Nürnberg has attempted to reduce the impact of high unemployment by re-training some workers in other fields. It has also supervised and subsidized a series of projects under the sponsorship of rural women's organizations. While some projects aimed to improve the quality of rural life by opening youth centers or landscaping village common areas, others produced goods for sale, such as handmade pottery or traditional clothing, or offered services such as gardening and housecleaning. Not all were intended to become profitable, but many were begun with the plan of founding women-owned businesses like YoYo Kid which would create new jobs in the region. One such attempt, described in Elke Goltz's research, was a project to teach unemployed rural women in the new federal state of Brandenburg to produce and market quality knitwear.

Northwest of Berlin lies the agricultural area targeted by this project, encompassing the small towns of Kyritz, Wusterhausen, and Neustadt. The region's population was shrinking even before 1989 as workers sought better opportunities in Berlin and other cities. By 1998 the area's population losses resulted less from emigration than from the increase of deaths over new births, a statistic which reveals that the older generation has stayed on while the younger people have moved away. In some regions the rural population is as much as 15% lower than it was in the days of the GDR. In the Ostprignitz-Ruppin district where the knitting project was located, there are only forty-seven inhabitants per square kilometer. Between 1993 and 1996 the number of working people in the region increased slightly, as some found jobs in civil service or opened their own businesses. Nonetheless, the overall unemployment rate, excluding the disabled and those in school or vocational training, reached 25-30%.

Before unification most of the area's 23,500 residents worked on huge collective farms raising grains, vegetables, and livestock. A fifth of all workers, mainly women, worked in industries such as a sewing machine factory in Wittenberge or a knitwear factory in Wittstock, both closed in the early nineties. Women were disproportionately represented here among the unemployed because they tended to be less educated than urban women, and bound to their homes because of the need to care for family members. By 1997 the employment office in Kyritz could place only one worker in thirty who came seeking another job.

Around 60% of the unemployed were women. The actual proportion of women in the ranks of the unemployed ranged from 72.7% in August 1994 to 50.7% in February 1996. The fact that women's fraction of the unemployed shrank was due not to any gains in their hiring, but to increases in the numbers of men who joined them in the unemployment lines. In a culture placing high premiums on women's attractiveness and tractability, older women found themselves at a disadvantage; while four-fifths of all workers under thirty found new jobs within a year, only half of those over forty-five had such good fortune. Rural women fared even worse. Farm workers tended to be older than the national average; they had clung to the land while younger people moved to the cities. While 70% of farm workers had completed vocational training, it was often specialized and geared to a technology which became out-dated with unification. Specific occupations like poultry breeder or tractorist were not recognized under the West German occupational classification. After unification some agricultural workers did learn new clerical or administrative skills, but then failed to find work because such positions were scarce in their rural area.

Elke Goltz's research showed that the loss of income that came with unemployment was not the only loss these women suffered. Family conflicts arose and many lost their self-esteem. In the GDR work meant not just a secure income, but social recognition. Being pushed out of the labor market reduced these women's chances for social interaction. Rural women who drove tractors and worked in the fields were confronted with a new, unfamiliar image of what a working woman should look like. These factors combined to make people feel they had lost ground with unification. While 49% of those surveyed who had held on to their jobs judged that they were better off after than before the Wende, only a fourth of those who lost their jobs agreed with this positive estimate of the huge changes after 1989.

Concerned about out-migration and the aging of the remaining population, the Federal Employment Office in Nürnberg decided to fund an experimental program. Seventeen women from the Kyritz area who had been out of work for more than a year were selected in 1997 to participate in the project "Knitting, Embroidery, Quilting, Jewelry-Making." In addition to learning to knit on computer-guided machines, these women were given training in management and sales. The intent was that they should be able to continue knitting and selling high quality garments as self-employed entrepreneurs after the project ended. Elke Goltz offered to take me to visit two women involved in the project, and we left East Berlin on a drizzly April morning.

We drove through the flat Brandenburg countryside northwest of Berlin. Endless flat fields stretched away like the wheat fields of America's Midwest. Some lay weedy and untended, and Elke explained that these were either lain fallow to obtain agricultural subsidies, or constituted property whose ownership remained entangled in litigation. In the small village of Wildberge I spotted a corner where Karl Marx Street met Friedrich Engels Street. Further along came Ernst Thälmann Street. Such street names were disappearing from cities like Leipzig and Neubrandenburg during my 1992 visit, but in the countryside they remained untouched. In other ways too the landscape had preserved vestiges of the old days of the GDR. Some house facades had been repainted and buildings repaired, but in other places little had been renovated. Huge empty warehouses stood on the outskirts of villages. Silos and farm buildings loomed up against the flat gray horizon, some still in use, and others empty and dilapidated. Here and there rusting farm machinery stood at the edge of a field as if the farmer had simply clambered down and walked away. Around Kyritz, a town of twelve thousand, several industries used to offer employment: grocery and soft drink producers, bakeries and slaughterhouses, an ice making plant, an electronics assembler, and the farm machinery repair, daycare, health clinic, large scale laundry, and industrial-sized kitchen attached to the collective farm. Most of these had their own administrative services, commonly staffed by women. All have closed or been dissolved since unification.

In Mechow, a tiny village which is now part of Kyritz, I met Frau Debbert and Frau Ullendorf who had joined the knitting project sponsored by the state and national labor offices. Frau Debbert, with bright blue eyes and gold-rimmed glasses, had trained as a poultry breeder. At eighteen she became an FDJ delegate for her district and later took a distance-learning course in government in Weimar which prepared her to become a small town mayor. For twenty-three years she served as mayor of Drewin. After unification she worked for two years in the district administration of the Deutscher Frauenbund counseling women. When she lost her job, she met Frau Ullendorf, a former elementary teacher who had worked in after school sports programs for children. Because she was considered a childcare worker rather than a teacher, Frau Ullendorf had no claim to return to a classroom job after the Wende came. "Home was no longer my world," she says. She and Frau Debbert worked together through the DFB on a series of endeavors to employ women: a young people's club in Ostprignitz, a tailor shop in Neuruppin, and a trash disposal project. She understood how badly women like herself needed to get out of their homes after losing their jobs.

Frau Ullendorf emphasizes that women initiated this knitting project themselves; the employment office got involved later and provided financial backing, instruction, and high-tech knitting equipment. She thinks the first version of the knitting project would have been best: it called for women to knit at home and come together once a week to fetch new raw materials and turn in their finished products. Two women would manage the business. But it didn't work out that way. The women who worked at knitting and those in management never really got together. A number of other factors halted the project when it came time for women to purchase the machines and found their own business. Even at favorable rates of interest, the machines' price of 4,500 DM was too expensive, and the financial risks too high. Frau Ullendorf and Frau Debbert visited the now defunct natural fiber clothing project in Zehdenick as part of their work with the DFB and were shocked to learn four weeks later that YoYo Kid had gone under. They knew that those women had staked their houses on the success of the venture and had been forced to obtain their husbands' backing. News of their failure had a sobering effect on any woman who contemplated launching a similar venture.

The women who were considering purchasing the knitting machines in Mechow never knew for certain when they would receive transitional payments to tide them over between the end of the labor office's subsidies and their own earnings. Four women survived the initial difficulties. One was the mother of three children who were in school or vocational training. When she applied for her usual housing subsidy, she had to declare her projected annual earnings of about three thousand marks. Right away she lost her housing subsidy and the subsidy for her children's training. She gave up.

Marketing their knitted products posed further difficulties. They sold some knitwear to a Berlin boutique that specialized in clothes from the countryside, but it would only pay them about thirty dollars a dress, and out of that they had to buy yarn. "Even a blind person with a cane could see that that wouldn't work," Frau Ullendorf says scornfully. They did purchase large lots of yarn, wooden buttons, and beads and resold them at retail prices in Pritzwalk and Frankfurt am Main, but they found it nearly impossible to both market their wares and continue producing at home. Right now they are trying to develop a product line and photographs to market it.

Frau Debbert figures that when she knits the sort of jacket and vest she is now making, she earns just 2.60 DM an hour; a woman with a child would need to earn at least ten marks an hour. She wouldn't be able to live on her earnings either, but she's still receiving the unemployment compensation she became eligible for when the project's funding expired last year. She and the other women still involved would need a loan of at least 25,000 DM to buy yarn and rent a room where they could knit together. "It's awful to sit home alone all day," she says. Her unemployment compensation will end soon, and she must work another seven years before she reaches the retirement age of sixty-five. Because of her age, she has no hope of getting a real job; her only chance is to find an ABM job.

Frau Ullendorf insists that she wants to show other women what they've learned and to stay active; it's not just a matter of money. She points out that if money were all that mattered, women wouldn't consider founding their own business at all. It's more advantageous for women to take a re-training course or an ABM job. The unemployed receive compensation based on 60% of their last net pay; thus they fare better if they've been laid off from a job with good earnings than if they take a lower-paying job just to keep working.

The supervisor of the knitting project is thirty years younger than Frau Debbert and Frau Ullendorf, and the information she volunteers suggests that the fate of younger women in rural areas may be somewhat brighter. She completed her studies as an agricultural engineer in 1986, and like so many East German women, she simply identifies her occupation by the masculine term. Her son was born in 1991 but she does not mention marriage or a husband. She welcomed the Wende as a chance to become active in politics, and was elected mayor of Neustadt, a small town we drive through after leaving her office. She worked as a social counselor in a home for political asylum seekers and then found a position in the local labor office which supports projects such as the knitters. The administration of the local LPG for animal and plant production employed five hundred people; today there are fifty left, and only one is a woman. The first time she herself was fired, it came as a terrible shock; she felt like a loser, but with time you get tougher, she says. People who lost their jobs early on fared better than those who have more recently become unemployed, she thinks, because there's less support for the jobless today. Furthermore, the workers the labor office sends her nowadays are really unmotivated. They arrive late for work and have no idea of the conventions of the workplace. "You have to ask them to put away the newspaper," she remarks. She worries about younger people; when they see there are no apprenticeships, they lose the motivation to work in school.

Elke Goltz's study of the Mechow knitting project suggests other factors which contributed to the project's failure. The women who participated knew imported knitwear was cheaper. In fact as consumers they took a dim view of the fairly high priced goods they were supposed to produce. For those who had spent decades as employees, the prospect of becoming self-employed was frightening:

taking on responsibility, seeking loans, heavy time commitments, the uncertainty of generating an income, and the reluctance to assume any leadership role hindered them from becoming entrepreneurs. Working at home had no tradition in this region, in contrast to areas such as the Erzgebirge, where hand-crafted ornaments and lace have been produced for centuries. Working at home was viewed as a way of supplementing one's income; Frau Debbert and Frau Ullendorf told us that village women knitted socks, made jams and jellies, or cemetery wreaths to bring in extra income. Work outside the home, on the other hand, brought women contact with non-family members; the desire to communicate with others was a powerful motivation for seeking work outside. Moreover, women lacked role models for becoming self-employed. Networking with women's organizations in tourism and other branches could provide positive examples of women who had made it on their own, but here there were few to be seen. Finally, women were unused to doing piecework. Under socialism's five-year plans, production quotas were set for factories and farms. But in a kind of catch twenty-two situation, the quotas themselves became a roadblock to productivity. Industries which reached their quotas were rewarded with higher quotas in the next five-year plan. Working hard just meant increased expectations, not greater rewards. Those who slacked off on the assembly line could not be fired, since it was illegal to be unemployed. Bonuses or premiums were seen as a capitalist trick. The only ways to reward highly productive workers were indirect: educational opportunities for their children, better housing, foreign travel, or vacation packages, and for the most part the same perks were handed out to party favorites as well as good workers. Workers just didn't understand how to make a profit from piecework.

After taking leave of Frau Debbert and Frau Ullendorf, Elke and I talk briefly with the woman who supervises the knitting project and she takes us downstairs to see the workroom. The machines with their complicated threadings of yarn and miniature computer screens would quickly intimidate the ignorant. The cardigans and pullovers they produce, however, look indistinguishable from Asian or Caribbean imports. Some women are creating beaded designs here, but their flowers and scrollwork look as if they could have been cheaply produced in China.

Some research characterizes rural women as fatalistic, resigned, willing to accept their lot and passive in seeking change (Dahms 1997, 36-37). Qualities formerly regarded as virtues–modesty, courtesy, and the willingness to accept what is given to them–work to their detriment in a capitalist job market which places a premium on competitiveness and personal initiative. These researchers find that rural women are not eager for further education, and must first be convinced of its value in qualifying them for a new job. They are unlikely to seize the initiative, and tend to wait for new opportunities to find them. Because they had no experience choosing a career or planning their own future, they are unable to conceive of doing so now.

Another hindrance is that two-thirds of these rural women have never held a driver's license or owned a car, something nearly impossible in the GDR. Now older women feel intimidated by increased traffic and higher speeds; in the old days speed was limited to a hundred kilometers and hour, and even that rate was dangerous on the poorly maintained two-lane roads. A further hindrance is the need to care for children or the elderly, now that daycare centers have closed and other social services have been eliminated.

The combination of factors adds up to the finding that women fare better in cities. In Dresden only 14% of women were unemployed in mid 1995, 15% in Potsdam (the capital of the federal state of Brandenburg), but over one fourth in rural areas. In Neuruppin, northwest of Berlin, every seventh unemployed person is a woman who has been out of work for more than a year and who worked in foods, retail sales, clerical work, or cleaning.

What is the long-term prognosis for these rural women? Government plans for northern Brandenburg call for development of the area as a tourist destination. Its sparsely populated countryside may attract weary city dwellers to enjoy boating, horseback riding, hiking, and open-air historical museums. With this image in mind, initiatives have been started to enhance the region's natural attractions by creating nature preserves and educational conservation areas. Its waterways are a resting ground for returning migratory cranes, swans, and storks. Therefore, some projects have begun employing farm women in landscaping, taking inventories of birds, and restoring the natural surroundings to their appearance in the era before collective agriculture, restoring streambeds, windbreaks, and hedgerows. Women who have labored in farm fields do not object to heavy labor, even under adverse weather conditions. Their knowledge of plants and animals can be put to good use here.

One novel project which has provided work for 140 people in season is a network of interrelated ecology initiatives. A herd of six hundred sheep, together with yaks, alpacas, and Scottish Highland cattle is used to graze on dikes and nature reserves, as well as for wool, milk and meat production. Another component of the scheme is a park to protect and propagate rare breeds of domestic animals; the site features a windmill to pump water and a display of antique farm machinery. An organic farm including a garden of plants which produce vegetable dyes markets its produce and bread in Berlin. Wool from the herd of sheep and other animals is spun, dyed, and woven into handmade textiles. Visitors can learn to bake bread, weave baskets, make pottery, or paint from nature. The park also offers hiking, bicycling, music, and harvest festivals.

There are difficulties, however, for women seeking to bridge the gap from such government subsidized projects to the so-called first labor market where free competition reigns. Researchers found that the older generation, women who had been socialized to work but unemployed for some time, like Frau Debbert and Frau Ullendorf, eagerly seized the opportunity of working again. Yet ironically it is precisely these women who have the poorest chance in the free labor market. On the other hand younger women, those most flexible and easiest to retrain, have begun to think of themselves as secondary earners with a husband or partner as the main provider (Dahms, Putzing, and Schiemann, 58). This kind of west-think may hold the key to contenting East Germany's younger rural women with the long term under-employment they will continue to experience for years to come.

Seeking evidence of new ventures in tourism in East Germany, I welcomed opportunities to visit the countryside during my stay in Berlin. I saw stork nests, huge wheels of sticks perched atop poles or chimneys, in Brandenburg villages. Friends treated me to a lunch of fresh asparagus and fried fish in Lübbenau in the Spreewald. We ate on a sunny terrace beside a shallow waterway where tourists can sit in flat-bottomed boats poled through the swamp. One person said that women from the region's Sorb minority (a Slavic people distinct from Serbs) wear native costumes and elaborately decorated hats as they pole boatloads of tourists through the tree-hung waterways.

Returning from our visit to Mechow and Kyritz Elke Goltz and I drove through the village of Neustadt, whose mayor supervised the knitting project. We stopped at an extensive horse-breeding farm, with long yellow barns, well-tended riding rings, and jumping courses. It remains unclear whether the farm's ownership, a holdover from East Germany's publicly owned land, will continue or be converted to some profit-oriented scheme.

Further on we parked in the hamlet of Kampehl, which marketed itself as a country vacation resort with bicycle paths, hiking trails, and farm lodgings for families. The attraction here lay in a crypt-like anteroom of the town's ancient stone church. Ducking our heads, we joined a handful of other curiosity-seekers around the dimly lit coffin of the Knight of Kahlbutz. His former residence lay behind the church, obviously converted long ago to more plebian uses. A guide to the bizarre exhibit in the church informed us that the knight himself seized his pleasures unchecked; legend told of his thirteen legitimate heirs and dozens of illegitimate children. He took a fancy to a young shepherdess who rebuffed his advances. Entitled as "nobleman" to claim a bride's wedding night, he surprised her one evening and took her by force. Shortly thereafter her young husband was found dead in the woods, but no one could prove the Knight of Kahlbutz to be the murderer. He swore that if he had killed the young man, his body should never decay. Three hundred years later, teeth, fingernails, and wispy bristles of hair attest to his guilt. Covered only by a loincloth, his gaunt cadaver lies in a simple coffin; his lance and armor stand nearby.

As we continued our journey toward Berlin, I mused on the tale of the Knight of Kahlbutz as a parable for the exploitation of rural women. His victim had no recourse for her own defense, but the centuries (assuming we choose to believe in the legend) reveal the perpetrator's heinous crime. Parallels suggest themselves between the Knight of Kahlbutz, ostensibly noble or superior to his peasants, and capitalist overlords who have dismantled the economic structure of Brandenburg. Will capitalism too prove moribund and antiquated in another century? Or was the hamlet of Kampehl and its grisly legend simply an example of the entrepreneurial spirit of the new East, where even the macabre and uncanny may be turned to a three-mark profit?

Chapter Eleven
Feminist Stepsisters

Stepsisters, What East-Women and West-Women Think of Each Other was the translation of the title of a book by Karin Rohnstock, published in Frankfurt in 1994. An exhibition contrasting women's lives on either side of the Wall, which I saw in Dresden in 1998, bore the title "Unequal Sisters" (*Ungleiche Schwestern*). These titles suggest on the one hand a wish for solidarity and cooperation, and on the other a sharp awareness of what differentiates women's lives and divides feminist movements in the East and West. To explore this issue, we will consider East Germany's official women's organization, the status and increasingly public role of lesbians, the emergence of a true feminist coalition, called the Independent Women's Association (*Unabhängiger Frauenverband*, or UFV) during the Wende, and differences between the East and West German feminist movements at the turn of the twenty-first century.

In the GDR the Demokratischer Frauenbund Deutschlands (DFD, now called simply Demokratischer Frauenbund, or DFB) officially represented women's interests. It was founded on International Women's Day, March 8, 1947 by 1,400 delegates from the communist women's movement coming from all sectors of occupied Germany. Its founders swore to unite "in sisterly solidarity above all philosophical, religious, and professional differences in order to eradicate militarism and fascism and to realize humanity's longing for lasting peace." These women consciously repudiated the political and military hierarchies that had brought on World War II (Schröter 1997, 15). The organization ceased to exist in the West in 1954.

One woman who belonged was a retired teacher I met at East Berlin's Gesellschaft zum Schutz von Bürgerrecht und Menschenwürde in 1998. Born in the mid-thirties, her education was interrupted by the war, and she completed her Abitur in 1955. After five years' study in Slavic languages and geography, she began teaching. Although childcare places to accommodate her children were scarce in the 1960s, she got a place through personal contacts, which the East Germans call

Vitamin B (*Beziehungen*). Even after her husband died in 1967, it was no problem to support her family. But after unification, schools no longer had to teach Russian, and her skills became superfluous. Because there were too many teachers in her school, she re-trained for the elementary school, where she taught music and biology. She worked till 1991, when she was fifty-five, and has been retired (a euphemism for unemployed) ever since.

This teacher belonged to the union for education and science (*Gewerkschaft für Erziehung und Wissenschaft*), and she belonged to the Demokratischer Frauenbund Deutschlands until 1964. Its purpose was to draw people into the political process, educate women, and promote exchange with other countries. She was contacted and asked to join it, perhaps because her teaching made her a positive role model for working mothers. The DFD was important in small towns and rural areas. In the post-war years, it represented women's interests in school reform and land ownership reform. It campaigned for part-time work for women in order to draw into the labor force those who remained at home. Later the DFD became less important as more women became employed and therefore integrated into socialism through institutions such as the Parteilehrjahr, (obligatory monthly political education programs). The DFD was also active on behalf of women away from the workplace during maternity and child-rearing leave. The DFD held thirty-two seats in the Volkskammer, the GDR's visible if fairly insignificant legislature, and claimed about a million and a half members in the late eighties.

At the time of the Wende the organization became independent of the Socialist Unity Party and reorganized under new leadership. It no longer claimed to be the exclusive representative of women's concerns, seeking instead to establish networks with other women's groups. Powered by highly educated, competent women like Frau Debbert and Frau Ullendorf who were forced into early retirement, the Demokratischer Frauenbund campaigns today for equitable pensions for women, publishes a newsletter, and sponsors over three hundred women's projects, such as cafés, meeting places, and shelters. The It functions in all the new federal states, has at its disposal about two thousand ABM jobs, and reports to the United Nations as an official non-government organization (Schröter 1997, 20).

The Socialist Unity Party established several bodies to address women's concerns. Affirmative action plans (Frauenförderpläne) were drawn up in the 1960s in every factory and district; their success was monitored, and most of the positions as affirmative action officers or women's officers (Gleichstellungsbeauftragte or Frauenbeauftragte) were held by women, who exercised real power. Since half the country's judges were women, chiefly in lower echelons of the justice ministry, the legal system heard women's voices too. East Berlin's Humboldt University had a women's commission already in 1959. In 1964 the Academy of Sciences established an office for women in socialist society (*Die Frau in der sozialistischen Gesellschaft*) to analyze the role of women as workers and mothers. For researchers within this group, women's equality was a forgone conclusion, and their studies stopped short of criticizing the socialist patriarchy. Nevertheless, much of the group's research was conducted by women, and its well-respected publications explored such issues as the lack of women in upper management, and did serve to raise women's consciousness.

Some aspects of the research formerly carried out by the Academy of Sciences (which was dissolved after unification) continue at the Center for Interdisciplinary Women's Studies at the Humboldt University. Feminist scholars from disciplines such as literature and sociology founded the Center in December 1989. Its goals are to create and sustain a network for feminist scholarship transcending the discipline boundaries that keep feminist researchers isolated from one another. By publishing lists of all university courses dealing with women's issues, sponsoring academic discussions, and bringing women scholars together, the Center promoted the establishment of Germany's first women's studies program at the Humboldt University.

In West Germany the University in Bielefeld had a center for women's research in 1980, and at West Berlin's Free University in 1981; the first professor of women's studies was appointed at the university in Frankfurt am Main in the mid 1980s (Jähnert, 48). The Center for Interdisciplinary Women's Studies at Humboldt University publishes bulletins and bibliographies, maintains an extensive library of materials related to East German women (including theses, pamphlets, and "gray" literature), and organizes workshops and colloquia. It supports the work of women's commissioners, documentation of the history of women in the GDR, and was instrumental in establishing a network of lesbian and women's archives in Berlin.

Women's studies programs at German universities resemble those in the US in status: courses are often taught over and above faculty's regular teaching loads, adequate funding is difficult to obtain, and most research concentrates on culture studies and humanities, with less emphasis on the natural and social sciences (Jähnert, 62).

East German feminists saw their goal as gaining greater power within the socialist state, rather than working to reject or overturn the political structure. Through women's high level of participation in the workforce and the equal pay mandate, the SED could declare that the country's women had achieved emancipation. International Women's Day recognized women's contributions to socialism, production, and motherhood. SED party functionary Inge Lange declared in 1979 that "we"–the Socialist Unity Party–opposed the sort of feminism which incites women to struggle against men and thereby hinders solidarity among workers. She explained that there was no feminist movement in the GDR because the revolutionary workers' movement had always held true to the comradeship and cooperation of women and men (Kuhrig 236-37; Schröter 1997, 27).

Recently this absence of an autonomous feminist movement in the GDR has become a bone of contention between East and West German feminists who disagree, for instance, about interpreting the introduction of abortion in the German Democratic Republic. West German feminists cite it as an example of the way East German women had their rights and privileges handed to them without needing to fight for them. It is worth noting that historians interpret the introduction of Germany's pension and insurance system in the 1880s as the government's way of granting the workers their demands before social unrest could arise. Today the infrequency of labor strikes in Germany is attributed to co-determination and the same wise guiding principle of granting people what they want rather than risking economic disruption and civil unrest. Why should not the same principle apply in granting women access to abortion?

Some East German women insist that because they were represented in the Socialist Unity Party, at least to a limited degree, and because they struggled alongside men for gains achieved by the peasants' and workers' state, they too can claim credit for advances in women's rights such as the abortion decision (Ockel, 41).

In the West, feminists rallied around campaigns for equal access to education and work, abortion, and gay and lesbian rights. While the East might claim to have solved the first three of these issues, gay and lesbian rights did not appear as a political question until the last ten years of the country's existence. Because the struggle for equal rights for homosexuals was one of the forces shaping the feminist movement which emerged in the last days of the German Democratic Republic, it is necessary to examine the historical and legal background of the treatment of sexual orientation in Germany.

Since 1851 Prussian and eventually German law forbade sexual intercourse (*widernatürliche Unzucht*) between two *males*. The law forbade such contact because it had no potential for procreation, the same rationale later used to justify prohibiting contraceptives and abortion. Because female homosexual acts did not produce sperm or "waste" procreative potential, the law did not concern itself with them (Ohms, 18-19). Ironically, this legal structure made lesbian homosexuality invisible and undefined (and thus less severely persecuted) for over a century. In the 1920s Germany's Communist Party fought unsuccessfully for the repeal of laws prohibiting male homosexual contact. The Nazi regime specified harsh penalties, including imprisonment from three months to ten years, for homosexual intercourse between males under twenty-one, and about 88,000 people were condemned under this law, which continued in effect in post-war West Germany (Schindler 2000). In 1969 West Germany eliminated penalties for consensual homosexual sex between males over twenty-one, and in 1973 lowered the age of consent to eighteen. Between 1950 and 1969, 59,316 people were condemned for homosexuality in the Federal Republic of Germany (Schindler 2000). The German Democratic Republic took a more liberal stance on homosexuality, reverting in 1949 to the pre-Nazi laws and in 1957 lifting all penalties for consensual homosexuality between adults. A reform of the GDR's penal code in 1968 for the first time specified homosexual intercourse between women, and lowered the age of consent to eighteen for both sexes (Schindler 2000).

While the legal framework demonstrates that homosexuality was a vastly different matter in East and West Germany, it tells us little about actual living conditions for gay couples in the German Democratic Republic, and their struggle for freedom from discrimination based on sexual orientation. I sought answers to these questions in an interview with Christina Schenk, who has championed lesbian and gay rights and other social issues in the German Bundestag since 1990. I found her office in an unprepossessing building more modest and more workmanlike than the corridors of power in America's congressional office building. Security precautions consisted of exchanging my American passport for a chit to be redeemed at the front office before leaving. As arrangements are completed for the settlement of Germany's capital in Berlin, the Bundestag's members will move to new offices closer to the rebuilt Reichstag building.

Christina Schenk comes from Ilmenau in Thuringia, but attended a special school for the hard of hearing in Berlin. She studied physics and worked at the Academy of Sciences until 1989. She planned a career change into the social sciences with the intention of writing about the sociological and psychological situation of lesbians in the GDR. Instead she plunged into politics via the newly formed Unabhängiger Frauenverband, and the treatment of homosexuals became one of her political causes. While German unification agreements made West German law valid for the new federal states, they exempted the law on homosexuality, which was finally repealed in the West in 1994. Although the Bundestag ruled in March 2000 that verdicts reached on the basis of Nazi ideology are invalid, it decided that cases of homosexuality must be examined individually. Thus homosexuals are not able to erase criminal charges from their records, and not entitled to compensation as are other victims of the Holocaust, unless they file suit as individuals. Christina Schenk is working to ensure that they receive equal treatment without the requirement that each case be tried individually. In the Bundestag debate she pointed out that more homosexuals had been condemned in the Federal Republic of Germany than in the Third Reich.

In its early days, the German Democratic Republic portrayed homosexuals as abnormal, pathological, and criminal, and subjected them to Stasi surveillance, although homosexuality was not illegal (Schenk, 160). Sex education materials offered no help to adolescents coming out, and those living outside of large cities found little understanding or support. Lesbians were nearly invisible; it was impossible for same-sex couples to obtain housing, personal ads were virtually unknown, and they found no way to meet and cooperate with one another. When gays and lesbians established the first support groups for people coming out in the early seventies, the Socialist Unity Party lacked any clear guidelines for registering such organizations, and viewed their calls for public debate as a criticism of socialist society. Thus the Stasi infiltrated their groups and spied on them.

Nevertheless, Christina Schenk believes lesbians were far more fairly treated in East Germany than in the West; she herself lived openly as a lesbian. She points out that homosexuals were no more severely hindered in their attempts to organize meetings or publish newsletters than other dissident groups. Because women had achieved economic independence and could support their own children, there was no economic disadvantage to lesbians. A 1985 conference in Jena published a report finding that heterosexuality and homosexuality were equally valid and natural, a judgment that had considerable authority in political circles. In 1989 the official film studio, DEFA, produced a film about homosexuality called *Coming Out*. Open discussion of AIDS and HIV began later in the East than in the West, but AIDS was never depicted as the scourge of homosexuals. In contrast to what Christina Schenk calls extreme prudery in the West, East Germans had an open attitude toward sexuality and nudity. While East Germany resembled Scandinavia in its sexual openness, she says that West Germany is a third world developing country when it comes to women's issues. West Germans find it difficult to separate themselves from the influence of Christianity and its traditional condemnation of homosexuality, a mind-set which played no role in the East.

Today lesbians enjoy freedom of movement, occupational choice, and a wide-open scene. Nevertheless Christina Schenk confirms that the overall status of women has declined since unification occurred under the leadership of the Christian Democrats. She points out that same sex couples are not recognized and not allowed to adopt children (although they may in some cases become foster parents, and single people can adopt). The 1998 turnover in Germany's government aroused new hopes because the Greens champion gay rights, but marriage is regulated by federal law, which is not likely to be liberalized. Germany's lesbian and gay alliance (*Lesben- und Schwulenverband Deutschlands*) is campaigning for recognition of same sex marriage, which Schenk favors, although she believes that no special tax or economic privileges should be granted for any type of marriage or civil union. The Greens and Social Democrats presented legislation in 1999 to recognize same sex marriage, and Hamburg (a federal state as well as a city) allows such couples to record their unions in its city marriage registry. Health coverage for domestic partners is not common, and the spouse of a deceased person may claim inheritance even if a will left property to a domestic partner.

The new federal states created new constitutions at the time of unification, and Thuringia, Saxony-Anhalt, and Brandenburg (and Berlin, as of 1995) included provisions against discrimination based on sexual orientation. Cases of such discrimination (like racial discrimination) can be prosecuted on grounds of creating a hostile work environment, but such instances are rare since victims have little to gain, even if they win. Job seekers need not answer questions about their sexual orientation; however if they are not hired because of it, they have no recourse to legal proceedings. Leipzig and Dresden have offices for lesbian issues, and ten federal states have offices for lesbian and gay equality: Thuringia, Saxony-Anhalt, Mecklenburg-Vorpommern, Brandenburg and Berlin in the East; and Schleswig-

Holstein, Hesse, Lower Saxony, Northrhine-Westphalia, and the Saarland in the West.

While such legal steps demonstrate greater social tolerance, discrimination and the very real risk of being attacked persist. One study of gay adolescents found that 18% had attempted suicide; 64% of young women and 56% of young men had at least considered it (Ohms, 4). Statistics suggest one lesbian in ten is the victim of a physical attack: pushing, shoving, or becoming the target of thrown objects. Sixty per cent of lesbians surveyed experienced verbal harassment. One-third have experienced sexual violence, i.e. grabbing breasts or buttocks or demanding sex (Ohms, 12-23). The magnitude of violence against lesbians is difficult to assess because homosexuality is not recognized as a hate crime; statistics are subsumed into violence against women.

Researchers in Berlin conducted another survey of 173 lesbians who had been attacked between 1996 and 1998. At the outset, male researchers assumed that such attacks were simply evidence of violence against women (the attitude reflected in police classification of such statistics), while women researchers believed that they were based on lesbians' sexual orientation (Faulseit and Müller, 3). Of the 305 people who attacked lesbians, 295 were male, 79% of them under twenty-five (Faulseit and Müller, 32). Women were most likely to be attacked when they were visibly recognized as lesbians: out together, in a lesbian bar or club, wearing symbols or jewelry, or expressing affection for their partners. Forty per cent of these attacks included physical violence, about half carried out by more than two men, making it unlikely that women could successfully defend themselves. Most physical attacks included shoving or being held forcibly, but in 17% of the attacks women were kicked or beaten (Faulseit and Müller, 11). Bystanders never intervened, although most attacks occurred in public places.

The viciousness and extent of violence against lesbians prompts us to look for deeper causes. Women who were mistaken for lesbians reported that their self-assured posture and confident body language seemed to have provoked the attack (Ohms, 19-20). Therefore the issue is not woman's sexual orientation per se, but her refusal to conform to the stereotypical female role: deferential, self-effacing, aware of men's eyes upon her, the object of male dominance and male sexuality. The attack aims to put her back in her place; therefore she is likely to be attacked by two or more men, and precisely by those who are unsure of their own power and place in society, those under twenty-five. Continued economic disorder in East Germany may well increase young males' sense of jeopardy and increase their proclivity to attack women. Christina Schenk raised the issue of measures to support lesbian women affected by violence, but received the reply that the federal government presently has no intentions of adopting any such measures (*Querblick*, 3).

My discussion with Christina Schenk returns at last to the genesis of the independent feminist movement in the final days of the German Democratic Republic. She recalls that lesbians played a key role in the movement because they recognized the power relationships inherent in patriarchy. However, she maintains that lesbian issues were not a focal point of the burgeoning feminist movement; rather women campaigned for equal treatment of all freely chosen forms of existence without preference for any model.

Paradoxically, early lesbian and feminist groups looked toward East German churches for assistance in their early days, and churches responded, reversing the historical role of Christianity in sanctioning only heterosexual marriage. Beginning around 1980 the Lutheran Church, exempt from requirements that any group of seven or more people must announce and register its meetings, offered meeting space and sometimes access to copying or printing facilities to such groups. The Lutheran Church did not demand nor expect that such people using its meeting facilities would necessarily be Christians. It opened its doors to peace groups such as *Frauen für den Frieden* (Women for Peace) organized in 1982 to protest legislation passed by the Volkskammer which would draft women into the military if necessary for the country's defense. This group was gathered women of disparate political views from lesbians to Christians, at first to petition against the new ruling, and later, as members were subjected to harassment and arrests, for support and solidarity (Miethe, 11). These peace activists included men, and only secondarily concerned themselves with women's issues. In 1984 the Halle group, Frauen für den Frieden, organized a national meeting, which was followed by yearly meetings in other cities to build a network. Gradually the more feminist groups of younger women born in the fifties and sixties began to criticize patriarchal structures, while more politically oriented groups encompassing women born in the thirties and forties instead aimed their criticism at the SED dictatorship. These politically oriented groups made common cause with the new political parties *Neues Forum* and *Demokratischer Aufbruch* at the time of the Wende and then disbanded after the fall of the dictatorship (Miethe 12-14).

The first semi-official gay and lesbian group appeared in Leipzig in 1982, and was followed by other groups in other cities, some of them infiltrated by the Stasi (Schenk, 161). Toward the end of the decade, other gay and lesbian groups were permitted to meet in cultural centers and public facilities, provided they paid lip service to socialist values, for example by condemning promiscuity. Their political conformity created friction with the more dissident groups meeting in churches. Feminists also bridled at patterns of male dominance emerging in joint lesbian and gay groups in the churches, and in 1983 the Berlin group split after its third joint meeting (Schenk, 163). Government-tolerated gay clubs were less likely to establish separate lesbian groups.

These lesbian groups, which affiliated with the more radical dissidents, feminists, and peace activists meeting in churches, comprised an autonomous feminist wave, separate from and developing much later than the state-sanctioned DFD and government women's offices. The final years of the German Democratic Republic saw a general loosening of political and social restrictions so that people tested what now appeared to be possible. In May 1989 two hundred feminists attended a national meeting in Jena and the Jena group founded an alternative newspaper, *frau anders* (Different Woman). The lesbian group *Lila Offensive* founded in October 1989, insisted, contrary to the tenets of socialism, that the elimination of capitalism was no guarantee that patriarchal repression had been eradicated, and that true equality of the sexes had not been achieved in the GDR (Nave-Herz, 115).

Lila Offensive called on all women to meet on December 3, 1989 in East Berlin's Volksbühne (People's Theater), where 1,200 lesbian and straight women founded the Unabhängiger Frauenverband or UFV. In her manifesto for an autonomous women's movement entitled "Ohne Frauen ist kein Staat zu machen" (you can't make a state without women) Ina Merkel boldly criticized the German Democratic Republic's social conditions, citing the high divorce rate, the declining number of births, the wage gap between women and men, and the environmental degradation which caused children's illnesses and allergies, obliging their mothers to leave work to care for them. Women, she declared, bore the burden of compensating for the economy's deficits. Because women were underrepresented in the higher echelons of politics and management, she laid the blame for these conditions squarely at the feet of men. "Women have no fatherland to lose, but rather a world to gain," she proclaimed (Merkel, 155). She warned that unification would mean three steps backward for women, a renewed struggle for the right to work, for daycare, for school meals. When someone asked whether the women present favored unification, they shouted "No!" Instead, Merkel demanded a new concept of paid labor, based not on the male model, but on recognition of time committed and results achieved, so that a nurse might earn as much as a truck driver. She advocated the institution of quotas in political reform and structural change, pointing out that her country had positive experience with using quotas to promote education and advancement of workers' and farmers' children to overturn the dominance of the wealthy after World War II. Ina Merkel called for a feminist movement based on widespread social reform, and warned that a movement oriented primarily to women's issues would become marginalized (Merkel, 159).

The UFV took Merkel's call, "Ohne Frauen ist kein Staat zu machen" as its motto and formed an umbrella organization encompassing over sixty smaller groups. For a few months after the Berlin Wall opened, it appeared that the German Democratic Republic might transform itself into a real democracy and continue its existence as an independent state. At the first meeting of a national Round Table on December 7, 1989, thirty-eight UFV members participated and voted–but only after women demonstrated in front of the meeting site, demanding that they be included together with established political parties and unions (Böhm, 155). In January 1990 the organization opened a central office in Berlin and regional offices in each of what would later become the new federal states.

Aware that West Germany's constitutional guarantees of equality for men and women had not proven effective, the UFV's representatives drafted a charter of social rights for a new East German constitution. This charter guaranteed affirmative action, quotas, an end to discrimination on the basis of sexual orientation, and continued access to abortion. It also demanded the creation of a Commissioner for the Equality of Women within the Ministry for Women and Families (who would have veto power over any legislation unfair to women), and the establishment of commissioners for the equality of women in every town over 10,000 residents. Although the Round Table meeting of March 5, 1990 unanimously adopted this charter of social rights and it was also passed by the Volkskammer, it was later cast aside in the rush to hasty currency union and unification.

At first members of the Unabhängiger Frauenverband expected their organization would take over the DFD's thirty-two seats in the Volkskammer, which briefly exercised real political power in the transition from the Honecker SED dictatorship through the provisional governments of Egon Krenz (General Secretary of the SED who held power from October 24 to December 3, 1989) and Hans Modrow. In the March 3, 1990 election for representatives to the Volkskammer, the Unabhängiger Frauenverband campaigned as a registered political body under the slogan "for women who have the courage to say 'I'," explicitly refuting socialist education's emphasis on the development of group consciousness, from "I" to "we" (Hampele, 180). One-fifth of that legislature's representatives were women. During the sweeping changes of 1989 and 1990, the UFV participated actively in the citizens' Round Tables in cities such as Leipzig and Jena, as well as on the national level in Berlin. However, attempts to make common cause with Neues Forum in Leipzig collapsed when that group rejected quotas for women, and feminists fought for a separate "Women's Caucus" presence at the Round Table there (Ferree 1994, 604).

Feminists also gained some access to the media during these months. Berlin women's groups briefly published a feminist newspaper called *Ypsilon* (Y) and a Leipzig group put out a newspaper called *Zaunreiterin* (fence sitter). Lila Offensive's sixteen women members briefly commandeered Berlin radio stations (Braun, 47). The UFV hoped to commandeer resources which belonged to the DFD, and did gain the use of its space in the officially sanctioned women's magazine, *Für Dich*. There feminists were instrumental in bringing articles on subjects which had so long been taboo, such as pornography and domestic violence (Dölling, 175).

In the fall 1990 elections, the UFV aligned itself with the Alliance 90/Greens political coalition, which won eight seats in the Bundestag, one of them held by Christina Schenk. The UFV also won seats in the state parliaments of Saxony, Saxony-Anhalt, and Berlin. West German law, which quickly became the law of the land, forced the UFV to choose whether to exist as a political party fielding candidates for election, or as an independent organization. Ever since small splinter parties contributed to the fracturing and demise of the Weimar Republic, political parties in Germany can send representatives to the Bundestag only if they garner 5% of the popular vote. While this provision was waived in the October 1990 Bundestag election to allow greater flexibility in the East, its subsequent wider application meant that it would be impractical for the UFV, with its small power base, to attempt to survive as a political party, and the organization chose instead in September 1991 to continue an independent existence.

Several factors contributed to the UFV's loss of power in the aftermath of the Wende. Conflicting interests developed within the organization between well educated women who had risen through loyalty to the SED and dissident women like the founders of Frauen für den Frieden who had sometimes lost out on educational and career opportunities because of their political beliefs (Miethe, 14). Negotiations on unification were led by Helmut Kohl's Christian Democrats, the only major West German party with offices, a network, and an independent power base in the East. The Christian Democrats, with the lowest proportion of women members of any West German party, set about eroding access to abortion. Like the Greens and the Social Democrats, the UFV pointed out what women were losing as a result of amalgamation into West Germany, and was consequently accused of being too loyal to the old SED regime. Like the Greens, the UFV rejected organizational hierarchy and professional functionaries, and committed itself to ensuring an open, democratic, flexible power structure. Unfortunately, like the Greens, it also experienced the ineffectiveness arising from such a commitment. Because it cooperated with various women's groups, whose members did not necessarily also join the UFV, it was unclear how many members the latter actually had (Hampele, 188). Its energies were divided between local feminist projects and the effort to represent women more forcefully on the national level. Feminist publications, unable to earn a profit, were forced to close. Even East Germany's oldest women's magazine, *Für Dich*, ceased publication in 1991.

The Unabhängiger Frauenverband continued its campaign for lesbian rights. In 1989, before its demise, the GDR lowered the age of consent for male homosexual relations to sixteen; for heterosexual and lesbian relations, the age was fourteen. Lesbian activists fear that maintaining eighteen as the West (and now united) German limit for consensual homosexual contact would harm adolescents whose parents wished to deny or repress their sexual orientation (Schenk, 165). They find that women's weaker position in the new economy increases male dominance and reinforces the West German view of the male as breadwinner. Attempts to re-Christianize the East, the institution of religious instruction in schools, the suppression of abortion, and efforts to reassert marriage as the norm will further harm lesbian rights.

The UFV campaigned hard to preserve access to abortion, which was important enough to be addressed separately in the unification agreement, guaranteeing each country's extant regulations would stay in effect through 1992. Initial victories which appeared to make the

East German law valid for the entire country would have constituted a liberalization of abortion access for West German women (who had to find two doctors to certify that an abortion was necessary to the health or social and psychological well-being of the woman). But women lost the fight in 1993, with a second decision from Germany's Supreme Court in 1995 confirming that abortion would henceforth be even more stringently controlled than had been the case in the old federal states. Disappointed and disillusioned, the UFV lost steam. Its defeat on this issue was compounded by East Germans' growing awareness that their new political system was no more responsive to their needs than the old had been.

To draw attention to their disadvantaged position in united Germany, women's groups East and West independently conceived of and jointly organized a Women's Strike Day on March 8, 1994, the International Women's Day celebrated yearly in the GDR. Over one million women participated and the event drew wide publicity, but hopes of founding a women's party, *Bundesweite feministische Bündnis* (Nationwide Feminist Alliance), based on this modest success soon faded. The women's party *Die Frauen*, founded in June 1995 attracted only about a thousand members, and has so far fallen short of the number of votes needed to qualify for federal campaign funds. (The group was still in existence as of 1999 with party headquarters in Frankfurt am Main).

One form of women's participation in the political process which remains from the days of the political turnaround are Round Tables, which exist at the town or city level, and in Berlin and Saxony at the state level. The Round Tables differ in their composition, organization, institutional connections, and financial provisions, but their purpose is to get publicity and to strengthen women's voice in political decision-making. They work not on the principle of majority rule, but by achieving consensus, seeking to overcome power plays or dominance by various participants. As such these Round Tables are less hierarchical and more democratic than is typical of West German organizations.

In the late nineties the UFV and all East German political groups faced rising costs for publicizing and lobbying to support their issues (Kamensita, 55). Higher prices for rent, telephone, faxes, printing, and staff salaries made it more difficult and costly for the group to function. The worsening economic situation impacted women in another way as well: they were told that their concerns would simply have to wait until the country's greater problems, such as economic restructuring and unemployment, had been solved. In short, women's issues were relegated to the back burner. The UFV maintains offices in East Berlin, where it publishes a newsletter *Infoblatt* and its *Weibblick*, a pun on the adjective "weiblich," meaning female; the title itself suggests a woman's viewpoint. The national organization was dissolved in June 1998 after an attempt to restructure it failed. Regional offices in Saxony-Anhalt and Mecklenburg-Vorpommern remained in existence in 1999.

Why was the feminist movement which emerged in the final days of the GDR unable to sustain itself after unification? To begin with, women, caught up in the chaos and euphoria of currency union, did not perceive the threats to the gains they had made under socialism. In fact 46% of the women who voted in the fall 1990 elections cast votes for the CDU/CSU coalition which campaigned for currency union and prompt unification with the West. Women who entered political activism with the founding of the UFV could scarcely keep pace with shifting needs. While they first gathered to oppose military or doctrinaire education in kindergarten, it did not occur to them that the kindergartens themselves might disappear. Prepared to campaign for conditions that made it easier for women to carry their double burdens, they only belatedly realized that half of these burdens—paid employment—might be endangered (Miethe, 16). East Germans knew that much of what they heard in the SED's obligatory monthly seminars was propaganda, and were surprised after unification to realize that some of the negative portrayal of the Federal Republic was accurate (Behrend 2000, 70). The erosion of abortion rights did not become apparent until the provisional arrangement governing abortion ended in 1992. By then most women were caught in the undertow as the social network of secure employment, housing, and childcare pulled away beneath their feet. Women exhausted their energies attempting to salvage not only their jobs and families but in some cases the very enterprises they had worked to create. Divisions among women widened in the sharp elbow competition for jobs and ABM positions. Older women confronted helplessly the dislocation of age as employers turned them away in favor of younger workers. Mothers whose daycare arrangements collapsed came to envy women without children. Some women, like Frau Fischer, consciously rejected new capitalist values while other women struggled to adapt to them. Highly educated women like Frau Bachmann and Frau Lindner remade themselves and relinquished the benefits their education had conferred. Women who worked in factories and farms could not easily identify with initiatives founded by well-educated women like the UFV and the new Center for Interdisciplinary Women's Studies. Some women embraced their new role as homemakers and full-time mothers, while others scorned them for doing so. In the long run, of course, the stresses which divide women and siphon away their collective strength serve the interests of patriarchy.

The Socialist Unity Party claimed that feminism was one way that capitalism (not patriarchy) diverts attention from the class struggle which exploits both sexes. If that is true, the question facing us today is why united Germany has no feminist movement. En route from Frankfurt to Paris I met an artist from Saarbrücken who described the pressures women face to conform to the West German stereotype of the *Hausfrauenehe*. She told me that people so often ask why she and her husband have no children that she has taken to replying that she can't. She described the situation of two academics, both with doctorates, who had a baby. The wife eventually returned to work, but only as a secretary. She professes herself happy. If a man were forced to accept such a demotion, the artist remarked, people would cry foul. In answer to my question about the existence of a German feminist lobby like America's National Organization for Women or the Feminist Majority working to promote abortion rights or affirmative action, she told me that there was none. Scattered initiatives existed, she assured me. She knew a woman involved in a coalition against the sexual exploitation of women and children, and she knew of a group called *Frauen helfen Frauen* (Women Helping Women) which provides shelters for victims of domestic violence. But there was no national women's lobby to repeal abortion restrictions, fight sexual harassment, or demand an end to sex discrimination in hiring.

Ten years ago, the prospects for a new German feminist movement looked far brighter. West German feminists watched with interest the emergence of a true feminist political lobby demanding a voice in the unification negotiations. Alice Schwarzer, West Germany's best-known feminist and publisher of *Emma*, attended the UFV's founding congress in February 1990. East and West German feminists met for the first broader discussion in April 1990 at the Berlin Sportforum, but could agree only on the campaign against the abortion law then in effect in the West. They met again for three days in November 1990, but the children of some East German participants disrupted the meeting and their presence irritated and distracted some women, particularly from the West. Discussions of relations between women and men and of motherhood failed to reach consensus. Other issues of concern in the

West, more part-time work and better pay for women, had been largely resolved in the East. Some West German feminist issues, such as domestic violence, had long been taboo in the East, or, like prostitution, pornography, and hostility toward foreigners, relatively unknown in East Germany's closed society. East German sociology was not accustomed to analyzing issues in terms of gender. Even now the western feminists' habit of analyzing race, gender, and social class as overlapping causes of women's oppression does not apply to East Germany (Schindler 1996, 153). The GDR was racially quite homogenous, and social class had not played much of a role in a society whose Marxist philosophy had nearly eradicated class distinctions. Some East German feminists found western feminist organizations competitive, riddled with personality conflicts, and undemocratic in their communications and ways of sharing power and information (Schindler 1996, 147). Not until September 1991 did the UFV open its membership to West Germans; thus it had little effect in bridging any gap between feminists in the old and new federal states.

East German women hoped that feminists in the West would support their efforts to prevent the expulsion of women from the labor force and the dismantling of the state childcare system. Some West German feminists wanted to begin with a more ideological approach, exploring broader issues of women's freedom, and considered their new stepsisters' concern with everyday issues a retreat into their private familial niche. They considered women in the East woefully ignorant of basic feminist scholarship, which had been unavailable to them. West Germans in turn knew little of Bebel's *Die Frau und der Sozialismus* and Engels' *Der Ursprung der Familie*.

The question of political power became a divisive issue as western feminists insinuated that East German women had their "emancipation" (working rights and access to abortion) handed to them by the SED and official organizations like the DFD. East Germans, on the other hand, insist that women's participation in politics after World War II gave them a voice in fighting for what they gained, and emphasize that women struggled to grant men the right to the monthly housework day and child-rearing leave. Furthermore, they find that the western feminists' view of them as passive objects replicates the traditional male perspective (Behrend 2000, 75). Other West Germans maintained that East German women shared responsibility for their country's decaying infrastructure, environmental damage, and unproductive industries. East Germans countered that what was needed was a critical examination and reform of both the capitalist and socialist systems, preserving the best features of each. What they got instead was the wholesale imposition of West German law and economics, with women as well as men appearing to reclaim real estate and take over agencies and jobs. They resist pressure to conform to western stereotypes of womanhood, which they do not accept without reservations.

Differences in gender relations and motherhood proved another huge obstacle for feminists. Westerners were shocked to realize that their counterparts in the East all had children and many were married, which radical feminists sometimes viewed as a betrayal of their cause. While some radical feminists might advocate lesbianism as a political statement, lesbians in the East considered it a matter of sexual orientation. Some West German women who had decided to forego children to pursue a career felt bitter comparing themselves to these working mothers who had been able to combine children with vocational training, earning a living wage, and professional satisfaction. The overwhelmingly negative portrayal of the GDR's daycare system in the media insulted the country's women, while it served capitalism's need to drive mothers back to their "duties" on the home front (Behrend 2000, 78). Some West German feminists saw a conflict between womanhood and motherhood, meaning that a woman can not fulfill her potential for self-realization if she becomes a mother, an attitude their eastern stepsisters could understand in the abstract, but not relate to their own experience. By contrast, many East German feminists believed that women achieve self-fulfillment only when they succeed in combining sexual and familial happiness with meaningful paid work. Some western theorists surmise that women had children in the GDR as an instrument to obtain apartments and child-rearing leave from monotonous and unsatisfying work. They contend that the sharp decline in the birthrate following unification shows that women are now able to satisfy their needs without children (cited by Schröter 1997, 49). In contrast, East German women choosing to have children within the framework of public patriarchy and often outside of marriage did not see themselves as sacrificing independence or self-fulfillment. As evidence of a fulfilling relationship with men as well as children, they point to a finding that 80% of East German fathers (compared to only half in the West) stay in touch with their children after separation or divorce (Wolff, 11).

East German women who explored feminism with new contacts in the West were alarmed to discover that these women identified men as their enemies and excluded them from feminist gatherings. East German feminists felt solidarity with men who worked alongside them.

The enemy, as they saw it, was an ossified political leadership that refused to hear its workers and citizens, a situation which unification did nothing to remedy. Overall they have had little success in bringing their particular concerns into a national feminist strategy: the alienation of youth, high unemployment for women over forty, and their ongoing struggle for the right to work (as opposed to the need for financial support) have not secured a firm place in any united German feminist agenda (Braun, 46).

Five years after unification East German feminist Christiane Schindler saw little hope of rapprochement with West German feminists: "We constantly renew our (pre)judgments of each other: western women are arrogant, know better about everything, are hostile to children and men, dogmatic and intolerant. Eastern women are accommodating, solid Moms, fixated on men, and not the least bit radical. Each considers the other less emancipated and independent than we are" (Schindler 1996, 147). She found that the relationships of the two groups of feminists are characterized by power and dominance, where the West Germans have the home court advantage and fully partake of the "victor" mentality. This relationship replicates the overall process of unification, where the East changes to become like the West, which is seen as the norm or standard.

Ten years after unification Hanna Behrend, professor of women's studies at Humboldt University, points out that the beginning of the twenty-first century is characterized by a widening gulf between rich and poor, between high-tech workers and the under-educated. This splintering into extremes serves capitalism because it plays off one group against another (Behrend 2000, 79). Thus for example the on-going criticism of East Germans as unmotivated, lacking creativity, devious, accustomed to attaining their ends by bribery, more interested in learning how to work the system than in learning how to work serves to legitimize their second-rate status and the take-over of the East by the West, which appears superior and deserving. The end result of such divisions between women and men or between different groups of women is to hinder any social movement against their exploiters. American slave owners' practice of mixing Africans from different ethnic and linguistic groups to prevent their mass uprising illustrates the efficacy of this principle. The divisions between East and West German feminists form part of this regrettable widespread trend in twentieth century world affairs to divide and conquer.

Yet despite these gloomy prospects, an examination of the feminist landscape reveals some positive initiatives. The beauty salon I visited in 1998 welcomed women from both halves of Berlin, and Frau Bachmann believed the counseling cum therapy that she offered appealed to all women. In April 2000 I visited an independent women's center which aims to break down barriers between East and West to serve and support all women. The EWA Frauenzentrum is located on Prenzlauer Allee not far from the Alexanderplatz. Its initials stand for *Erster weiblicher Aufbruch* (first women's uprising) but also evoke the name Eve. Women founded the center in December 1989 at the same gathering in the Volksbühne where the UFV was born. Its meeting rooms and library (called *Hex libris*–Hexe means witch) are housed on the top floor of an adjacent building in former Stasi offices. The Center offers lectures, a film series, poetry readings, courses in computer training, self-defense, communication and job-hunting skills, and counsels women on a variety of issues. It was one of the initiators of the study on violence against lesbians cited earlier and sponsors a lesbian club. The project manager who received me at EWA comes from West Berlin and the counselor who joined our conversation is from the East, a former editor of *Für Dich*. EWA strives to avoid the separatism which otherwise characterizes so many women's issues. The Center receives some state and city funding, but its directors also go out "polishing doorknobs," as they call it, to raise money.

There are centers like EWA in most large cities, and several in the various districts of Berlin, most of them staffed partially by women in temporary ABM jobs or working as volunteers. Many women's centers were founded by feminists working against the handover of political patriarchy from one group of old men to another during the Wende. However, these projects do not necessarily serve to advance women's emancipation because they focus on acute needs and local initiatives. Their staff may come together because of ABM opportunities rather than feminist convictions. And the ABM positions are temporary at best.

At EWA and at the Center for Interdisciplinary Women's Research I asked women how they reacted to the use of the –in suffix designating women's occupations. A West German sociologist who interviewed women doctors in Cottbus found that they identified themselves simply as doctors, shunning the –in suffix that specified their gender (Lützenkirchen, 83). She questioned whether the lack of literature about the socialization of women doctors was evidence of their equality. Were they so widely accepted as equal that there was simply no impetus to study women in professions? Or did socialism reject any such differentiation and thereby stifle recognition of women as different? While West German feminists view this suffix as a symbol of emancipation, because it draws attention to their presence in various occupations, critics maintain that it draws attention to how women differ from men and affirms the male as the norm in a profession. Like Eve's creation from Adam's rib, the suffix starts from the male as norm and designates woman as the derivative, the other. The women I spoke with at EWA and at the Center for Interdisciplinary Women's Research welcomed the use of the –in suffix. One woman considered it one of the achievements of West German feminists, who oblige speakers and writers to recognize gender and acknowledge the presence of women in occupations. Another, who championed its use and insisted upon it, remarked that as guidelines for non-sexist language become more widespread, feminist linguistics was gaining interest as a field of research. Overall my informal survey produced the conclusion that older East German women seldom think about the question, while younger women tend to favor the use of the feminine derivative suffix.

In the end it seems that the West German emphasis on the differences between the sexes is slowly gaining ground in the East. Yet while East German women readily agree that their gains in employment and childcare fell short of true emancipation as long as men did not change, they also expect that West German women will recognize and concede their own dependency under a patriarchal capitalist system which imposes their occupational choices within a homemaker-marriage. One feminist analyst points out that the struggle over the differences between feminists has kept both East and West Germans from a critical examination of their respective political and social systems (Miethe, 21).

A decade after the two systems came together, it becomes apparent that communism and capitalism evolved different ideas of what it meant to be a woman. In the GDR's real existent socialism, being a woman meant working for wages and working a second shift at home, having children, and running a household. In united Germany's capitalist democracy, it appears to mean chiefly being sexually involved with a male, buying as a status-conscious consumer, aspiring to the media's images of femininity, and playing second fiddle on the job or at home. Which of these roles will predominate in the coming century remains to be seen.

Chapter Twelve
Looking Forward

Intoxicated by their new liberty and power, Berliners tore down the Wall that had divided their city for twenty-eight years. Streams of Trabbis and Wartburgs poured through the newly opened streets. Water, electricity, and communications services flowed East. Families carrying their belongings in plastic bags fled West and sought refuge in temporary shelters. Others came to look around the Kaufhaus des Westens on the Kurfürstendamm, and then went home. Older West Germans went East to search for their childhood homes, and to try to understand how it all used to be.

Belatedly the city's inhabitants discovered that tourists visited Berlin precisely because they wanted to see the Wall. Before it was altogether destroyed, they salvaged some sections of the crude old barricade, although so much cement had been chipped away that rusty rebar shows through. I set out to see what was left of it one April Saturday in 2000 accompanied by a mail carrier who sought me out to practice her English. She and her second husband had weathered the political turnaround together. Proudly she showed me a spanking new hotel near the Pariser Platz which he had helped to build. She survived the re-structuring and mechanization of her local post office, although many of her friends were laid off. To keep up with the faster work pace, she goes in at seven in the morning to begin sorting letters. Today she is eager to learn English because the Japanese and American tourists who see her in uniform delivering mail often ask directions, and she wants to be able to help them. She and her husband have traveled to Africa and plan a trip to Mallorca, where she will pursue her hobby of photography.

The letter carrier belonged to the optimists of the younger generation, women who take the advantages which their new situation presents such as exotic travel and better photography equipment. We climbed the spiral ramp of the new glass dome of the Reichstag together, and admired the new buildings going up along the former no-man's land that bordered the Wall. She pointed out the television tower at the Alexanderplatz and the old buildings of La Charité. My companion said she felt at home in all of Berlin and delighted in exploring the unfamiliar West. She loves the exciting new architecture at the Potsdamer Platz and likes to go to the movies there with her husband, or to stroll through its public spaces where there is an experimental pond complete with frogs and ducks. We visited the last vestiges of the Berlin Wall and then I suggested we tour the museum at Checkpoint Charlie. Its exhibits of escape vehicles and failed attempts left her subdued and pensive; she had never seen such things before.

Several older East Germans told me they only went to West Berlin on special occasions, such as to hear a concert at the Philharmonic. The bustle and hubbub of the Zoo train station or the Ku'damm made them uneasy, or they recounted incidents when they had been insulted or snubbed in West Berlin. This sometimes hostile awareness of the differences between East and West has been dubbed "the wall in their heads" (*die Mauer im Kopf*).

This persisting division between East and West fascinates the country's observers. Journalists, reporters, and Germans themselves often seem to take pride in pointing out what differentiates Germans from one another, instead of what unites them. They remind us that the country's inhabitants have considered themselves for generations not as citizens of Germany, but as Hessians, Bavarians, or Rhinelanders. In fact the word "deutsch," Germans' name for themselves and their culture, means not the inhabitants of a geographic entity, but the people who use that language the word refers to. In that sense, German literature encompasses works of Swiss and Austrian authors too. Franz Kafka, a recognized master of German prose, spent most of his life in his birthplace, Prague, and died in Vienna. Even today people who may claim German citizenship cannot do so based solely on their birthplace. Rather, descendants of Germans born (or living for decades) in Russia or America can still hold German citizenship. Thus culture rather than geographic boundaries determines what is German.

While German unification accomplished the papering over of a political fault line, the cultural unification of Germany has not yet taken place. In interviews, East Germans often qualified their observations on German unity by admitting that their best friends were still all East Germans. Young women in their twenties and thirties said that when and if they married, it would have to be someone "from here," meaning from the East. A survey of 9,000 students at the University of Constance found that half were not interested in contact with the other part of Germany (*DAAD Letter* 3/99, 20). Almost immediately after unification the terms *Ossi* and *Wessi* appeared as the popular way to designate easterners and westerners.

Everywhere I ask how easterners tell the difference between West Germans and East Germans. One teacher replies that she can hear the differences in dialect. Another woman asserts that the westerners all take pains to speak standard German, while the more genuine easterners retain their Saxon, Brandenburg, or Berlin dialects. Herr Voigt takes umbrage at the West Germans' use of English words, such as team and teamwork instead of the East German *Kollektiv* or collective. Someone asserts that West Berlin concert-goers wear their coats to the performance to save the one mark fee for the cloakroom.

But it seems that distinctions are gradually becoming harder to perceive. In the spring of 2000 I reconnect with two younger women I met in 1998 and learn that both now have boyfriends from the West, relationships they entered with some trepidation. One woman says her boyfriend just can't believe she wasn't unhappy in the old days and didn't long to escape to the West. He doesn't know anything about the kind of books she read, or her vacation camp experiences, or the songs she learned either. She gets tired of trying to explain things to him. "We just have to agree not to talk about some things," she says.

Compared to my visit in 1998, I notice other changes. The Gesellschaft zum Schutz von Bürgerrecht und Menschenwürde has moved into new offices, a visible symbol of its increasing confidence and strength. The older people who comprise most of its members seem more self-assured, more critical of the West. Compact discs of FDJ and Young Pioneer songs are for sale in sidewalk displays. The woman who owns a small bookstore in Marzahn tells of a customer in her thirties, like herself, who bought one, and the two women listened to it together, tears streaming down their cheeks. People talk about a new East German mentality called *Abgrenzungsidentität*, which means roughly defining themselves as different from others, in this case, from westerners. That concept seems more negative than necessary. In fact what seems to be happening is a trend toward preserving the separateness of East German society even after the demise of the GDR. At the time of the Wende, feminists such as Ina Merkel advocated preserving a socialist state independent from the West. Politically and economically that aspiration collapsed, yet separate values and beliefs persist.

East Germans, whose education trained them to submerse individual egos into the collective, hesitate to put themselves forward. They find West Germans pushy and arrogant. Creativity, thinking in a novel or non-conforming way, got people into trouble in the GDR, and its inhabitants remain wary of it now. They shun confrontation and conflict, a behavior which West Germans interpret as waiting for others to take the initiative, or expecting others to fight their battles for them.

Some of these behavioral differences can be traced to differences between what have been called East Germany's public patriarchy and West Germany's private patriarchy (Ferree 1997, 526-29). While the GDR freed women from dependence on a male provider, it made them dependent on the social provisions and protections of *Vater Staat* instead. By contrast, West Germany's capitalist market economy tied women to dependence on individual men, whom they must attract and bind in a lasting intimate relationship. Therefore in East Germany individuality and personal initiative, which had no value in women's relationship to the patriarchal state, were not cultivated, whereas in the West they might prove valuable in securing a personal relationship.

Today other behavioral styles that continue to differentiate East and West German women can be viewed as rooted in their historical dependence on these two different kinds of patriarchy. For example West German women say that easterners dress less elegantly, or perhaps they simply can't afford to spend so much on clothing. East German women respond that fashionable clothing isn't versatile and durable enough for workers whose schedule takes them from a directors' meeting to the parents' group at the daycare center. They don't see a woman's dress or appearance as the basis of her identity because for decades they had no pressing need to make themselves attractive to men. Furthermore in the old socialist economy shopping for clothes and cosmetics was a time-consuming chore, not a means of establishing and projecting personal identity and prestige.

The transition to private patriarchy has other repercussions as well. One woman defined as a glaring contrast between official protocol and what really goes on in hiring interviews the fact that employers look last at women's qualifications and instead base their decisions on subjective factors such as age, attractiveness, and mobility (Wolff, 11). Older women have been forced to recognize age, which often increased their value in the socialist workforce, as a liability which makes them less employable in a capitalist patriarchy that prizes youth and sexual attractiveness. The *Versorgungsausgleich* which credits West but not East German divorced mothers with higher pension allotments is also geared to the private patriarchy of West Germany.

At the time of unification, West German analysts assumed that East German women would be happy to devote themselves to full-time home-making, something they had never had the opportunity to do. The next few years proved the error of these predictions. By the mid-nineties, people spoke of these women as the losers of German unification, and at the same time regretted their undiminished desire to work: *ununterbrochene Erwerbsneigung*. By the end of the decade, East German women not only rejected the possibility of full-time housewifery, but the suggestion that their doing so resulted from a "desire" to work. They claimed it as a right. Gradually attention has shifted from the economic effects of their unemployment to the personal, psychological, and social effects. While capitalism measures work in monetary terms, women (and probably male workers as well) claim work as a necessary component of self-worth.

The shift from public to private patriarchy also shapes changes in family relationships. The East German women interviewed regret that the progress they had made in sharing housework has gone backwards. In the fifties and sixties, sons of working mothers learned to wash and iron. Yet men who become unemployed do not take over the housework. Half of the East German respondents to a 1999 survey about housework indicated that the amount of time it takes has remained unchanged, and almost two-thirds of both men and women said nothing has changed in the distribution of housework (*Sozialreport 1999*, 294). Some women, however, believe that unemployment is easier for women to accept because they can fall back on their traditional role of homemaker, while man sink into depression, or as one woman said, "Sie ergeben sich dem Fernsehen, oder dem Suff" (They get addicted to television, or to drinking).

Behind the rocky transitions from public to private patriarchy, some hopeful signs surface that patriarchy itself may be growing weaker. First, the women I interviewed at Schloß Hasenwinkel form part of a statistically significant trend: there are more women entrepreneurs than ever before. Women, more strongly represented in the East than in the West, started about a third of new businesses in the 1990s. Lesbians are freer to live openly than ever before. Increasing attention to domestic violence and sexual harassment should result in greater protection for women. Some researchers believe that men themselves have become more aware of the drawbacks of patriarchal societies. They realize that higher suicide rates, a lower life expectancy, and more high-risk behavior such as road rage all indicate that societal pressures overwhelm some men. Some fathers bemoan the lack of time to spend with their families in a society which devalues emotional commitment and places a premium on toughness, aggressiveness, competitiveness, and perseverance, all traditional male traits (Schröter 1997, 63-64).

Some see increasing evidence that males themselves feel threatened, and that their aggressive reactions prove indeed that their hegemony is weakening. According to such logic, hostility toward foreigners (as well as domestic violence and sexual harassment) demonstrates male tendencies to re-assert their power. Thus even the 2000 election of Jörg Haider's right-wing Freedom Party (which won 27% of the popular vote in Austrian federal elections) might be taken as a sign that Austrian as well as German males need to dominate a weaker enemy. Even the popularity of Viagra can be interpreted as a strike against male impotence (Geisler, 12-13). Fathers' rights groups also clamor for attention in Germany, although they are not linked to traditional Christian teachings of "family values" or male-dominant groups like the American Promise Keepers.

On the national scene there are further signs that historically male-dominated hierarchies may be disintegrating. The campaign funds scandal in the Christian Democratic Union which erupted in the fall of 1999 plunged Helmut Kohl, the architect of German unification, into disgrace. Even the debate on abortion counseling within the Catholic Church brought forth new questions about its unity. Militarism also appeared to be losing its sway; the 1995 decision to deploy Bundeswehr troops on foreign soil for the first time since the Second World War drew the opposition of 108 delegates, half of them women (although women comprised only a fourth of Bundestag delegates at the time.) Increasingly Germany and its European neighbors have been plagued by troubles in which military force is useless. The year 2000 saw the first ruling by the European Court that the Bundeswehr must open its ranks to women, a verdict which will further challenge its role as a bastion of male power.

A decade after unification, East German women *and* men question whether adopting the western capitalist market economy as the norm is wise or desirable. Their criticisms cut to the heart of capitalism itself and inevitably call private patriarchy into question as well. A 1997 survey asked what women should do if their husbands earn enough to support them comfortably. Forty per cent of West, but only 11.3% of East German women would forego working themselves. Thus most women feel (albeit more strongly in the East) that money is not the point of working.

After unification East Germans gradually took another look at the richer variety of consumer goods. One woman commented, "Es ist erstaunlich, was es alles gibt, was man nicht braucht." (It's amazing how many things there are that one just doesn't need.) Susanne W. said that it was senseless to have so many varieties of hand towels, as long as there are some people who have none at all. Now buyers must compare prices and quality: "Vorher sind wir herumgerannt, um etwas zu bekommen. Heute rennen wir herum, um es billig zu bekommen," one woman said. (In the old days we chased around to obtain something. Today we chase around to get it cheaper.)

In the political democracy of united Germany, some East German women complain of the lack of freedom of expression. In earlier days, it was verboten to say "Der Honecker ist ein Schwein" (Honecker is a pig). They could, however, complain that the factory boss was "ein Schwein" if he failed to provide a hot meal for workers on the night shift. Today the freedoms are reversed. 'Schröder ist ein Schwein" would not put them in jeopardy, they say, but complaining about the boss would cost them their jobs. "Today people swallow everything" Jutta Freiberg commented. "Who would dare today to argue with the boss?"

The end of political restrictions on speech and travel does not necessarily mean freedom: as several women pointed out, if they lack money to travel, they're no better off than they were before. They would agree with Ivan Ilyich's concept of economic democracy; in united Germany, freedom does not depend on the political regime in power; instead access to money ensures individual liberty to choose one's residence, education, and work. Susanne W. spoke of the dictatorship of capitalism, meaning that economic strictures can limit personal freedom as much as political censorship and the exercise of power by a small group of men who are not accountable to the public. I thought of her phrase, "die Diktatur des Kapitals" when I revisited the residential section of Erfurt near the College of Education dormitory where I had lodged in 1985. The 1950s style GDR apartment blocks had been repainted and spruced up with some green spaces paved over to make more parking spaces. Each apartment had its own balcony, and the residents, both before and after the Wende, enjoyed the expansion of living space that balconies offered. They furnished them with sun shades, chairs, tables, and plants. Now each balcony has been further equipped with identical metal plant boxes hanging from the railing, as if to dictate that the residents must ornament their facades with flowers.

In capitalism we learn to revere political freedom, because it's what we have and what others (whom we pity or look down upon) do not. However, we never learn to question economic freedom or economic security, which is not a given in a capitalist society that produces a middle class that enjoys freedom and security, and an increasingly large underclass which does not. These values were reversed in East Germany, where everyone had basic economic security but no one had political freedom. Today East Germans continue to value economic and social security for all above the possession of status-conferring material goods which capitalism encourages them to compete for.

East German women in particular remain skeptical of the value and even the existence of political freedom; they feel that government is in the hands of male-dominated political parties which ignore them. One woman, comparing to the old SED regime in the GDR to united Germany's political democracy, said scornfully, "As much democracy as there is now, we had that much then too."

One further demarcation between East and West is the continued strong showing of the Party of Democratic Socialism, East Germany's old Socialist Unity Party, which carries no weight in the West. Schröder's Social Democrats, Kohl's Christian Democrats and the Party of Democratic Socialism each attract 20-25% of the East German vote, but women are less likely to engage in political activity than men are. A look toward the future raises more questions than it answers. At the end of the twentieth century, Germany had spent about six and one-half billion dollars rebuilding the East in the initiative called *Aufschwung Ost*. Optimists at least would consider this a one-time expense which would not have to be repeated. But the country lost two million jobs in industry and construction between 1992 and 1997, most of them in the East. The unemployment rate, 11.5% nationwide in July 1999, differs sharply in the West, where the rate of 9.6% is serious but not alarming, and in the East, where it was 18.8% (*Sozialreport 1999*, 156). There is no downward trend. In December 1999, 4,047,000 Germans were out of work. In some sectors such as mining, energy, and chemical production, 85-90% of jobs have been eliminated. Unemployment in regions dependent on these sectors runs as high as 40% (Lhaik, 69). Those who blame the high cost of labor for the lack of new jobs seem to disregard the discrepancy between East and West: while skilled industrial workers earn on average 45.92 DM an hour in the West (including fringe benefits), their East German counterparts earn only 32.97 DM, yet jobs are not flowing into the new federal states. In Poland, Hungary, or Slovakia, wages of about five marks an hour tempt employers to move production into these countries. The 53% tax on German corporate profits further discourages companies from expanding and creating new jobs.

But those who conclude that Germany's high unemployment characterizes an economy on the skids are in error. United Germany's gross national product grew in every recent year except 1975, 1982, and 1993 and was higher at the end of the twentieth century (both in total amount and amount per capita) than ever before (Schröter 1997, 63). Among the one hundred wealthiest people in the world, twenty-five are German, but here as in other capitalist countries the trend moves toward increasing wealth in fewer hands: 10% of united Germany's population controls half of its wealth (Schröter 1997, 63). The gross domestic product per capita doubled in the East between 1991 and 1997 (Lhaik, 69), and salaries in the East, which amounted to just 48% of West German levels at the time of unification, have now risen to about 77%. More efficient production methods reduced the need for workers when Volkswagen took over the former Trabant plant in Zwickau and when Opel assumed ownership of the old Wartburg factory in Eisenach. Of course the use of robots and computer-driven production machines ultimately creates savings–at least for the corporation, though not for its displaced workers.

What is afoot here can also be detected in international mergers and takeovers led by German firms in the late nineties. Car manufacturers led the way: Bavarian Motor Works and British Rolls Royce, and Daimler-Benz and America's Chrysler. Bertelsmann publishing took over Random House and Deutsche Bank bought out Bankers Trust. Other German firms merged with or took over French firms: insurance giant Allianz and AGF, pharmaceuticals leader Hoechst and Rhône-Poulenc. Deutsche Telekom merged with British Vodafone and made a bid to purchase American Voicestream. These developments indicate economic strength, not weakness.

But do such mergers and takeovers benefit workers? Increasingly, Germans doubt it. They have become aware that what is good for business does not coincide with what is good for the population at large. Awareness has increased of the ecological damage caused by the primacy of economic gain over the preservation of nature. East Germans, particularly see the growth of corporate profits and executive salaries with alarm. In the old days, the factory manager earned less than twice the wages of the average hourly worker. Capitalism broadens the gulf between rich and poor, so that the manager may take home literally hundreds of times as much money as the assembly line worker.

Who will come out on top? In the aftermath of unification, studies of East German women as losers in the process abounded. Ten years later it is time to re-phrase the question. What success and what setbacks can East German women expect on the road into the twenty-first century?

Surveys of these women conducted between 1990 and 1993 identified two groups which stood out: those who described themselves as "without hope" and those identified as "more active" than they were under the GDR (Schröter 1997, 55-61). In 1990 few common features characterized those without hope, as fear and confusion swept through women of every social strata. By 1991 this group stood out as over fifty years old, women who had lost their jobs or were about to, were unmarried, widowed or divorced, living in small or mid-sized cities primarily in the north of the former GDR, and having an income of a thousand marks per month or less. These women felt excluded from social changes, regretted the loss of their workmates, and withdrew as much as possible into their families. By May 1993 when last surveyed, the proportion of these women had risen from 29% to 35% of those surveyed. Many had worked in publicly owned industries or agriculture where job losses were particularly drastic, and some were enrolled in retraining or ABM make-work schemes. Now the group grew broader and included younger women, forty-five or older, more women living in Thuringia and Saxony, and those whose incomes were as high as 1,500 DM per month. Feeling disillusioned and helpless, such women were unlikely to seek help from women's centers or to protest their situation.

Far brighter were the futures of the second group studied, those who described themselves as more active after unification. Like the women I met at Hasenwinkel, and like Frau Bachmann and Frau Lindner in the Berlin beauty salon, these women saw opportunities rather than risks in their new situation. Most were under forty when the Berlin Wall opened, better educated than average, single, and living in the north of the GDR. They looked toward the future rather than the past; like the women I interviewed, they had no wish to revive socialism, and were less critical of the Federal Republic. They accepted political and economic changes as for the best, and took part in or at least believed they had a voice in politics. Under the socialist regime, such women were more likely to have worked in trade, administration or government or for a private company than in a publicly owned factory. They were better off than average, and more likely to save for a specific purchase rather than just for a rainy day. Not content with pursuing a career alone, they sought sexual fulfillment, including having children and a family. The sad news is that while the proportion of women without hope increased between 1990 and 1993, the proportion of these more optimistic and more active women decreased from 20% of those responding in October 1991 to just 12% of those surveyed in May 1993. Taken together, however, these two groups constituted less than half of all women surveyed (Schröter 1997, 61). Thus most women assess their situation as somewhere between these two groups.

Although the surveys cited ended in 1993, my own research suggests some indications for women's success or failure. Of first importance are age and education. Women under thirty at the time of unification, particularly those still studying, seized the opportunity to change course and train for the new system. Many, like Karin destined for plant chemistry on a large collective farm, welcomed the chance to follow their own tastes and aspirations. Flexibility was another key predictor of success; countless women subsisted through a whole series of ABM jobs and retraining programs before they could stand on their own. Another precious advantage was the ability some women had to put their fingers on the country's pulse and divine what services or commodities its next generation would prize, as Regina Werner had done with her donkey farm. Obviously family situations were also key to success, although there was no single pattern of family support. Some women, unmarried and childless, were able to travel toward their opportunities. Others counted on the loyal help of husbands and children, like Frau Fähnrich in her Arko candy store in Schwerin. Some mothers like Frau Graumann in her secondhand boutique continued to juggle childcare and work as they had done for years. It is young people who tend most strongly to see themselves as citizens of united Germany (which one-third of them affirm) rather than clinging to their East identity (*Sozialreport 1999*, 54). Sixty-four per cent of the over twelve hundred East Germans of all ages surveyed responded that they neither felt themselves as citizens of united Germany nor wished for the return of the GDR.

The situation of single mothers will continue as a large question mark on the country's future. The percentage of children born outside of marriage in 1998 ranged from 44-55% in the new federal states, over twice as high as the rates of 13-21% in the West German states (Hempel, 88). West German rates in the cities of Bremen and Hamburg were higher than in more conservative and Catholic regions such as Baden-Württemberg with 13% and Bavaria at 15%. These disparate trends parallel different expectations about who is responsible for taking care of children. While only 36% of East German mothers cared for children under four at home in 1995, the rate was 84% in the West (Pfitzner, 45). If East German women succeed in lowering their rate of unemployment, even fewer mothers will be available to care for children at home. To continue the slightly upward tendency in the birthrate which has predominated since 1997, the country will need to return to better provisions for childcare.

Older women are less likely than the young to embrace their status as part of united Germany. Those closely tied to the SED regime by political belief or party loyalty, like Frau Fischer, Jutta Freiberg, and Susanne W. faced the greatest unhappiness, regret, and emotional as well as financial insecurity upon its demise. If we follow the thesis of public versus private patriarchy one step further, we could say that such women lost their provider. When I ask women of this generation how they assess the chances for the country growing together, they concede that opening the mental wall which divides them may take longer than a decade. A short time ago, they spoke of a rapprochement within their daughters' lives. Yet while they describe their daughters' new careers proudly, they concede that these young women are childless, and often unmarried; there have been great sacrifices too. Others say that perhaps their grandchildren will be able to identify themselves simply as German. Dr. Christa Anders concurred with this point of view; she identified herself as East German or a Berliner, but felt no ties to the Federal Republic. Within her activity at the Gesellschaft zum Schutz von Bürgerrecht und Menschenwürde, however, she attended a peace conference in the West German city of Münster and came away newly inspired by the spirit of solidarity in working for a cause which could unite both East and West.

A survey of one thousand East and West Germans aged fourteen to fifty conducted in April 1999 does not augur well for the two halves of the country growing together. East Germans felt they were second-class citizens and were more "pessimistic, passive, and mistrustful" than West Germans. Both East and West Germans assumed that social tensions would increase, as would the gap between rich and poor. While East Germans believed that in five years they would be more dissatisfied, West Germans assumed the opposite, and were and planned to continue to be more content with their work, income, and health. For East Germans, children, a partner, and sexuality were more important than they seemed to be in the West. Professor Elmar Brähler of the University of Leipzig, co-author of the study, stated that East Germans divide the world into a personal, intimate sphere and unfriendly, hostile surroundings (*DAAD Letter* 3/99, 20). The former tends to harbor their happiness and satisfaction, while the latter appears threatening.

This gulf, rather than geographic divisions, will continue to bedevil Germans' attempts to see themselves as a unified nation. East Germans' definition of their homeland as a *Beitrittsgebiet*, or annexed territory likewise resists the notion of unity. Perhaps gradually Germany will become integrated into the European Union, so that the old boast of "Deutschland über alles" (Germany above all) will be replaced by "Deutschland unter anderem" (Germany among others). Women, who are better at cooperation than defending territory may better suit the new spirit of Europe.

I visit an adult English conversation class in East Berlin's Prenzlauer Berg and ask about German versus East German identity. One aspiring actress, whose existence would have been easier in the old days of state support for the arts responds, "I think it's time the East stopped blaming West Germany for all its troubles." Someone else volunteers, "I think it's time the West stopped expecting the East to feel grateful for being taken over." Another student sounds an optimistic note: "I've had the experience of living under socialism before and under capitalism now," he says. "That's an enormous advantage." And like many who share this experience, he concludes that capitalism may not have the final word.

What conditions for women's equality and success are lacking in the Federal Republic of Germany at the beginning of the twenty-first century? What measures could advance their status toward true equality? Working conditions are of paramount importance, according to the old socialist ideals which have informed our inquiry thus far. In June 2000 Germany loosened immigration restrictions to attract foreign workers with badly needed computer skills, a move that highlights the need for better technology training for women. Affirmative action quotas, as Ina Merkel demanded in the UFV's manifesto, are needed to overturn the gender imbalance in education, training programs and in highly paid occupations. The right to legal prosecution, class action lawsuits, and serious penalties for sex discrimination in hiring and for sexual harassment in the workplace must be available to women. Asking a job seeker about her childcare arrangements or a possible pregnancy should become so legally risky for employers as to be unthinkable. Widely publicized lawsuits prosecuting sexual harassment offenders should elevate consciousness of its insidious effects. Encouraging women to found their own businesses is no substitute for changing the climate of male-dominated workplaces.

Paradoxically, generous provisions for child-rearing place women at a disadvantage in the workplace. To ensure that motherhood does not relegate women to a second tier of underpaid, short-term, part-time labor, affordable daycare and all-day schools must become a priority. More important, the image of daycare needs to change, so that it is recognized as part of the educational system and thus not only a public responsibility, but a means of enriching the environment of children, who may otherwise spend their formative years without siblings and unsocialized to the group behavior standards that become the norm once they enter school. No woman should be obliged to leave work because she is pregnant, nor be prevented from returning as soon as she has given birth, if she chooses to do so. It goes without saying that men's willingness to assume their half of parenting must be encouraged. One means of doing so is to ensure that women earn at least as much as their partners, so that the choice of which parent stays home with a new baby does not automatically fall to the mother because she earns less. Women who return to work, at least within a brief span of time, must be guaranteed their jobs.

Those who wish to protect the unborn's right to life must turn their attention to the children who are already with us. One-fourth of all children in California live in poverty as the new century opens, and one-third of all children of single mothers in Germany. For those who truly love children, there is plenty to be done. The repeal of all restrictions on timely abortions would ensure that every child is a wanted child; *Wunschkinder*, as East Germans say (wanted children) is a beautiful expression.

The continuing existence of the East within the Federal Republic of Germany leaves open two important questions for feminists: what will be the long-term result of the uncoupling of motherhood and marriage? As 47% of all births in the East are to unmarried women, the phenomenon comes to resemble teen pregnancy in the United States. Here sociologists suspect that powerless, under-educated poor American teenagers have babies because they need to feel loved and wanted. Is the same true of East German women? Or does the social welfare system in united Germany (like the old socialist system) simply make it possible for women to raise children independently of men? Or do women seek a loving interpersonal relationship free of the pattern of dominance and subservience which characterizes so many marriages?

The second unresolved social question concerns the return of Christianity as a historical underpinning of patriarchy. Ten years after unification, it would be inaccurate to speak of a re-Christianization of the East. Nonetheless a confluence of East with West German culture and the search for transcendent ideals in a society where reality falls short of its promises may contribute to an increase in interest in religion.

Even as the German Democratic Republic is folded into the archives of history, feminists should pay homage to its two great achievements. On a scale unmatched by any other modern industrial society, it enabled women to combine motherhood with meaningful work. Three-fourths of the East German women and men responding to a survey a decade after unification judged that the conditions for combining work and motherhood have worsened (*Sozialreport 1999*, 294). And finally, the country demonstrated the possibility of a model of feminism which does not exclude men. For to paraphrase Ina Merkel, "Ohne Männer ist kein Staat zu machen."

Sources

"ABM Ost; 90 000 Frauen stehen vor der Tür," *Neues Deutschland* 13 February 1997.

Arbeitslosenreport 1999, edited by Siegfried Frister, Holger Lijeberg, and Gunnar Winkler. Berlin: Sozialwissenschaftliches Forschungszentrum Berlin-Brandenburg e.V., 1999.

Bauermann, Susanne. "Frauen und Technik: die unsichtbaren Mauern des Kapitalismus." *Marxistische Blätter* 38 (March-April 2000): 17-21.

Behrend, Hanna. "Die ostdeutschen Schwestern als die neuen 'Anderen': Beziehung der Differenz zwischen sozial Ungleichen oder gleichwertige Partnerinnen?" *Beiträge zur feministischen Theorie und Praxis* 54 (April 2000): 69-86.

___, ed. *Die Abwicklung der DDR; Wende und deutsche Vereinigung von innen gesehen* Cologne: ISP, 1996.

Bittorf, Wilhelm. "Das Glitzern in der Wüste." *Spiegel* 39 (1993): 42-58.

Böhm, Tatiana, "The Women's Question as a Democratic Question: In Search of a Civil Society." In *Gender Politics and Post-Communism*, edited by Nanette Funk, 151-59. New York: Routledge, 1993.

Braun, Anneliese. "Ost-West Kontakte der eher (noch) seltenen Art; Feministische Denkweisen als Klammer und als Überlebenshilfe." *Beiträge zur feministischen Theorie und Praxis* 54 (April 2000): 37-50.

Braun, Annaliese, Gerda Jasper, and Ursula Schröter. "Rollback in der Gleichstellung der Geschlechter: Trends in der Erwerbsentwicklung ostdeutscher Frauen." In *Die Abwicklung der DDR; Wende und*

Umbruch–Beiträge zur sozialen Transformation, Band 14. Berlin: Sozialwissenschaftliches Forschungszentrum Berlin-Brandenburg e.V., Hans Böckler Stiftung, 1998.

Buddin, Gerd. "Berufsverbot in the United Germany." In *Human Rights in East Germany,* 8-10. Berlin: Society for the Protection of Civil Rights and Human Dignity, 1994.

Bundesamt für Finanzen, Bundesanstalt für Arbeit. *Kindergeld.* Bonn: Bundesamt für Finanzen, Bundesanstalt für Arbeit, 1997.

Bundesministerium für Familie, Senioren, Frauen und Jugend. *Programm Frau und Beruf, Aufbruch in der Gleichstellungspolitik.* Bonn: Bundesministerium für Familie, Senioren, Frauen und Jugend, 1999.

Childs, David. *The GDR: Moscow's German Ally.* London: Allen & Unwin, 1983.

Cromm, Jürgen. "Familie, Familienbildung und Politik in der DDR, Anmerkungen eines Wessis." In *Geburtenentwicklung nach der Wende,* 39-62. Umbruch–Beiträge zur sozialen Transformation, Band 14. Berlin: Sozialwissenschaftliches Forschungszentrum Berlin-Brandenburg e.V., Hans Böckler Stiftung, 1998.

Dahms, Vera, Monika Putzing, and Frank Schiemann. "Aktive Arbeitsmarktpolitik im ländlichen Raum." Potsdam: Landesagentur für Struktur und Arbeit, 1996.

____. "Evaluierung von Frauenprojekten in Trägerschaft der Landfrauenverbände der neuen Bundesländer." Berlin: Sozialökonomische Strukturanalysen, SÖSTRA, 1997.

Dahn, Daniela, *Westwärts und nicht vergessen; vom Unbehagen in der Einheit.* Berlin: Rowohlt, 1996.

Davidson, Louise K. "Women in East Germany Today." *Off Our Backs, a Women's Newsjournal* 20 (July 1990): 8-10.

Dennis, Mike. *German Democratic Republic: Politics, Economics and Society.* London: Pinter, 1988.

Deutscher Gewerkschaftsbund. "Schwerpunkt: Sexuelle Belästigung am Arbeitsplatz." Frauen-Info-Brief (1998): 5-16.

Dodds, Dinah. "Five Years After Unification: East German Women in Transition." *Women's Studies International Forum* 21 (1998): 175-82.

Dodds, Dinah and Pam Allen-Thompson, eds. *The Wall in My Backyard; East German Women in Transition.* Amherst: University of Massachusetts Press, 1994.

Dölling, Irene, "'But the Pictures Stay the Same ...' The Image of Women in the Journal Für Dich Before and After the 'Turning Point'." *Gender Politics and Post-Communism,* edited by Nanette Funk, 168-79. New York: Routledge, 1993.

"Dokumentation: Qualifiziert, weiblich und ohne Arbeit." *Neues Deutschland,* 7 February 1997.

Drauschke, Petra and Margit Stolzenburg. "Zurück an den Familienherd –neue Orientierungen der Ostfrauen?" *Frauen in den neuen Bundesländern – Go West?, Tagungsreader der 6. Tagung 'Sozialunion in Deutschland' am 4.10.199,* edited by Katrin Andruschow, Renate Hürtgen and Rita Mersmann, 99-129. Umbruch–Beiträge zur sozialen Transformation in den alten und neuen Bundesländern, Band 11. Berlin: Sozialwissenschaftliches Forschungszentrum Berlin-Brandenburg e.V., Hans Böckler Stiftung, 1996.

Engelbrech, Gerhard, "Zwischen Wunsch und Wirklichkeit, Einstellungen ostdeutscher Frauen zur Erwerbstätigkeit zwei Jahre nach der Wende–Ergebnisse einer Befragung." IAB Werkstattbericht Nr. 8. Nuremberg: Institut für Arbeitsmarkt- und Berufsforschung der Bundesanstalt für Arbeit, 1993.

Engler, Wolfgang. *Die Ostdeutschen; Kunde von einem verlorenen Land.* Berlin: Aufbau-Verlag, 1999.

Faulseit, Andrea and Karin Müller. "Dokumentation der Fragebogenauswertung Gewalt gegen Lesben in Berlin 1996/97." Berlin, 1998.

Ferree, Myra Marx. "Patriarchies and Feminisms: The Two Women's Movements of Post-Unification Germany." In *Feminist Frontiers IV,*

edited by Laurel Richardson, Verta Taylor, and Nancy Whittier, 526-35.
New York: McGraw Hill, 1997.

___. "The Time of Chaos Was the Best, Feminist Mobilization and
Demobilization in East Germany." *Gender & Society* 8 (December
1994): 597-623.

Festraëts, Marion, "Oecuménisme et liberté de conscience," *L'Express*,
nr. 2522 (November 1999): 23.

Frauen in Deutschland; auf dem Weg zur Gleichstellung. Information
zur politischen Bildung Nr. 254. Munich: Franzis-Druck, 1997.

Frister, Siegfried, Holger   Lijeberg, and Gunnar Winkler, eds.
Arbeitslosenreport   1999.   Berlin: Sozialwissenschaftliches
Forschungszentrum Berlin-Brandenburg e.V., 1999.

Funk, Nanette. "Abortion and German Unification." In *Gender Politics
and Post-Communism*, edited by Nanette Funk, 194-200. New York:
Routledge, 1993.

___. "Feminism Meets Post-Communism: The Case of the United
Germany." *Feminist Nightmares: Women At Odds; Feminism and the
Problems of Sisterhood* (1994): 310-20.

Geisler, Magdalena. "Erbarmen mit den Männern." *Fakta für Frauen* 3
(1998): 12-13.

German Academic Exchange Service. "Überholspur zur Professur."
DAAD Letter 3 (1999): 13.

German Democratic Republic. *The German Democratic Republic*
Berlin: Panorama DDR, 1986.

___. Statistisches Taschenbuch der   Deutschen Demokratischen
Republik 1988.   Berlin: Staatsverlag der Deutschen Demokratischen
Republik, 1988.

___. Statistisches Taschenbuch der   Deutschen Demokratischen
Republik 1990. Berlin: Rudolf Haufe Verlag, 1990.

Goltz, Elke. "Aufbau einer Wollmanufaktur," unpublished paper. Berlin, 1998.

Hampele, Anne. "The Organized Women's Movement in the Collapse of the GDR: The Independent Women's Association (UFV). In *Gender Politics and Post-Communism*, edited by Nanette Funk, 180-93. New York: Routledge, 1993.

Haug, Frigga, "Boys' Games and Human Work: on Gender Relations as Relations of Production." *Rethinking Marxism* 6 (Fall 1993): 49-65.

Haupt, Hanna, Heidrun Schmidtke, and Heidemarie Wille, eds. *Materielle Alterssicherung von Frauen im Land Berlin*. Umbruch–Beiträge zur sozialen Transformation, Band 10. Berlin: Sozialwissenschaftliches Forschungszentrum Berlin-Brandenburg e.V., Hans Böckler Stiftung, 1994.

Hempel, Marlies. "'Und eine Arbeit soll meine Frau haben und sie soll Chefin sein'. Lebensentwürfe von Mädchen und Jungen in Ost und West." *Beiträge zur feministischen Theorie und Praxis* 54 (April 2000): 69-86.

Hessisches Ministerium für Umwelt, Energie, Jugend, Familie und Gesundheit. "Rechtsinformation für gleichgeschlechtliche Partnerschaften." Wiesbaden: Hessisches Ministerium für Umwelt, Energie, Jugend, Familie und Gesundheit, 1998.

Hofmann, Friedrich. "Fachverband Philologen führte Gespräch im Kultusministerium." *Neue sächsische Lehrerzeitung* 11 (2000): 9.

Hosken, Fran, "Reports from Around the World: Europe; Germany; Only 5% of Top Positions Held by Women." *Women's International Network* WIN News 24, no. 1, 71-72.

Igney, Claudia. "Zwischen westlichen Vorurteilen und verklärender Ostalgie, ein persönlicher Rückblick." *Beiträge zur feministischen Theorie und Praxis* 54 (April 2000): 51-68.

Institut für Demoskopie Allensbach. *Frauen in Deutschland: Lebensverhältnisse, Lebensstile und Zukunftserwartungen; die Schering-Frauenstudie '93*. Cologne: Fund Verlag, 1993.

Jähnert,   Gabriele.   "Zehn   Jahre   danach: Zum   Stand   der
Institutionalisierung der Frauen- und Geschlechterforschung in den
neuen Bundesländern," 47-63. ZiF Bulletin 19: Institutionalisierung und
Interdisziplinarität, Frauen und Geschlechterforschung an der Humboldt
Universität. Berlin: Zentrum für interdisziplinäre Frauenforschung,
1999.

Jansen, Mechthild M., Sigrid Baringhorst, and Martine Ritter, eds.
Frauen in der Defensive? Zur Backash-Debatte in Deutschland.
Perspektiven aktueller Frauenforschung, vol. 3. Münster: Lit, 1995.

Kamensita, Lynn. "East German Feminists in the New German
Democracy: Opportunities, Obstacles, and Adaptation." *Women &
Politics* 17 (1997): 41-68.

Kebir, Susanne. "Frauenemanzipation in Ost und West. Zwei
gegensätzliche Sozialisationen." *Marxistische Blätter* 38 (March-April
2000): 28-31.

Kischke, Martina I. Review of *"Mythen von Solidarität und
Gerechtigkeit–Gewalt gegen Frauen in Ostdeutschland vor und nach
der Wende,"* by Elke Amberg. *Frankfurter Rundschau* 12 June 1999,
ZB 5.

Kuhrig, Herta. "'Mit den Frauen'—Für die Frauen': Frauenpolitik und
Frauenbewegung in der DDR." In *Geschichte der deutschen
Frauenbewegung,* edited by Florence Hervé, 209-48. Cologne:
PapyRossa, 1998.

Landesarbeitsamt Rheinland-Pfalz – Saarland. *Frauen und
Arbeitslosigkeit,* 2d ed. Saarbrücken: Landesarbeitsamt Rheinland-
Pfalz-Saarland, 1996.

Leipziger Gesellschaft für Politik und Zeitgeschichte e. V. "Frauen im
Umbruch, Feminismus im Aufbruch." Einspruch. Leipziger Hefte 4.
Leipzig: Leipziger Gesellschaft für Politik und Zeitgeschichte e. V.,
1992.

Lhaik, Corinne, "Dur, dur d'être une modèle." *L'Express* nr. 2522
(November 1999): 68-69.

Lützenkirchen, Anne. "'Wir wollten das so!' Die Frauenemanzipation der DDR-Ärztinnen." *Zeitschrift für Frauenforschung* 17 (1999): 73-89.

McCardle, Arthur W. and A. Bruce Boenau, eds. *East Germany: A New Nation Under Socialism?* Lanham, MD.: University Press of America, 1984.

Menning, Sonja. "Leben mit Kindern–ein Auslaufmodell in den neuen Bundeslandern?" *Frauen in den neuen Bundesländern–Go West? Tagungsreader der 6. Tagung 'Sozialunion in Deutschland' am 4.10.1995,* edited by Katrin Andruschow, Renate Hürtgen and Rita Mersmann, 130-144. Umbruch–Beiträge zur sozialen Transformation in den alten und neuen Bundesländern, Band 11. Berlin: Sozialwissenschaftliches Forschungszentrum Berlin-Brandenburg e.V., Hans Böckler Stiftung: 1996.

Merkel, Ina. "Ohne Frauen ist kein Staat zu machen . . . Manifest für eine autonome Frauenbewegung." *Metis; Zeitschrift für historische Frauenforschung und feministische Praxis* 16 (1999): 152-61.

Miethe, Ingrid. "Frauenbewegung in Ostdeutschland—Angekommen in den neuen Verhältnissen?" *Beiträge zur feministischen Theorie und Praxis* 54 (April 2000): 9-22.

Nave-Herz, Rosemarie. *Die Geschichte der Frauenbewegung in Deutschland.* Opladen: Leske + Budrich, 1994.

Nickel, Hildegard Maria. "Women in the GDR: Will Renewal Pass Them By?" *Women in German Yearbook* 6 (1991): 99-107.

___. Women in the German Democratic Republic and in the New Federal States: Looking Backward and Forward (Five Theses)." In *Gender Politics and Post-Communism,* edited by Nanette Funk, 138-50. New York: Routledge 1993.

Ockel, Edith. *Die unendliche Geschichte des Paragraphen 218, Erinnerungen und Erlebnisse.* Berlin: Edition Ost, 2000.

Ohms, Constance. "Gewalt gegen Lesben, eine vergleichende Studie." Frankfurt, 1999.

Ottow, Silvia. "Verordnet und doch in Ordnung; Hanna Behrend . . ." *Neues Deutschland,* 26 February 1997.

___. "Die Durchschnittsrentnerin ist eine Pappkameradin." *Neues Deutschland,* 10 December 1999.

Panzig, Christel. "Die Wende auf dem Lande." In *Die Abwicklung der DDR; Wende und deutsche Vereinigung von innen gesehen,* edited by Hanna Behrend, 159-90. Cologne: ISP, 1996.

Pelkner, Anna-Katharina. "Feministische Wissenschaft und politische Einmischung—die Geburtsstunde des ZiF der Humboldt-Universität Berlin." In *Frauen und Geschlechterforschung an der Humboldt Universität,* 28-41. ZiF Bulletin 19: Institutionalisierung und Interdisziplinarität. Berlin: Zentrum für interdisziplinäre Frauenforschung, 1999.

Pfitzner, Heike. "Auf dem Weg zueinander—Praxiserfahrungen aus einem Seminar zu Problemen und Perspektiven in der Kommunikation von Frauen aus Ost- und Westdeutschland." *Beiträge zur feministischen Theorie und Praxis* 54 (April 2000): 23-26.

Pinzler, Petra. "Die mageren Jahre, Warum vier hochqualifizierte Frauen nicht in die Topetagen aufstiegen." *Die Zeit,* 18 October 1996.

Querblick, Infoblatt des Arbeitskreises Feministische Politik der PDS-Bundestagsfraktion. Berlin: Partei des demokratischen Sozialismus, 1999.

Rastetter, Daniela. "Sexuelle Belästigung am Arbeitsplatz–ein betriebliches Problem." *Zeitschrift für Frauenforschung* 17 (1999): 90-108.

Richter, Wolfgang. "The Human Rights of Academics in East Germany." In *Human Rights in East Germany.* Berlin: Society for the Protection of Civil Rights and Human Dignity, 1994.

Roether, Diemut. "Stipendien statt Stellen?" *Deutsche Universitäts-Zeitung* 15-16 (1992): 24-27.

Rogers, Ingrid. *Recollections of East Germany: Biographical Essays of Women Church Leaders.* New York: McGraw-Hill, 1996.

Rohmann, Eva. Untitled lecture on the Demokratischer Frauenbund, Paper read at the Kongreß gegen Renten- und Versorgungsunrecht, 13 January 1996, Berlin. Berlin: Gesellschaft zum Schutz von Bürgerrecht und Menschenwürde, 1996.

Rohnstock, Katrin, *Stiefschwestern; was Ost-Frauen und West-Frauen voneinander denken*. Frankfurt: Fischer, 1994.

Rosenberg, Dorothy. "Introduction" to *Daughters of Eve; Women's Writing from the German Democratic Republic*, translated and edited by Nancy Lukens and Dorothy Rosenberg, 1-22. Lincoln: University of Nebraska Press, 1993.

Schäfer, Simone. "Schwangerschaft, Geburt und Mütterberatung in der DDR—unter den Aspekten gesetzlicher Regelungen und Eigenverantwortlichkeit." *Beiträge zur feministischen Theorie und Praxis* 49/50 (1998): 129-38.

Schenk, Christina. "Lesbians and Their Emancipation in the Former German Democratic Republic: Past and Future." In *Gender Politics and Post-Communism*, edited by Nanette Funk, 160-67. New York: Routledge, 1993,.

Schindler, Christiane, "Demokratieerfahrung ostdeutscher Frauen in der Frauenbewegung," *Frauen in den neuen Bundesländern – go West? Tagungsreader der 6. Tagung 'Sozialunion in Deutschland' am 4.10.1995*, edited by Katrin Andruschow, Renate Hürtgen and Rita Mersmann, 145-56. Umbruch–Beiträge zur sozialen Transformation in den alten und neuen Bundesländern, Band 11. Berlin: Sozialwissenschaftliches Forschungszentrum Berlin-Brandenburg e.V., Hans Böckler Stiftung, 1996.

____. "Geschichte des Paragraphen 175." Unpublished working paper. January 24, 2000.

____. "Keine Privatsache!"*Landeszeitung der PDS Berlin* (March 2000): 7.

Schröter, Ursula. "Die DDR Frau und der Sozialismus und was daraus geworden ist." In *Als ganzer Mensch leben; Lebensansprüche ostdeutscher Frauen,* 13-86. Auf der Suche nach der verlorenen Zukunft Band 5. Berlin: Trafo Verlag, 1997.

___. "Ostdeutsche Frauen–die widerständigen Verliererinnen." *Marxistische Blätter* 38 (March-April 2000): 22-27.

___. "DDR sozialisierte Frauen in Deutschland." *Metis; Zeitschrift für historische Frauenforschung und feministische Praxis* 16 (1999): 131-51.

Seeland, Suzanne. "Yo Yo Kid: von der Produktidee zur Gründung." Berlin: athene, n.d.: 51-70.

Sieg, Katrin. "Sex, Subjectivity, and Socialism: Feminist Discourses in East Germany. *Genders* 22 (1995): 105-21.

Städter, Helga. "Women–Where are They?" In *Meet United Germany; Perspectives,* edited by Susan Stern, 152-64. Frankfurt: Atlantik-Brücke, 1992/93.

Vaskovics, Laszlo A. "Kinderwunsch junger Ehepaare in West- und Ostdeutschland nach der Wende." In *Geburtenentwicklung nach der Wende,* 81-103. Umbruch–Beiträge zur sozialen Transformation, Band 14. Berlin: Sozialwissenschaftliches Forschungszentrum Berlin-Brandenburg e.V., Hans Böckler Stiftung, 1998.

Versieux, Nathalie. "Les blues des Allemandes de l'Est," *L'Express,* nr. 2522 (November 1999): 20.

Volkhard, Peter. "Dokumentiert: Die Sturzgeburt." *Journal für Recht und Würde* 4+5 (1992): 5,

von Ankum, Katharina. "Political Bodies: Women and Re/Production in the GDR." *Women in German Yearbook* 9 (1993): 127-41.

Wander, Maxie. *Guten Morgen, Du Schöne, Frauen in der DDR.* 5th ed. Berlin: Luchterhand, 1978.

Winkler, Gunnar, ed. *Frauenreport 90.* Berlin: Verlag die Wirtschaft, 1990.

___, ed. *Sozialreport 1995; Daten und Fakten zur sozialen Lage in den neuen Bundesländern.* Düsseldorf: Hans-Böckler Stiftung; Berlin: Sozialwissenschaftliches Forschungszentrum Berlin-Brandenburg e. V., 1995.

___, ed. *Sozialreport 1999; Daten und Fakten zur sozialen Lage in den neuen Bundesländern.* Düsseldorf: Hans-Böckler Stiftung; Berlin: Sozialwissenschaftliches Forschungszentrum Berlin-Brandenburg e. V., 1999.

___. Untitled lecture on the Volkssolidarität. Paper read at the Kongreß gegen Renten- und Versorgungsunrecht, 13 January 1996, Berlin. Berlin: Gesellschaft zum Schutz von Bürgerrecht und Menschenwürde, 1996.

Wolff, Christiana. "Frau, quo vadis?" *Fakta für Frauen* 6 (1997): 10-11.

Zentrum für interdisziplinäre Frauenforschung. *Bulletin 13: DDR-Frauen-Wende.* Berlin: Humboldt University, 1999.

Index